STUDY GUIDE

MANAGEMENT SCIENCE

MODELING, ANALYSIS AND INTERPRETATION

JEFFREY D. CAMM
University of Cincinnati

JAMES R. EVANS
University of Cincinnati

PREPARED BY
SCOTT M. SHAFER
Auburn University

SOUTH-WESTERN College Publishing

An International Thomson Publishing Company

Acquisitions Editor: Jack C. Calhoun
Publisher/Team Director: Valerie Ashton
Developmental Editor: Dennis Hanseman
Production Manager: Rebecca Roby
Cover Design: Craig LaGesse Ramsdell
Team Assistants: Ronda Faulkner, B.J. Parker, Cory Broadfoot

MI61AD

ISBN: 0-538-82739-4
1 2 3 4 5 6 7 PN 1 0 9 8 7 6 5
Printed in the United States of America

International Thomson Publishing
South-Western College Publishing is an ITP Company. The ITP trademark is used under license.

PREFACE

It is widely acknowledged that the revolution in personal computers has dramatically changed the way businesses operate. As an example, widespread use of personal computers has permitted performing a variety of analyses that were previously impractical or uneconomical to perform. Without a doubt, today's highly competitive global marketplace with the added challenges of rapidly advancing technology and dramatically shorter product life cycles, demands that decision makers have a solid working knowledge of computers beyond simple literacy.

One of the most significant developments associated with personal computers was the creation of the spreadsheet. Arguably, the spreadsheet is the most powerful decision support tool available today due to its flexibility to model a wide variety of decision making situations. To illustrate, most spreadsheets have built in capabilities to perform a variety of statistical, financial, mathematical, database, sensitivity, and optimization analyses. Indeed, the combined availability and power of spreadsheets makes learning about management science tools relevant to all decision makers.

Given management science's orientation of applying the scientific method to analyze and solve complex decision problems and given the spreadsheet's power and flexibility to model a wide variety of situations, it is natural to combine the two and demonstrate how spreadsheet's can be used to solve a variety of decision problems. This is especially true since most decision makers already have access to a spreadsheet program.

The purpose of this study guide is to help you master the topics presented in your management science textbook with particular emphasis on using spreadsheets to model, analyze, and solve complex decision making problems. Each chapter in this study guide contains three sections: a 1-2 page summary of the major points in the corresponding textbook chapter, one or more illustrated problems, and true/false questions with answers.

This study guide is meant to help you master the material in the textbook. To accomplish this objective, it is recommended that the study guide be used in the following way. First, the short summary in the study guide should be used to test your understanding of the major concepts presented in the text. As such, the summary highlights the major concepts but does not explain them. Thus, as you read the summary, if you are unable to explain a particular point, this indicates that you need to go back to the textbook and study the concept in more detail.

Once you feel comfortable with the concepts in the summary section you can move on to the illustrated problems. Typically, the illustrated problems present a problem and then explain the solution to the problem. Since the only way to learn to solve management science problems is by doing it, it is strongly recommended that you attempt to solve the problem prior to reading the solution. Once you have completed the problem or have invested sufficient time and are truly convinced you cannot move forward, read the solution to the problem. Using the study guide in this fashion will help you when you get stuck, reinforce your learning when you successfully solve a problem, and may even demonstrate a different solution strategy which provides you with even more knowledge.

Finally, the last section of each chapter in the study guide provides a number of true/false questions with answers. It is recommended that these questions be used after you have completed your study of the chapter to gage your final understanding of the material.

Scott M. Shafer

TABLE OF CONTENTS

CHAPTER 1

REVIEW

Management science is the application of the scientific discipline to the analysis and solution of complex decision problems. It uses the language of mathematics and the power of computers to help decision makers determine how to best design and operate systems where the allocation of scarce resources is required.

Management science is a relatively new discipline and was formally spawned through efforts to improve military operations during World War II. In fact, the term *operational research* was coined to describe the application of scientific principles to improving military operations. After the war, it was recognized that the mathematical tools and techniques developed to improve military operations could also be applied to problems faced by businesses. As the view of operations researchers enlarged to include business applications, the term *management science* was adopted. Today, the terms operations research and management science are used interchangeably.

Management science principles are applicable to all industries and all sectors of the economy. The chapter provides examples of management science applications for scheduling airline crews, telecommunications planning, transportation planning, the search for sunken treasure, and telephone network planning.

Management science is primarily concerned with *problem solving*, i.e., selecting an appropriate solution that resolves or improves the situation. Problem solving consists of the following six steps: 1) recognizing the problem, 2) defining the problem, 3) structuring the problem, 4) analyzing the problem, 5) interpreting the results and selecting a solution, and 6) implementing the solution.

Problem recognition occurs when a "gap" is identified between the present and desired state. Identifying the "true" problem is critical to successful problem solving. Managers have to guard against identifying the symptoms of the problem and thus making a "type III error" (solving the wrong problem).

Once a problem has been identified, the goals and objectives to be achieved need to be determined. Often multiple objectives may be developed and the manager may need to make tradeoffs between these objectives. Also, it is important to involve the people who are affected by the decision in the problem definition phase.

A model is a representation or abstraction of a real object, idea, or system and is used to structure a problem after it is defined. Models are classified into three categories: 1) descriptive models, 2) predictive models, and 3) prescriptive models. *Descriptive models* are useful primarily for describing relationships. *Predictive models* are used to forecast future events. *Prescriptive models* are used to recommend the best decision given the objectives and constraints associated with the situation.

Models consist of *parameters* and *variables*. Parameters are constant whereas variables can change. Furthermore, variables that are under the control of the decision maker are called *controllable variables* (or *decision variables*) while variables that cannot be directly controlled by the decision maker are called *uncontrollable variables*.

Prescriptive models contain four components: 1) controllable (or decision) variables, 2) uncontrollable variables and parameters, 3) constraints, and 4) an objective function. *Constraints* limit the range of acceptable values for the decision variables. An *objective function* is a mathematical statement of the objective associated with a given decision making situation. Usually, the decision maker seeks to maximize or minimize the value of the objective function. Such problems are called *optimization problems*. In an optimization problem, the assignment of specific values to the decision variables is referred to as a solution to the problem. Any solution that satisfies all the constraints is called a *feasible solution*. A feasible solution that maximizes or minimizes the value of the objective function is called an *optimal solution*.

Another way to categorize models is based on whether they include randomness or not. *Deterministic models* are models where all the input information is assumed to be known with certainty and thus do not allow for randomness. *Stochastic models* are models where one or more of the inputs to the model are not known with certainty and are therefore described probabilistically.

Management science uses models to:

1. To study the behavior of systems.

2. To find acceptable or optimal solutions to problems.

3. To examine the sensitivity of solutions to changes in the data.

An *algorithm* is a systematic procedure that finds a feasible or an optimal solution to a problem. *Exact algorithms* are guaranteed to find an optimal solution to a problem. *Heuristic algorithms* or simply *heuristics* are rules that generally provide good, but not necessarily optimal, solutions.

One of the most important management science activities is sensitivity analysis. *Sensitivity analysis* allows the decision maker to see what happens to the results when changes are made in the model data.

The increasing availability and power of computers has increased the use of management science tools and decision support systems (DSS) in industry. A *decision support system* is a set of computer-based tools used by a manager in connection with his or her problem-solving and decision-making duties. Decision support systems include three components: 1) data management, 2) model management, and 3) a communication system.

SOLVED PROBLEMS

Example Problem 1: Descriptive Model

A simple economic model suggests that housing starts depend on interest rates and demographic factors such as population size, family income, and number of people that are 25-55 years old. Further analysis suggests that interest rates depend on inflation, federal reserve policies and government borrowing. Government borrowing depends on government spending and tax revenues. Develop an influence diagram that shows the relationships among the factors that influence housing starts.

Solution:

We begin with the factors that directly affect housing starts: interest rates, population size, family income, and the number of people 25-55:

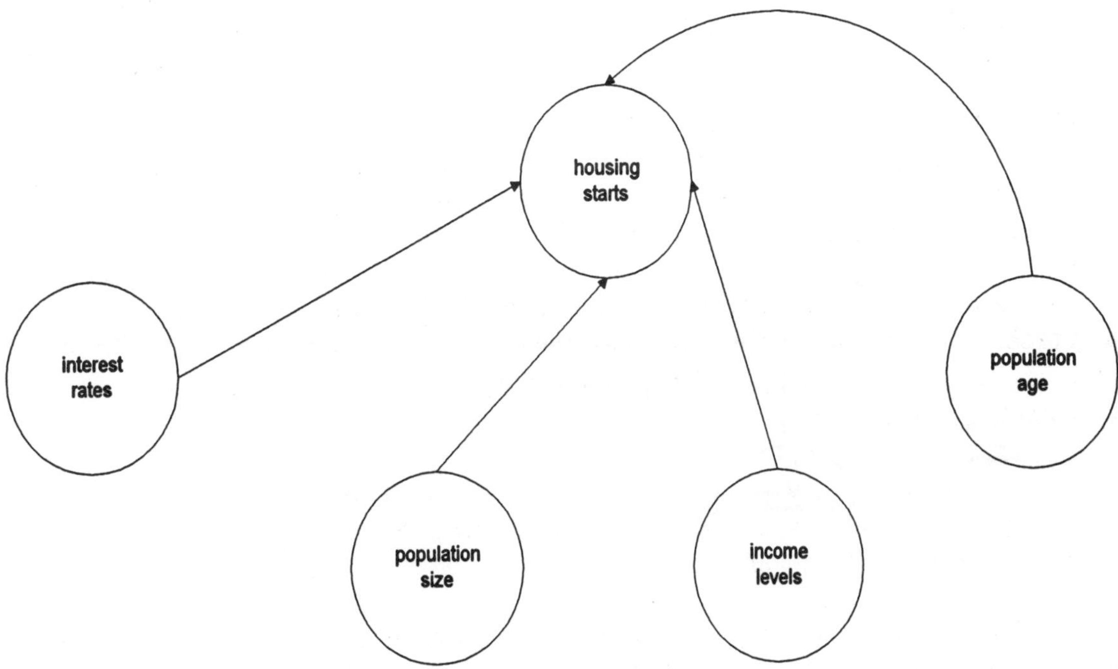

Next we add the factors that affect interest rates:

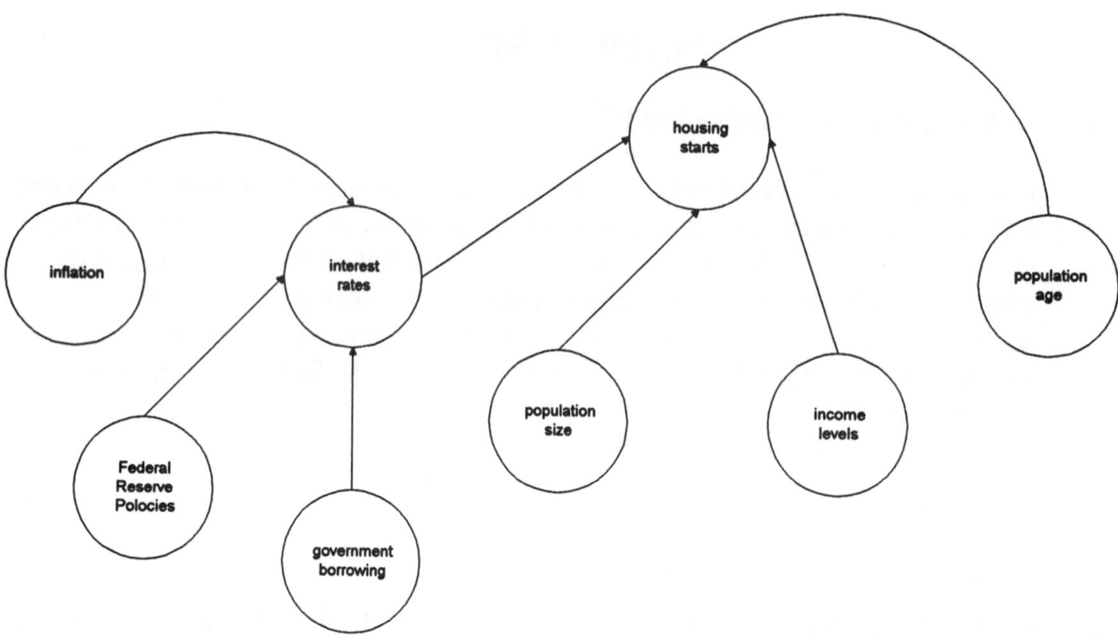

Finally, the factors that determine government borrowing are added to complete the influence diagram:

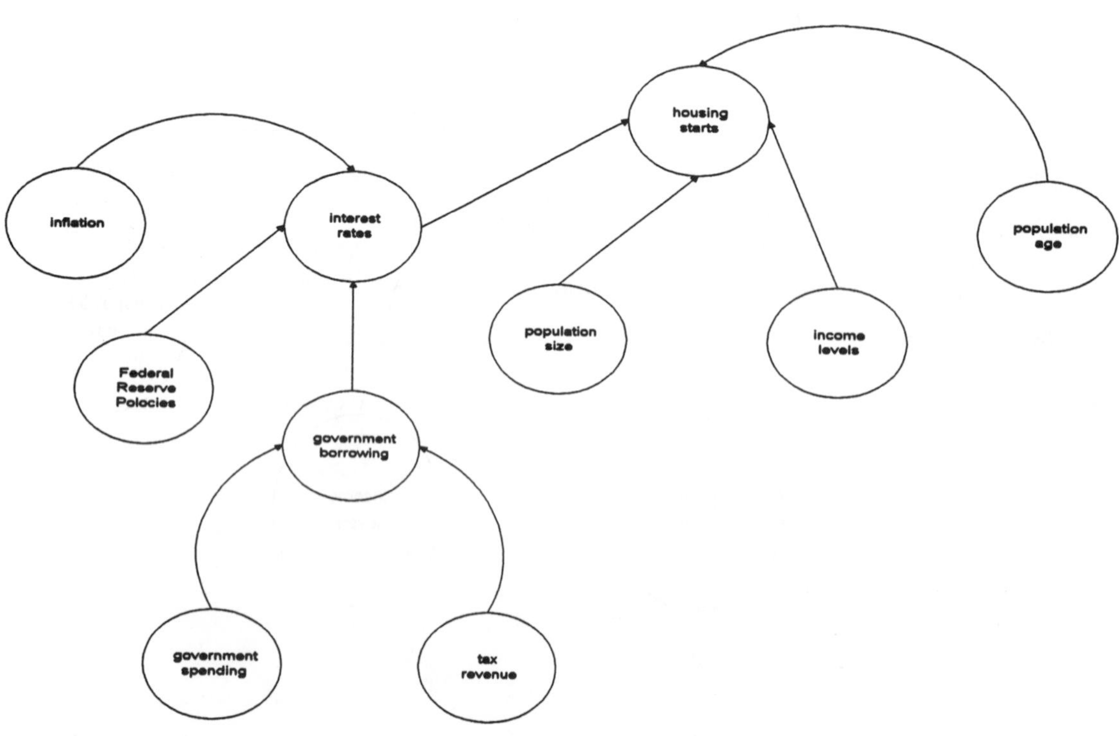

Example Problem 2: Predictive Model

Referring to example problem 1, develop a predictive model for government borrowing assuming all government expenditures can be categorized as either discretionary spending, entitlements, or interest.

Solution:

Let:

GB = government borrowing,

TFR = total federal revenue,

DS = discretionary spending,

E = entitlements,

I = interest payments.

Then a predictive model for government borrowing would be:

$$GB = TFR - (DS + E + I)$$

Using this model a decision maker could "plug in" alternate values of TFR, DS, E, and I to predict the amount of government borrowing required.

Example Problem 3: Prescriptive Model

A manufacturer of guitars makes three models: an acoustic model, a classical model, and an electric model. Producing the guitars requires six major operations: cutting and crafting the wood, assembling the wood components, applying the finish to the guitars, installing the hardware, testing and adjusting, and packaging. Additional information for this manufacturer are given in the following table.

	Acoustic Guitar	Classical Guitar	Electric Guitar
Profit Per Guitar	\$25	\$55	\$75
Time to Cut and Craft	2 hours	3 hours	1 hour
Time to Assemble	3 hours	3 hours	1 hour
Time to Finish	1 hour	1.5 hours	0.5 hours
Hardware Installation	1 hour	1 hour	2 hours
Testing and Adjusting	1.5 hours	1 hour	2 hours
Packaging	0.5 hours	0.75 hours	0.25 hours
Forecast Demand	175 Guitars	30 Guitars	100 Guitars

The cutting and crafting department has 800 hours of labor available. Likewise, the assembly, finishing, hardware installation, testing, and packaging departments have 640, 500, 500, 340, and 200 hours available, respectively. Formulate a model to help managers determine how may guitars should be produced given its desire to maximize profits.

Solution:

We begin by defining the decision variables. In this case management must decide how many of each type of guitar to manufacture. Thus, we have the following decision variables:

Let A = the number of acoustic guitars to manufacture,

C = the number of classical guitars to manufacture, and

E = the number of electric guitars to manufacture.

Next, we need to state the objective mathematically. Recall, a mathematical statement of the objective for a given problem is called the objective function. Since our objective in this problem is to maximize profits we need a mathematical statement that reflects the amount of profits made based on the number of guitars manufactured:

$$\textit{Profit} = 25A + 55C + 75E$$

This equation states that the total profit made is the number of acoustic guitars manufactured at \$25 each plus the number of classical guitars made at \$55 each plus the number of electric guitars at \$75 each. Since management desires to maximize this, the objective function would be:

$$\textit{Maximize Profit} = 25A + 55C + 75E$$

We next need to consider the limitations or constraints associated with this decision. If there were no limitations or constraints in this problem the solution would be easy. Management would simply produce an infinite number guitars and make infinite profits. Unfortunately, in the real world mangers must deal with scarce resources and other constraints. In the present example, the guitar manufacturer is limited by the number of labor hours available in each production department and by the demand for its guitars.

Let's first address the limitation associated with the number of hours available to cut and craft the guitars. Recall that there are 800 hours available to cut and craft guitars. We also know that the time to cut and craft the acoustic, classical, and electric guitars is 2, 3, and 1 hour, respectively. Thus, what is needed is a mathematical statement that says that the number of hours spent cutting and crafting guitars must not exceed the 800 hours available. Such as statement is the following:

$$2A + 3C + 1E \leq 800$$

The left side of this equation represents the total number of hours that will be needed to cut and craft all the guitars manufactured since 2A is the time it will take to cut and craft the acoustic guitars, 3C is the time it will take for the classical guitars, and 1E is the time for the electric guitars. Thus, the above constraint says that the total number of hours needed to cut and craft the three different guitars must not exceed the 800 hours of labor time available.

In a similar fashion, we can develop constraints for the other departments:

$$3A + 3C + 1E \leq 640 \text{ (Assembly Department)}$$

$$1A + 1.5C + 0.5E \leq 500 \text{ (Finishing Department)}$$

$$1A + 1C + 2E \leq 500 \text{ (Hardware Installation)}$$

$$1.5A + 1C + 2E \leq 340 \text{ (Testing and Adjustment)}$$

$$0.5A + 0.75C + 0.25E \leq 200 \text{ (Packaging)}$$

Furthermore, since the company does not make any profit on guitars manufactured over and above what is demanded in the marketplace, we add the following constraints:

$$A \leq 175 \text{ (demand for acoustic guitars)}$$

$$C \leq 30 \text{ (demand for classical guitars)}$$

$$E \leq 100 \text{ (demand for electric guitars)}$$

Finally, since it is not possible to produce a negative number of guitars we add the following non-negativity constraints:

$A \geq 0$

$C \geq 0$

$E \geq 0$

Therefore, the complete model is:

$$\textit{Maximize Profit} = 25A + 55C + 75E$$

subject to the constraints

$2A + 3C + 1E \leq 800$

$3A + 3C + 1E \leq 640$

$1A + 1.5C + 0.5E \leq 500$

$1A + 1C + 2E \leq 500$

$1.5A + 1C + 2E \leq 340$

$0.5A + 0.75C + 0.25E \leq 200$

$A \leq 175$

$C \leq 30$

$E \leq 100$

$A \geq 0$

$C \geq 0$

$E \geq 0$

In the above model A, C, and E are the decision variables while the profits per guitar, operation times, and forecasted demands are parameters.

TRUE/FALSE QUESTIONS

1. __ Management science is typically only applicable to large multi-million dollar corporate projects.

2. __ As a formal discipline, management science was spawned by efforts to improve military operations prior to and during World War II.

3. __ The terms operations research and management science can be used interchangeably.

4. __ For models to be useful, they must capture every detail of the real problem.

5. __ The term "type III error" refers to solving the right problem using the wrong methodology.

6. __ The complexity of a problem increases when the potential number of courses of action is large.

7. __ Structuring a problem involves developing some type of model.

8. __ Descriptive models are aimed at forecasting or predicting future events.

9. __ An influence diagram is an example of a prescriptive model.

10. __ Controllable variables are called decision variables.

11. __ An objective function represents limitations or requirements imposed on acceptable values of the decision variables.

12. __ Problems where it is desired to minimize or maximize some objective function are called optimization problems.

13. __ Any solution that satisfies all constraints is called an optimal solution.

14. __ Models that include randomness are called deterministic.

15. __ Heuristics are rules that always find optimal solutions.

16. __ Sensitivity analysis involves investigating the effect to model results to changes in model data.

17. __ Since models include all important considerations, managers should implement model solutions without further consideration and not bias the results with human subjectivity.

18. __ The more well-structured a problem is, the more a manager can rely on management science model results.

19. __ Because management science is a relatively new discipline, it is deemed acceptable that the cost of solving the problem may exceed the benefits.

20. __ The operational research group that analyzed convoys in the early 1940s discovered that large convoys lost fewer total ships than small convoys.

Answers:

1. F, 2. T, 3. T, 4. F, 5. F, 6. T, 7. T, 8. F, 9. F, 10. T, 11. F, 12. T, 13. F, 14. F, 15. F, 16. T, 17. F, 18. T, 19. F, 20. T

CHAPTER 2

REVIEW

This chapter demonstrates that spreadsheets are excellent tools for working with mathematical management science models. A spreadsheet consists of cells in which numeric constants, text, and formulas can be entered. Cells exist at the intersection of all rows and columns. Typically, the rows in a spreadsheet are identified with numbers and the columns are identified with letters. By convention, each cell is given a unique name or address combining the letter of the column the cell is in with the number of the row the cell is in. For example, a cell in the fifth row of a spreadsheet and in the second column has the cell address B5 (or b5 since cell addresses are not case sensitive).

Well designed spreadsheets should have the following properties:

- They should provide accurate results.
- They should be understood by both the creator and users of the spreadsheet.
- They should be designed so that changes in the model are easily accommodated.
- They should be efficient in the sense that the user should be able to readily locate and observe important areas of the worksheet.

When designing and building a spreadsheet model it is helpful to keep the following in mind:

- Planning saves time and trouble. It is particularly helpful to plan the layout of a worksheet on paper before working on the computer.
- Document your worksheet.
- Use an effective layout. In general vertical layouts are preferred to horizontal layouts. Also the spreadsheet should begin with an easily viewed identification. Furthermore, separate sections of the worksheet should be defined for the data, work area, assumptions, definitions and formulas, and output.
- Pay attention to alignment and format. For example, all columns should be labeled.
- Use the printer wisely.
- Write clear formulas. Complex formulas should be divided into several cells.
- Always keep flexibility in mind.
- Learn to use the **Copy** command.
- Use the advanced spreadsheet capabilities such as the @functions and macros.
- Protect your worksheet from hardware and software failures by backing up your work frequently.

@Functions are used to perform special calculations. Useful Lotus 1-2-3 @functions include: @MIN, @MAX, @SUM, @AVG, @STD, @STDS, @NORMAL,

@POISSON, @SQRT, and @RAND. Another useful @function is the @IF(CONDITION,A,B). If the specified condition is true, the value A is put in the cell. If the condition is false, the value B is put in the cell. Note A and B can be either constants or formulas. For example,

B2: @IF(A1=2,C1*2,0)

states that if the value in cell A1 is 2, then the value of C1 times 2 is placed in cell B2, otherwise a zero is placed in cell B2. Conditions can include =, >, <, >=, <=, and <>.

The @VLOOKUP(A,X..Y,C) and @HLOOKUP(A,X..Y,C) functions allow you to look up a value in a table. The three arguments in this function correspond to the value to look up, the table range, and then number of the column whose value we want to use, respectively.

What-if tables allow you to investigate the results of substituting different values into formulas. Creating a what-if table requires that you fill a range with values for the variables you want to evaluate. The spreadsheet then evaluates the formula for every combination of values you specified and displays the results in the worksheet.

Spreadsheet use in management science is employed to perform: 1) data analysis, 2) what-if analysis, 3) goal seeking and optimization, or 4) risk analysis. Data analysis is concerned with organizing, summarizing, and displaying data that is used to develop management science models. What-if analysis is probably the most important use of spreadsheets and involves investigating how model results are affected by alternate decision strategies and changes to the inputs. Optimization involves seeking solutions that maximize or minimize the decision maker's objective. Two types of search processes used to seek good or optimal solutions are enumerative or heuristic search. Risk analysis involves repeated sampling from a probability distribution that describes the inputs to generate distributions for other variables of interest.

SOLVED PROBLEMS

Example Problem 1: Using the @IF Function and Absolute Cell Addresses

A wholesaler has decided to reevaluate the way it manages the inventory of one of its products. The company has determined that it costs $2 to hold this particular item in inventory for one week and it costs $3 per unit on backorder per week. Backorders occur when demand for the product exceeds the wholesaler's on-hand inventory. The manager evaluating the ordering policy has decided to test various ordering policies with the actual weekly demands for the last ten weeks. These demands are as follows: 72, 91, 96, 67, 35, 83, 78, 66, 65, and 77. The wholesaler wishes to determine what how much should be order each week so that the sum of inventory holding costs and shortage costs are minimized. Assume there is no beginning inventory, nor any shortages.

Solution:

A spreadsheet to facilitate the analysis of this problem is given in Figure 2-1. This spreadsheet has been divided into four areas: an input data section, an area where alternate values for the decision variable can be entered, a work area that keeps track of weekly ending inventory and backorders, and an output section that calculates the cost associated with the specified order quantity.

The weekly unit holding and shortage costs are entered in the input section. Entering these parameters as inputs provides maximum flexibility because the cost formulas refer to these input cells. Thus, if we need to change these parameters, we simply enter the new values over the old values. By using this approach, no changes are needed to the cost formulas should these parameters change.

In this example, the only decision variable is the amount to order each week. This quantity is entered in cell B9 in the spreadsheet shown in Figure 2-1. Entering alternate values for the order quantity and then observing the effect on costs should permit the decision maker to quickly identify good solutions to this problem.

The work area contains five columns. The actual formulas entered into the spreadsheet are shown in Figure 2-2. Labels identifying each week have been entered in column A. In column B the weekly demands for the last ten weeks have been entered. In column C a formula has been entered for the order quantity. Specifically, the formula +B$9 was entered in cell C15. The dollar sign in front of the 9 means that the 9 will remain constant when this formula is copied. Thus, by making use of absolute cell addressing in our formula we are able to enter the formula once in cell C15 and then copy it down to cells C16 to C23. If we had not placed the dollar sign in front of the 9, when we copied the formula from cell C15 to cell C16, the order quantity for week 2 would have used the value in cell B10, not cell B9.

In columns D and E formulas that calculate the ending inventory and ending backorders were entered, respectively. The logic for calculating ending inventory is: if the ending inventory from the prior period plus the amount ordered in the current period is greater than the current weekly demand plus the ending backorders from the prior period, then ending inventory equals (the ending inventory from the prior period plus the amount ordered in the current period) minus (the current weekly demand plus the backorders from the prior period), otherwise ending inventory equals zero. The same logic applies to calculating ending backorders. Specifically, if current weekly demand plus the prior period's ending backorders are greater than this week's order quantity plus the prior period's ending inventory, then backorders equal (current weekly demand plus the prior period's ending backorders) minus (this week's order quantity plus the prior period's

Figure 2-1

A	A	B	C	D	E
1	**Inventory Cost Calculation**				
2					
3	**Input Data:**				
4	Holding Cost				
5	Shortage Cost				
6					
7					
8	**Decision Variable**				
9	Order Quantity				
10					
11	**Work Area**				
12					
13		Weekly	Order	Ending	Ending
14	Week	Demand	Quantity	Inventory	Backorders
15	1	72	0	0	72
16	2	91	0	0	163
17	3	96	0	0	259
18	4	67	0	0	326
19	5	35	0	0	361
20	6	83	0	0	444
21	7	78	0	0	522
22	8	66	0	0	588
23	9	65	0	0	653
24	10	77	0	0	730
25					
26	**Model Outputs**				
27	Inventory Cost	$0.0			
28	Backorder Cost	$0.0			
29	Total Cost	$0.0			

Figure 2-2

A	A	B	C	D	E
1	**Inventory Cost Calculation**				
2					
3	**Input Data:**				
4	Holding Cost				
5	Shortage Cost				
6					
7					
8	**Decision Variable**				
9	Order Quantity				
10					
11	**Work Area**				
12					
13		Weekly	Order	Ending	Ending
14	Week	Demand	Quantity	Inventory	Backorders
15	1	72	+B$9	@IF(C15>B15,C15-B15,0)	@IF(B15>C15,B15-C15,0)
16	2	91	+B$9	@IF(C16+D15>B16+E15,C16+D15-B16-E15,0)	@IF(B16+E15>C16+D15,B16+E15-C16-D15,0)
17	3	96	+B$9	@IF(C17+D16>B17+E16,C17+D16-B17-E16,0)	@IF(B17+E16>C17+D16,B17+E16-C17-D16,0)
18	4	67	+B$9	@IF(C18+D17>B18+E17,C18+D17-B18-E17,0)	@IF(B18+E17>C18+D17,B18+E17-C18-D17,0)
19	5	35	+B$9	@IF(C19+D18>B19+E18,C19+D18-B19-E18,0)	@IF(B19+E18>C19+D18,B19+E18-C19-D18,0)
20	6	83	+B$9	@IF(C20+D19>B20+E19,C20+D19-B20-E19,0)	@IF(B20+E19>C20+D19,B20+E19-C20-D19,0)
21	7	78	+B$9	@IF(C21+D20>B21+E20,C21+D20-B21-E20,0)	@IF(B21+E20>C21+D20,B21+E20-C21-D20,0)
22	8	66	+B$9	@IF(C22+D21>B22+E21,C22+D21-B22-E21,0)	@IF(B22+E21>C22+D21,B22+E21-C22-D21,0)
23	9	65	+B$9	@IF(C23+D22>B23+E22,C23+D22-B23-E22,0)	@IF(B23+E22>C23+D22,B23+E22-C23-D22,0)
24	10	77	+B$9	@IF(C24+D23>B24+E23,C24+D23-B24-E23,0)	@IF(B24+E23>C24+D23,B24+E23-C24-D23,0)
25					
26	**Model Outputs**				
27	Inventory Cost	@SUM(D24..D15)*B4			
28	Backorder Cost	@SUM(E24..E15)*B5			
29	Total Cost	@SUM(B28..B27)			

ending inventory, otherwise backorders are equal to zero. To capture this logic, the @IF function is needed.

Recall the format of the @IF function is: @IF(CONDITION,A,B). The way this function works is if the condition is true then the value of A is placed in the cell, otherwise B is placed in the cell. Note, both A and B can be either constants or formulas.

The formulas that calculate the ending inventory and backorders for period one are different from the other weeks since in week one there are no backorders or inventories from the prior period. The following formula to calculate the ending inventory in period 1 was entered in cell D15:

@IF(C15>B15,C15-B15,0)

This formula says that if the amount received in period 1 (cell C15) is greater than the amount demanded in period 1 (cell B15) the amount of inventory left over at the end of period 1 is the difference between the available inventory and what was demanded (i.e., C15-B15). On the other hand, if the amount demanded exceeds the amount available, then no inventory would be left over at the end of the period. A similar formula was entered in cell E15 that calculates the ending backorders for period 1 as follows:

@IF(B15>C15,B15-C15,0)

The formulas for the ending inventory levels and ending backorders for periods two through ten are entered in a similar fashion except that the previous period's inventory level and backorders need to be considered. Inventory from the previous period can be used to meet the current period's demands, while backorders from the previous period serve to increase the current period's demand. Thus, in cell D16 ending inventory in period 2 is calculated as:

@IF(C16+D15>B16+E15,C16+D15-B16-E15,0)

and in cell E16 ending backorders in period 2 is calculated as:

@IF(B16+E15>C16+D15,B16+E15-C16-D15,0)

Once these formulas are entered in cells D16 and E16, respectively, they can be copied to cells D17..E24.

Finally, the model outputs section contains formulas that calculate the inventory cost, backorder cost and total cost over the ten weeks investigated. Since the cost to hold one unit in inventory one week was entered in cell B4, the total inventory holding cost (cell B27) was calculated as the sum of the ending inventory values in column D times the quantity entered in B4. Likewise, the cost of being short one unit for per week is entered in cell B5 and thus the backorder cost (cell B28) was calculated as the sum of the backorder values in column E time the quantity entered in cell B5. A formula for the total costs was entered in cell B29 as the sum of the total inventory and backorder costs. While it was not necessary to break the total costs down into total inventory costs and total backorder costs, the process of entering long and/or complex formulas is greatly simplified if such formulas can be broken down into logical chunks and entered into separate cells. Not only is it easier to enter formulas this way, but it is also easier to identify the source of errors when formulas are split up and entered in separate cells. Furthermore, in this case, the decision maker might be interested in knowing what the inventory and backorder costs are in addition to knowing what the total costs are.

In Figure 2-3 the weekly unit holding cost and backorder costs were entered in cells B4 and B5, respectively. Also, since the total demand over the ten weeks adds up to 730 units, a weekly order quantity of 73 units (730 units/10 weeks) was first investigated and entered into cell B9. The cost associated with this order quantity is $354 (cell B29 in Figure 2-3). Looking at the other outputs, we see that the backorder costs are much larger than the inventory costs. Thus, we might be able to lower total costs by increasing the order quantity. This will have the effect of increasing inventory costs and decreasing backorder costs. In Figure 2-4 the order quantity was increased by five units to 78. We observe that our total costs have increased to $574. As can be seen by comparing Figures 2-3 and 2-4, inventory costs increased more than backorder costs decreased. In Figure 2-5 we investigate an order quantity of 74. As is illustrated in Figure 2-5, an order quantity of 74 provides the lowest total costs of the three order quantities investigated. The decision maker could continue entering other order quantities until he/she was satisfied with the solution obtained.

Example Problem 2: Using the @VLOOKUP Function

> The supplier of the manufacturer discussed in Example Problem 1 above has decided to offer quantity discounts on orders. Specifically, the unit cost of the item is $15 if 1-74 units are ordered, $12 if 75-99 units are ordered, and $10 if 100 or more units are ordered. Given this development, modify the previous spreadsheet to help this manufacturer decide how much to order.

Solution:

Only a few changes to the spreadsheet shown in Figure 2-1 are required. First, in the input data section the quantity discount information will be entered in a form so that the @VLOOKUP function can be used to determine the appropriate price to use in calculating the total purchase cost. This information was entered in cells D5..E7 and is shown in Figure 2-6. The formulas for the worksheet are shown in Figure 2-7. When the range D5..E7 is specified as the range in the @VLOOKUP function with an offset of 1, an order quantity between 1 and 74, will return 15. Likewise, an order quantity of 75-99 will return 12. Finally, an order quantity of 100 or more returns 10.

Figure 2-3

A	A	B	C	D	E
1	**Inventory Cost Calculation**				
2					
3	**Input Data:**				
4	Holding Cost	2			
5	Shortage Cost	3			
6					
7					
8	**Decision Variable**				
9	Order Quantity	73			
10					
11	**Work Area**				
12					
13		Weekly	Order	Ending	Ending
14	Week	Demand	Quantity	Inventory	Backorders
15	1	72	73	1	0
16	2	91	73	0	17
17	3	96	73	0	40
18	4	67	73	0	34
19	5	35	73	4	0
20	6	83	73	0	6
21	7	78	73	0	11
22	8	66	73	0	4
23	9	65	73	4	0
24	10	77	73	0	0
25					
26	**Model Outputs**				
27	Inventory Cost	$18.0			
28	Backorder Cost	$336.0			
29	Total Cost	$354.0			

Figure 2-4

A	A	B	C	D	E
1	**Inventory Cost Calculation**				
2					
3	**Input Data:**				
4	Holding Cost	2			
5	Shortage Cost	3			
6					
7					
8	**Decision Variable**				
9	Order Quantity	78			
10					
11	**Work Area**				
12					
13		Weekly	Order	Ending	Ending
14	Week	Demand	Quantity	Inventory	Backorders
15	1	72	78	6	0
16	2	91	78	0	7
17	3	96	78	0	25
18	4	67	78	0	14
19	5	35	78	29	0
20	6	83	78	24	0
21	7	78	78	24	0
22	8	66	78	36	0
23	9	65	78	49	0
24	10	77	78	50	0
25					
26	**Model Outputs**				
27	Inventory Cost	$436.0			
28	Backorder Cost	$138.0			
29	Total Cost	$574.0			

Figure 2-5

A	A	B	C	D	E
1	**Inventory Cost Calculation**				
2					
3	**Input Data:**				
4	Holding Cost	2			
5	Shortage Cost	3			
6					
7					
8	**Decision Variable**				
9	Order Quantity	74			
10					
11	**Work Area**				
12					
13		Weekly	Order	Ending	Ending
14	Week	Demand	Quantity	Inventory	Backorders
15	1	72	74	2	0
16	2	91	74	0	15
17	3	96	74	0	37
18	4	67	74	0	30
19	5	35	74	9	0
20	6	83	74	0	0
21	7	78	74	0	4
22	8	66	74	4	0
23	9	65	74	13	0
24	10	77	74	10	0
25					
26	**Model Outputs**				
27	Inventory Cost	$76.0			
28	Backorder Cost	$258.0			
29	Total Cost	$334.0			

Figure 2-6

A	A	B	C	D	E
1	**Inventory Cost Calculation With Quantity Discounts**				
2					
3	**Input Data:**			Order	
4	Holding Cost			Quantity	Cost
5	Shortage Cost			1	15
6				75	12
7				100	10
8	**Decision Variable**				
9	Order Quantity				
10					
11	**Work Area**				
12					
13		Weekly	Order	Ending	Ending
14	Week	Demand	Quantity	Inventory	Backorders
15	1	72	0	0	72
16	2	91	0	0	163
17	3	96	0	0	259
18	4	67	0	0	326
19	5	35	0	0	361
20	6	83	0	0	444
21	7	78	0	0	522
22	8	66	0	0	588
23	9	65	0	0	653
24	10	77	0	0	730
25					
26	**Model Outputs**				
27	Inventory Cost	$0.0			
28	Backorder Cost	$0.0			
29	Purchase Cost	ERR			
30	Total Cost	ERR			

Figure 2-7

	A	B	C	D	E
1	**Inventory Cost Calculation With Quantity Discounts**				
2					
3	**Input Data:**			Order	
4	Holding Cost			Quantity	Cost
5	Shortage Cost			1	15
6				75	12
7				100	10
8	**Decision Variable**				
9	Order Quantity				
10					
11	**Work Area**				
12					
13		Weekly	Order	Ending	Ending
14	Week	Demand	Quantity	Inventory	Backorders
15	1	72	+B$9	@IF(C15>B15,C15-B15,0)	@IF(B15>C15,B15-C15,0)
16	2	91	+B$9	@IF(C16+D15>B16+E15,C16+D15-B16-E15,0)	@IF(B16+E15>C16+D15,B16+E15-C16-D15,0)
17	3	96	+B$9	@IF(C17+D16>B17+E16,C17+D16-B17-E16,0)	@IF(B17+E16>C17+D16,B17+E16-C17-D16,0)
18	4	67	+B$9	@IF(C18+D17>B18+E17,C18+D17-B18-E17,0)	@IF(B18+E17>C18+D17,B18+E17-C18-D17,0)
19	5	35	+B$9	@IF(C19+D18>B19+E18,C19+D18-B19-E18,0)	@IF(B19+E18>C19+D18,B19+E18-C19-D18,0)
20	6	83	+B$9	@IF(C20+D19>B20+E19,C20+D19-B20-E19,0)	@IF(B20+E19>C20+D19,B20+E19-C20-D19,0)
21	7	78	+B$9	@IF(C21+D20>B21+E20,C21+D20-B21-E20,0)	@IF(B21+E20>C21+D20,B21+E20-C21-D20,0)
22	8	66	+B$9	@IF(C22+D21>B22+E21,C22+D21-B22-E21,0)	@IF(B22+E21>C22+D21,B22+E21-C22-D21,0)
23	9	65	+B$9	@IF(C23+D22>B23+E22,C23+D22-B23-E22,0)	@IF(B23+E22>C23+D22,B23+E22-C23-D22,0)
24	10	77	+B$9	@IF(C24+D23>B24+E23,C24+D23-B24-E23,0)	@IF(B24+E23>C24+D23,B24+E23-C24-D23,0)
25					
26	**Model Outputs**				
27	Inventory Cost	@SUM(D24..D15)*B4			
28	Backorder Cost	@SUM(E24..E15)*B5			
29	Purchase Cost	+B9*10*@VLOOKUP(B9,D5..E7,1)			
30	Total Cost	@SUM(B29..B27)			

The other change that was made was that purchase cost was added as a model output and the formula that calculates the total cost was modified to sum up inventory cost, backorder cost, and purchase cost. The logic to calculate purchase cost is to add up the total number of units purchased over the ten weeks and multiply this quantity by the appropriate unit cost. Recall, the appropriate unit cost depends on the amount ordered each time. Since the amount ordered each time is entered in cell B9, we can use the @VLOOKUP function as follows to determine the appropriate unit cost:

@VLOOKUP(B9,D5..E7,1)

Thus, the value entered in cell B9 is used to find the appropriate unit cost in the range D5..E7. To illustrate, if 35 were entered in cell B9, then 15 would be returned since 35 is greater than 1 but less than 75. Similarly, if 88 were entered in cell B9, then 12 would be returned since 88 is greater than 75 but less than 100.

The complete formula for calculating the purchase price of all units ordered over the ten weeks was entered in cell B29 as:

+B9*10*@VLOOKUP(B9,D5..E7,1)

Thus, the total purchase price is equal to the amount ordered each week as entered in cell B9 times the ten weeks times the appropriate unit price as determined with the @VLOOKUP function.

In Figure 2-8 our previous best order quantity of 74 units was entered. This results in a total cost of $11,434. In Figure 2-9 the smallest order quantity that qualified for the first price break was entered. This action reduced total costs to $9,379. Finally, in Figure 2-10, the smallest order quantity that qualified for the lowest unit cost was entered. Because inventory cost increased more than purchase cost decreased, ordering 100 units or more per week is not cost effective.

Example Problem 3: Enumerative Analysis of Guitar Manufacturer Production Mix Decision

In Example Problem 3 of Chapter 1, information about a guitar manufacturer was given. Develop a spreadsheet that will allow the decision maker to experiment with and determine the implications associated with alternate values of the decision variables.

Solution:

The spreadsheet shown in Figure 2-11 was created to help this manufacturer decide how many of each guitar to make. The formulas for this spreadsheet are shown in Figure 2-12.

Figure 2-8

	A	B	C	D	E
1	**Inventory Cost Calculation With Quantity Discounts**				
2					
3	**Input Data:**			Order	
4	Holding Cost	2		Quantity	Cost
5	Shortage Cost	3		1	15
6				75	12
7				100	10
8	**Decision Variable**				
9	Order Quantity	74			
10					
11	**Work Area**				
12					
13		Weekly	Order	Ending	Ending
14	Week	Demand	Quantity	Inventory	Backorders
15	1	72	74	2	0
16	2	91	74	0	15
17	3	96	74	0	37
18	4	67	74	0	30
19	5	35	74	9	0
20	6	83	74	0	0
21	7	78	74	0	4
22	8	66	74	4	0
23	9	65	74	13	0
24	10	77	74	10	0
25					
26	**Model Outputs**				
27	Inventory Cost	$76.0			
28	Backorder Cost	$258.0			
29	Purchase Cost	$11,100.0			
30	Total Cost	$11,434.0			

Figure 2-9

A	A	B	C	D	E
1	**Inventory Cost Calculation With Quantity Discounts**				
2					
3	**Input Data:**			Order	
4	Holding Cost	2		Quantity	Cost
5	Shortage Cost	3		1	15
6				75	12
7				100	10
8	**Decision Variable**				
9	Order Quantity	75			
10					
11	**Work Area**				
12					
13		Weekly	Order	Ending	Ending
14	Week	Demand	Quantity	Inventory	Backorders
15	1	72	75	3	0
16	2	91	75	0	13
17	3	96	75	0	34
18	4	67	75	0	26
19	5	35	75	14	0
20	6	83	75	6	0
21	7	78	75	3	0
22	8	66	75	12	0
23	9	65	75	22	0
24	10	77	75	20	0
25					
26	**Model Outputs**				
27	Inventory Cost	$160.0			
28	Backorder Cost	$219.0			
29	Purchase Cost	$9,000.0			
30	Total Cost	$9,379.0			

Figure 2-10

	A	B	C	D	E
1	**Inventory Cost Calculation With Quantity Discounts**				
2					
3	**Input Data:**			Order	
4	Holding Cost	2		Quantity	Cost
5	Shortage Cost	3		1	15
6				75	12
7				100	10
8	**Decision Variable**				
9	Order Quantity	100			
10					
11	**Work Area**				
12					
13		Weekly	Order	Ending	Ending
14	Week	Demand	Quantity	Inventory	Backorders
15	1	72	100	28	0
16	2	91	100	37	0
17	3	96	100	41	0
18	4	67	100	74	0
19	5	35	100	139	0
20	6	83	100	156	0
21	7	78	100	178	0
22	8	66	100	212	0
23	9	65	100	247	0
24	10	77	100	270	0
25					
26	**Model Outputs**				
27	Inventory Cost	$2,764.0			
28	Backorder Cost	$0.0			
29	Purchase Cost	$10,000.0			
30	Total Cost	$12,764.0			

Figure 2-11

A	A	B	C	D	E
1	**Guitar Manufacturer Production Mix Decision**				
2					
3	**Model Inputs:**				
4		Acoustics	Classicals	Electrics	Available
5	Profit/Guitar	$25	$55	$75	
6	Cutting Time	2.00	3.00	1.00	800
7	Assembly Time	3.00	3.00	1.00	640
8	Finishing Time	1.00	1.50	0.50	500
9	Hardware Install.	1.00	1.00	2.00	500
10	Testing	1.50	1.00	2.00	340
11	Packaging	0.50	0.75	0.25	200
12	Demand Forecast	175	30	100	
13					
14	**Decision Variables:**				
15					
16	Acoustics				
17	Classicals				
18	Electrics				
19					
20	**Model Outputs:**				
21					
22		Value	Limit	Slack	
23	Profit	0			
24	Cutting Time	0	800	800	
25	Assembly Time	0	640	640	
26	Finishing Time	0	500	500	
27	Hardware Install.	0	500	500	
28	Testing	0	340	340	
29	Packaging	0	200	200	
30	Acoustics Made	0	175	175	
31	Classicals Made	0	30	30	
32	Electrics Made	0	100	100	

Figure 2-12

A	A	B	C	D	E
1	**Guitar Manufacturer Production Mix Decision**				
2					
3	**Model Inputs:**				
4		Acoustics	Classicals	Electrics	Available
5	Profit/Guitar	$25	$55	$75	
6	Cutting Time	2.00	3.00	1.00	800
7	Assembly Time	3.00	3.00	1.00	640
8	Finishing Time	1.00	1.50	0.50	500
9	Hardware Install.	1.00	1.00	2.00	500
10	Testing	1.50	1.00	2.00	340
11	Packaging	0.50	0.75	0.25	200
12	Demand Forecast	175	30	100	
13					
14	**Decision Variables:**				
15					
16	Acoustics				
17	Classicals				
18	Electrics				
19					
20	**Model Outputs:**				
21					
22		Value	Limit	Slack	
23	Profit	(B$16*B5)+(B$17*C5)+(B$18*D5)			
24	Cutting Time	(B$16*B6)+(B$17*C6)+(B$18*D6)	+E6	+C24-B24	
25	Assembly Time	(B$16*B7)+(B$17*C7)+(B$18*D7)	+E7	+C25-B25	
26	Finishing Time	(B$16*B8)+(B$17*C8)+(B$18*D8)	+E8	+C26-B26	
27	Hardware Install.	(B$16*B9)+(B$17*C9)+(B$18*D9)	+E9	+C27-B27	
28	Testing	(B$16*B10)+(B$17*C10)+(B$18*D10)	+E10	+C28-B28	
29	Packaging	(B$16*B11)+(B$17*C11)+(B$18*D11)	+E11	+C29-B29	
30	Acoustics Made	+B16	+B12	+C30-B30	
31	Classicals Made	+B17	+C12	+C31-B31	
32	Electrics Made	+B18	+D12	+C32-B32	

The top of the worksheet contains cells where the model inputs were entered. The model inputs include the profit margins for the three guitars, the operation times for each guitar in each department, the amount of time available in each department, and the demand forecasts for each guitar.

The next section of the worksheet contains cells where alternate values can be entered for the three decision variables. Recall, the decision variables were how many acoustic, classical, and electric guitars to manufacture. The values for the three decision variables are entered in cells B16, B17, and B18, respectively.

In the model outputs section, the first row calculates the value of the objective function, or profit in this case. As is shown in Figure 2-12, this was accomplished by multiplying the value entered for each decision variable times the respective profit margin stored in the Models Input section. The remaining rows correspond to the constraints developed for the prescriptive model. To illustrate, consider row 24. In the *value* column of row 24, a formula that calculates the total amount of time required to cut all the guitars specified in cells B16..B18 has been entered. This formula is based on the values of the decision variables entered in cells B16..B18, and the parameters entered in the Model Inputs section. Entering the formula in this fashion facilitates investigating how changes to either the decision variables or model parameters affect the model results because none of the formulas would need to be modified should such a change be made. The *limit* column for row 24 contains a formula that refers to the available time in the cutting department entered in cell E6. Finally, the *slack* column in row 24 represents the amount of unused time that is still available in the cutting department. Slack is computed by subtracting the *value* column from the *limit* column. Because of the way the input data was organized, once the formulas were entered in row 24, they were then copied to rows 25 through 29. Thus, thinking about how the input data was going to be used ahead of time greatly facilitated the development of the model outputs.

Figures 2-13 through 2-16 illustrate the enumerative procedure. In Figure 2-13, it was decided to make as many electric guitars as possible since they have the highest profit margin. Given the demand forecast for electric guitars, 100 was entered in cell B18. This results in a profit of $7,500 and all of the resources have slack. Next, since classical guitars are the next most profitable, 30 was entered in cell B17 as shown in Figure 2-14. This results in a profit of $9,150 and still all resources have slack. Therefore, it was decided to add 175 acoustic guitars to the solution. However, as shown in Figure 2-15, adding 175 acoustic guitars is not a feasible solution since it would require 75 more assembly hours than are available and 153 more testing and packaging hours than are available. Since each acoustic guitar requires 1.5 hours of testing, and since we are short by 153 hours in testing, we need to reduce the number of acoustic guitars by at least 100. In Figure 2-16 the number of acoustic guitars has been reduced to 73 and we now have a feasible solution that generates a profit of $10,975.

Figure 2-13

	A	B	C	D	E
1	**Guitar Manufacturer Production Mix Decision**				
2					
3	**Model Inputs:**				
4		Acoustics	Classicals	Electrics	Available
5	Profit/Guitar	$25	$55	$75	
6	Cutting Time	2.00	3.00	1.00	800
7	Assembly Time	3.00	3.00	1.00	640
8	Finishing Time	1.00	1.50	0.50	500
9	Hardware Install.	1.00	1.00	2.00	500
10	Testing	1.50	1.00	2.00	340
11	Packaging	0.50	0.75	0.25	200
12	Demand Forecast	175	30	100	
13					
14	**Decision Variables:**				
15					
16	Acoustics	0			
17	Classicals	0			
18	Electrics	100			
19					
20	**Model Outputs:**				
21					
22		Value	Limit	Slack	
23	Profit	7500			
24	Cutting Time	100	800	700	
25	Assembly Time	100	640	540	
26	Finishing Time	50	500	450	
27	Hardware Install.	200	500	300	
28	Testing	200	340	140	
29	Packaging	25	200	175	
30	Acoustics Made	0	175	175	
31	Classicals Made	0	30	30	
32	Electrics Made	100	100	0	

Figure 2-14

A	A	B	C	D	E
1	**Guitar Manufacturer Production Mix Decision**				
2					
3	**Model Inputs:**				
4		Acoustics	Classicals	Electrics	Available
5	Profit/Guitar	$25	$55	$75	
6	Cutting Time	2.00	3.00	1.00	800
7	Assembly Time	3.00	3.00	1.00	640
8	Finishing Time	1.00	1.50	0.50	500
9	Hardware Install.	1.00	1.00	2.00	500
10	Testing	1.50	1.00	2.00	340
11	Packaging	0.50	0.75	0.25	200
12	Demand Forecast	175	30	100	
13					
14	**Decision Variables:**				
15					
16	Acoustics	0			
17	Classicals	30			
18	Electrics	100			
19					
20	**Model Outputs:**				
21					
22		Value	Limit	Slack	
23	Profit	9150			
24	Cutting Time	190	800	610	
25	Assembly Time	190	640	450	
26	Finishing Time	95	500	405	
27	Hardware Install.	230	500	270	
28	Testing	230	340	110	
29	Packaging	47.5	200	153	
30	Acoustics Made	0	175	175	
31	Classicals Made	30	30	0	
32	Electrics Made	100	100	0	

Figure 2-15

	A	B	C	D	E
1	**Guitar Manufacturer Production Mix Decision**				
2					
3	**Model Inputs:**				
4		Acoustics	Classicals	Electrics	Available
5	Profit/Guitar	$25	$55	$75	
6	Cutting Time	2.00	3.00	1.00	800
7	Assembly Time	3.00	3.00	1.00	640
8	Finishing Time	1.00	1.50	0.50	500
9	Hardware Install.	1.00	1.00	2.00	500
10	Testing	1.50	1.00	2.00	340
11	Packaging	0.50	0.75	0.25	200
12	Demand Forecast	175	30	100	
13					
14	**Decision Variables:**				
15					
16	Acoustics	175			
17	Classicals	30			
18	Electrics	100			
19					
20	**Model Outputs:**				
21					
22		Value	Limit	Slack	
23	Profit	13525			
24	Cutting Time	540	800	260	
25	Assembly Time	715	640	-75	
26	Finishing Time	270	500	230	
27	Hardware Install.	405	500	95	
28	Testing	492.5	340	-153	
29	Packaging	135	200	65	
30	Acoustics Made	175	175	0	
31	Classicals Made	30	30	0	
32	Electrics Made	100	100	0	

Figure 2-16

	A	B	C	D	E
1	**Guitar Manufacturer Production Mix Decision**				
2					
3	**Model Inputs:**				
4		Acoustics	Classicals	Electrics	Available
5	Profit/Guitar	$25	$55	$75	
6	Cutting Time	2.00	3.00	1.00	800
7	Assembly Time	3.00	3.00	1.00	640
8	Finishing Time	1.00	1.50	0.50	500
9	Hardware Install.	1.00	1.00	2.00	500
10	Testing	1.50	1.00	2.00	340
11	Packaging	0.50	0.75	0.25	200
12	Demand Forecast	175	30	100	
13					
14	**Decision Variables:**				
15					
16	Acoustics	73			
17	Classicals	30			
18	Electrics	100			
19					
20	**Model Outputs:**				
21					
22		Value	Limit	Slack	
23	Profit	10975			
24	Cutting Time	336	800	464	
25	Assembly Time	409	640	231	
26	Finishing Time	168	500	332	
27	Hardware Install.	303	500	197	
28	Testing	339.5	340	1	
29	Packaging	84	200	116	
30	Acoustics Made	73	175	102	
31	Classicals Made	30	30	0	
32	Electrics Made	100	100	0	

TRUE/FALSE QUESTIONS

1. ___ Because formulas entered into spreadsheets are more susceptible to undetected errors than standard computer programs, the user must exercise extra care when developing spreadsheets.

2. ___ While lengthy formulas are particularly vulnerable to undetected errors, there is nothing that can be done to help reduce these errors.

3. ___ Spreadsheets should be efficient in the sense that the user should be able to readily locate and observe critical areas of the worksheet.

4. ___ Since it is easy to retrieve spreadsheet files and observe their contents, descriptive file names do not need to be used.

5. ___ In general, a good layout should be horizontal rather than vertical.

6. ___ For efficiency reasons, complex calculations should not be divided into several cells.

7. ___ What-if tables can be used to show the results of substituting different values in formulas.

8. ___ Conducting sensitivity analyses to answer a variety of what-if questions is one of the most important uses of spreadsheets in management science.

9. ___ The automatic recalculation feature of spreadsheets allows a decision maker to evaluate a variety of scenarios and interactively seek solutions to a given problem.

10. ___ Enumerative search depends on intelligently modifying solutions to work towards the best solution.

Answers:

1. T, 2. F, 3. T, 4. F, 5. F, 6. F, 7. T, 8. T, 9. T, 10. F

CHAPTER 3

REVIEW

This chapter provides additional information on developing and using management science models. It is noted that the process of developing a model is highly intuitive and is more of an art than science. Often models are developed by imitating the modeling efforts of others. However, a drawback associated with imitation is it limits creativity and the ability to develop models for unique situations. It is also worth noting that developing mathematical models requires more logical thinking than mathematical skills.

A model is used to provide structure to an ill-defined situation. There is always more than one correct way to model a given problem. Models should be simple, complete, robust, consistent, and flexible.

The first step in model development is to understand the system and environment in which the model will be used. This is often best accomplished by drawing some kind of picture such as an influence diagram, flowchart, or a picture of the physical system itself.

After the system and environment are understood, attention focuses on determining the purpose of the modeling and gaining an understanding of the problem assumptions. This is then followed by identifying what data are available. Next, available solution methods and software are explored. In general, there are two types of software available for solving problems: special purposed packages and general purpose modeling packages. Finally, the quality of the solution obtained is assessed. In general, the more detailed a model, the better it will reflect reality. However, it is important to first determine how accurate the solution needs to be.

Guidelines for developing management science models include:

- Organize the information and define the variables.
- If possible, draw a picture.
- Define the symbols. Typically, decision variables are denoted by letters at the end of the alphabet while uncontrollable variables and parameters are denoted by letters at the beginning of the alphabet.
- Construct the model by writing down the relationships among variables in mathematical terms.
- Solve and/or analyze the model.

Modelers must also evaluate models in terms of their appropriateness and validity. Validity refers to how well a model represents reality. It is important that a model be able to predict performance that would be observed in the actual system.

Often modeling is used more to obtain insight into a situation than in obtaining actual numbers. Sensitivity analysis is useful for achieving such insights. Also, modeling can be viewed as a process of enrichment and elaboration. Typically, the modeling process begins with simple models that are subsequently enhanced to better capture the complexity of the real situation. Models are enhanced by changing constants into variables, adding new variables, relaxing some of the assumptions, and adding randomness to the model. Indeed, recognizing that many models are simply minor variations or extensions of other models greatly facilitates the modeling process.

SOLVED PROBLEM

Example Problem: Using the Guidelines for Developing Management Science Models

A manufacturer has two plants that supply its four warehouses. Plant 1 can produce 500 units per year and plant 2 can produce 400 units per year. The demand forecast for the four warehouses is 250, 150, 200, and 300 units, respectively. The cost to ship one unit from a given plant to a particular warehouse is given in the table below:

Plant	Warehouse 1	Warehouse 2	Warehouse 3	Warehouse 4
1	$1	$2	$4	$5
2	$3	$1	$2	$4

Applying the Guidelines:

The first step is to organize the information and to define the variables. We can organize all the relevant information into the following table:

Cost to Ship One Unit from a Given Plant to a Given Warehouse

Plant	Warehouse 1	Warehouse 2	Warehouse 3	Warehouse 4	Capacity
1	$1	$2	$4	$5	500
2	$3	$1	$2	$4	400
Demand	250	150	200	300	

The information in this table are the parameters for this situation. Also we must define the decision variables. In this situation the decision variables are the amount to ship from each plant to each warehouse.

It is helpful to draw a picture that shows the relationships among our variables and parameters. One way to represent this situation with a picture is as follows:

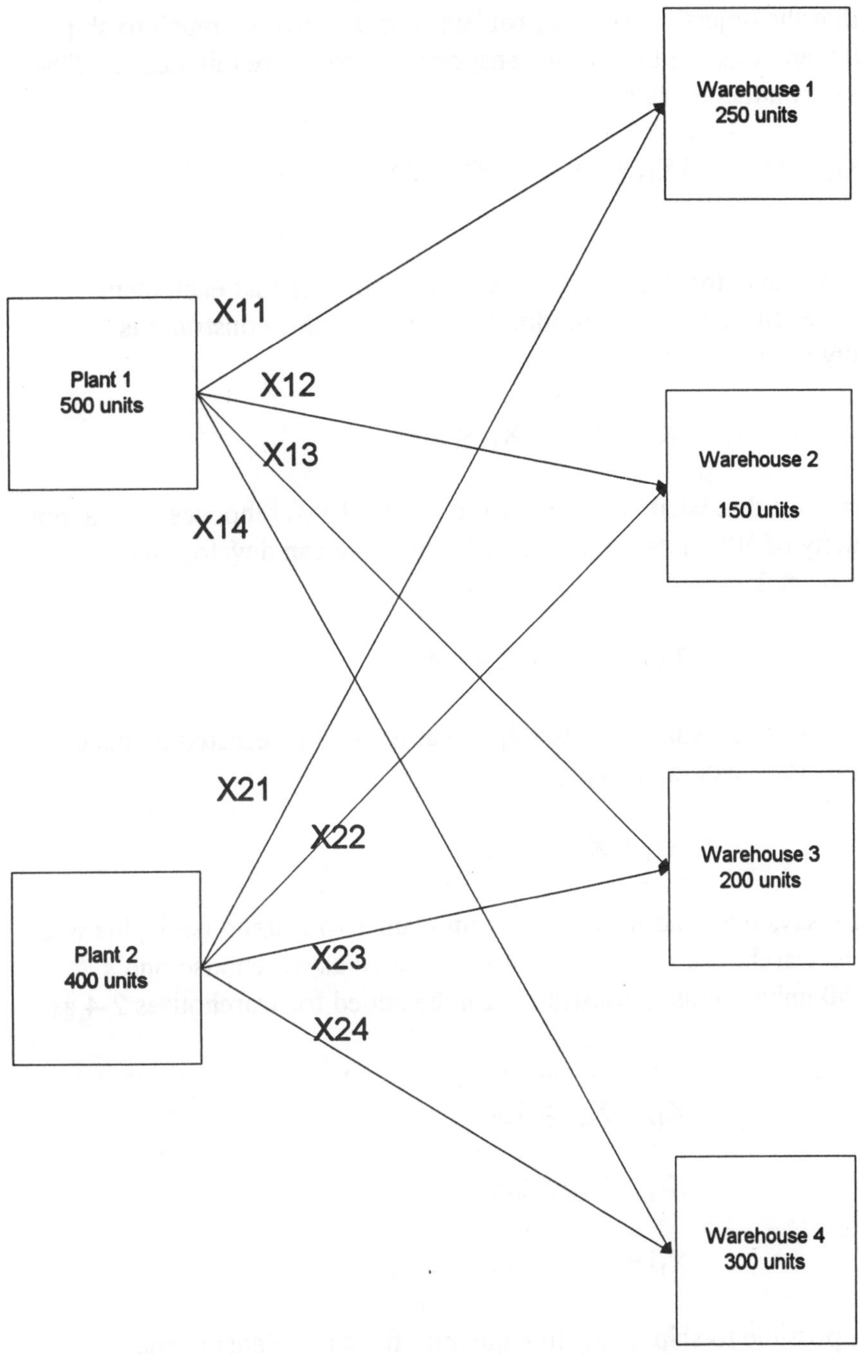

The next step is to establish symbols. In keeping with convention, we will use letters toward the end of the alphabet to represent our decision variables. One way to symbolically define the decision variables is as follows:

Let X_{ij} = the amount to ship from plant i to warehouse j, for i = 1, 2, and j = 1, 2, 3, 4.

The next step is to construct a model by writing down all the relationships among the variables in mathematical terms. Although it was not stated explicitly, it is clear from the nature of the problem that the objective for this problem is to decide how much to ship from each plant to each warehouse so that total transportation costs are minimized. This objective can be expressed mathematically as:

$$\text{Min Costs} = 1X_{11} + 2X_{12} + 4X_{13} + 5X_{14} + 3X_{21} + 1X_{22} + 2X_{23} + 4X_{24}$$

Next, we can add the constraints for this situation. One constraint is that each plant cannot ship more than it has the capacity to produce. For plant 1 this constraint is expressed mathematically as:

$$X_{11} + X_{12} + X_{13} + X_{14} \leq 500$$

In English this constraint says that what is shipped from plant 1 to warehouses 1-4 cannot exceed plant one's capacity of 500 units. In a similar fashion, we can develop the following constraint for plant 2:

$$X_{21} + 2X_{22} + X_{23} + X_{24} \leq 400$$

Next, we want to ensure that each warehouse is shipped at least its forecasted demand. For warehouse 1 this constraint would be expressed as:

$$X_{11} + X_{21} \geq 250$$

In English, this constraint says that what is shipped from plant 1 to warehouse 1 plus what is shipped from plant 2 to warehouse 1 must be at least as much as warehouse one's forecasted demand of 250 units. Similar constraints can be added for warehouses 2-4 as follows:

$$X_{12} + X_{22} \geq 150$$

$$X_{13} + X_{23} \geq 200$$

$$X_{14} + X_{24} \geq 300$$

Finally, because it is not possible to ship a negative quantity from the plants to the warehouses, we add the following non-negativity constraints:

$$X_{11} \geq 0$$

$$X_{12} \geq 0$$

$$X_{13} \geq 0$$

$$X_{14} \geq 0$$

$$X_{21} \geq 0$$

$$X_{22} \geq 0$$

$$X_{23} \geq 0$$

$$X_{24} \geq 0$$

The last step is to solve the problem. Figure 3-1 shows a spreadsheet that can be used to analyze this problem. The formulas that were entered into this spreadsheet are shown in Figure 3-2.

The top area of the worksheet shown in Figure 3-1 contains the parameters or model inputs for this situation. Changes in the parameters are easier to execute by having the formulas in the Model Output section refer to the parameters in the Model Input section as opposed to entering the values for the parameters directly into the formulas.

The middle of the worksheet contains an area for the decision maker to enter values for the eight decision variables. To facilitate the calculations in the Models Output section, the Lotus 1-2-3 command /RangeNameLabelRight was used in conjunction with the range A11..A18. This command gives the cells to the right of the specified range the range name of the labels entered in the specified range. Thus, cell B11 has the range name X_11, cell B12 has the range name X_12 and so on. Because range names can be used in formulas just like cell addresses, naming each cell permits entering the formulas in the model output section in a form almost identical to the form used above in the mathematical model. The only difference was we could not give the cells the exact name of the decision variables as they were defined in the mathematical model because these names are identical to cell addresses. For example, we defined the decision variable X_{11} as the amount to ship from plant 1 to warehouse 1. We could not use X11 as a range name since cell X11 is the name of a cell in the spreadsheet and thus it would not be clear in a formula containing X11 if we were referring to a cell or a range name.

The bottom area of the worksheet in Figure 3-1 contains the model outputs. The first column in this section (column A) contains labels for the rows. Thus, row 24 corresponds to the objective function of cost, row 25 corresponds to plant one's capacity, and so on. The second column contains formulas that calculate the value of the objective function or the value of a constraint. The formulas entered in this column are almost identical to the way they were specified in the mathematical model thanks to the use of range names. The third column contains the limit for each constraint. Finally, the fourth column contains the

Figure 3-1

A	A	B	C	D	E	F
1	**Plant Production Allocation Model**					
2						
3	**Model Inputs:**					
4		W1	W2	W3	W4	Capacity
5	Plant 1	1	2	4	5	500
6	Plant 2	3	1	2	4	400
7	Demand	250	150	200	300	
8						
9	**Decision Variables**					
10						
11	X_11					
12	X_12					
13	X_13					
14	X_14					
15	X_21					
16	X_22					
17	X_23					
18	X_24					
19						
20	**Model Outputs:**					
21						
22						
23		Value	Limit	Slack/Surplus		
24	Cost	0				
25	Plant 1 Capacity	0	500	500		
26	Plant 2 Capacity	0	400	400		
27	Warehous 1 Dem.	0	250	-250		
28	Warehous 2 Dem.	0	150	-150		
29	Warehous 3 Dem.	0	200	-200		
30	Warehous 4 Dem.	0	300	-300		

Figure 3-2

A	A	B	C	D	E	F
1	**Plant Production**	**Allocation Model**				
2						
3	**Model Inputs:**					
4		W1	W2	W3	W4	Capacity
5	Plant 1	1	2	4	5	500
6	Plant 2	3	1	2	4	400
7	Demand	250	150	200	300	
8						
9	**Decision Variables**					
10						
11	X_11					
12	X_12					
13	X_13					
14	X_14					
15	X_21					
16	X_22					
17	X_23					
18	X_24					
19						
20	**Model Outputs:**					
21						
22						
23		Value	Limit	Slack/Surplus		
24	Cost	1*X_11+2*X_12+4*X_13+5*X_14+3*X_21+1*X_22+2*X_23+4*X_24				
25	Plant 1 Capacity	+X_11+X_12+X_13+X_14	+F5	+C25-B25		
26	Plant 2 Capacity	+X_21+X_22+X_23+X_24	+F6	+C26-B26		
27	Warehous 1 Dem.	+X_11+X_21	+B7	+B27-C27		
28	Warehous 2 Dem.	+X_12+X_22	+C7	+B28-C28		
29	Warehous 3 Dem.	+X_13+X_23	+D7	+B29-C29		
30	Warehous 4 Dem.	+X_14+X_24	+E7	+B30-C30		

slack or surplus for each constraint. Constraints that have to be less than or equal to a limit have slack to the extent that the amount of the resource used is less than the limit specified whereas constraints that have to be greater than or equal to a limit have surplus to the extent that the amount of the resource exceeds the limit. In the case of both slack and surplus, these values must be non-negative for the solution to be feasible.

Figure 3-3 contains an example feasible solution to this problem. According to this solution 250 units where shipped from plant 1 to warehouse 1, 200 from plant 1 to warehouse 3, 50 from plant 1 to warehouse 4, 150 from plant 2 to warehouse 2, and 250 from plant 2 to warehouse 4. The cost of this solution is $2,450. Other solutions could be easily investigated by entering alternative values for the decision variables and observing the cost associated with the solution and ensuring that the slack and surplus values all remain non-negative.

Figure 3-3

	A	B	C	D	E	F
1	Plant Production Allocation Model					
2						
3	Model Inputs:					
4		W1	W2	W3	W4	Capacity
5	Plant 1	1	2	4	5	500
6	Plant 2	3	1	2	4	400
7	Demand	250	150	200	300	
8						
9	Decision Variables					
10						
11	X_11	250				
12	X_12					
13	X_13	200				
14	X_14	50				
15	X_21					
16	X_22	150				
17	X_23					
18	X_24	250				
19						
20	Model Outputs:					
21						
22						
23		Value	Limit	Slack/Surplus		
24	Cost	2450				
25	Plant 1 Capacity	500	500	0		
26	Plant 2 Capacity	400	400	0		
27	Warehous 1 Dem.	250	250	0		
28	Warehous 2 Dem.	150	150	0		
29	Warehous 3 Dem.	200	200	0		
30	Warehous 4 Dem.	300	300	0		

TRUE/FALSE QUESTIONS

1. ___ Developing models is more of an art than a science.

2. ___ One draw back associated with modeling by imitation is that it can inhibit creativity.

3. ___ Developing a mathematical models has more to do with mathematical skills than logical thinking.

4. ___ There is often more than one correct way to model a given problem.

5. ___ A flexible model is one where it is difficult to obtain bad answers from.

6. ___ A flow chart is a picture of the sequence of steps in a process.

7. ___ Typically, it is best to start by developing a prescriptive model and then develop a descriptive model to develop a better understanding of the system.

8. ___ Assumptions are often necessary to account for unavailable information or to simplify the model so that it can be solved.

9. ___ In order to keep the model simple, it is best not to complicate it by making the assumptions explicit.

10. ___ As a general rule, the minimum amount of data that is necessary should be used.

11. ___ In general, the more detailed a model, the better it will reflect reality.

12. ___ Since mangers always need the most accurate solution possible, it is not important to determine how accurate the solution needs to be.

13. ___ In a correctly constructed influence diagram, the outputs will have no arrows point into them.

14. ___ One way to determine if a model is complete is to determine if all quantities that are not influenced by others are either decision variables or known values.

15. ___ In developing models, it is considered good practice to break the problem down into smaller prices, develop detailed models for each piece, and then combine the pieces into the overall model.

16. ___ Whenever possible, an exact solution method should be used rather than a heuristic procedure.

17. ___ Models must first appeal to management scientists before they can appeal to managers.

18. ___ Validity refers to how well a model predicts reality.

19. ___ It is impossible to include every detail in one model.

20. ___ Management scientists often state that the purpose for modeling is to obtain insight, not numbers.

21. ___ Many models are minor variations or extensions of others.

Answers:

1. T, 2. T, 3. F, 4. T, 5. F, 6. T, 7. F, 8. T, 9. F, 10. T, 11. T, 12. F, 13. F, 14. T, 15. T, 16. T, 17. F, 18. T, 19. T, 20. T, 21. T

CHAPTER 4

REVIEW

This chapter overviews issues related to linear programming (LP) modeling. A mathematical programming problem is a problem where the maximization or minimization of some objective function is desired and where restrictions which can be represented mathematically with inequalities and equalities are present. A wide variety of planning and operational problems can be expressed as mathematical programming problems. The term programming was originally coined because these models find the best program or course of action to follow.

In mathematical programming models, the quantities that the decision variables are multiplied by in the objective function are called the *objective function coefficients*, and the quantities that the decision variables are multiplied by in the constraints are called *constraint coefficients*.

Linear programming models can be characterized as mathematical, prescriptive, and deterministic. To be a linear program, the following three conditions must be met:

1. The constraints must be of a $\leq$, $\geq$, or $=$ type.
2. The objective function must be a linear function of the decision variables.
3. Variables may assume any fractional numerical value.

The first condition means that all decision variables can be raised only to the first power and can only be multiplied by a constant term. The second condition requires that constraints be represented with inequalities ($\leq$ or $\geq$) or equalities ($=$) and not strict inequalities ($<$ or $>$). The third condition states that decision variables are allowed to assume any fractional values. A solution method that forces the variables to assume integer values is referred to as an integer linear programming model.

Before undertaking the task of developing a mathematical model, the estimated cost associated with model development, debugging, data collection, and verification should be weighed against the potential benefits associated with using the model. Three helpful questions to assist you in developing LP models are:

1. What am I trying to decide?
2. What is the objective to be maximized or minimized?
3. How is the problem restricted?

In developing LP models, only variable costs relative to the decision being made should be included in the model. Fixed costs (or sunk costs) will not effect the optimal strategy since these costs have already been incurred. Thus, only those variable (or incremental) costs incurred based on the decision should be included in the model.

Explicit constraints are restrictions which are explicitly stated in the scenario while implicit constraints are those which are not explicitly stated in the problem, but must be included in the model for it to accurately represent the scenario.

A quick verification check for LP models is to check the dimensionality of the model. Inconsistencies in dimensions within the objective function or within a particular constraint indicate an error has been made in constructing the model.

There are a number of general classes that LP models commonly fall into such as product mix problems, knapsack problems, diet problems, the transportation problem, and the assignment problem. Because of its special structure, as long as the capacities and demands are integers, the solution to the LP transportation problem will also have an integer optimal solution. Also, because the assignment problem is a special case of the transportation problem, its optimal solution will yield only zeros and ones for the decision variables.

LP models provide a framework to identify solutions that satisfy all of the constraints. Thus, the power of linear programming comes from the ability of the linear programming solution algorithms to systematically consider the tradeoffs among the constraints and between the constraint and the objective. Such linear programming solution algorithms have the added advantage over the trial-and-error approach in that they guarantee an optimal solution will be found if one exists.

For large models, subscripted variables and summation notation is used to write LP models in shorthand. The symbol Σ is used to signify the addition of elements. Double subscripted variables can be used when it is natural to think of the modeled entities in pairs.

SOLVED PROBLEMS

Example Problem 1: An Application of LP Models - The Nurse Scheduling Problem

Get Well Hospital has the following nurse staffing needs:

Period	Time	Minimum Number of Nurses Needed
1	8 AM - 12 PM	70
2	12 PM - 4 PM	30
3	4 PM - 8 PM	60
4	8 PM - 12 AM	40
5	12 AM - 4 AM	20
6	4 AM - 8 AM	35

Nurses are scheduled to begin work at the beginning of these periods and they work for 8 consecutive hours. Nurses that start their shift in period 1 or 2 are paid the base rate. Nurses that start in periods 3 or 4 are paid one-and-half times the base rate. Nurses that begin in periods 5 or 6 are paid double the base rate.

Solution:

What is the hospital trying to decide? The hospital must decide how many nurses should begin work in each of the six periods. Thus, we define the following decision variables:

X_i = *the number of nurses starting their shift in period i* i=1,2,3,...,6

What is the objective to be maximized or minimized? The hospital wishes to minimize the labor cost associated with staffing the six periods. Mathematically, this can be expressed as an objective function as follows:

$$Min \quad 1X_1 + 1X_2 + 1.5X_3 + 1.5X_4 + 2X_5 + 2X_6$$

How is the problem restricted? The only explicit restriction is that the minimum number of nurses be available in each period. In addition, we have to recognize that nurses that begin in a given period are also available in the next period. To illustrate, a minimum of 30 nurses are needed to staff period 2. Since nurses work 8 consecutive hours, in addition to the nurses that begin their shift in period 2, nurses that began their shift in period 1 will also be available in period 2. Mathematically this can be expressed as follows:

$$X_1 + X_2 \geq 30$$

Since it is not possible for a nurse to work a negative number of hours, nonnegativity constraints are implicit constraints for this situation. Thus, the complete LP model for this problem is as follows:

$Min \quad 1X_1 + 1X_2 + 1.5X_3 + 1.5X_4 + 2X_5 + 2X_6$

subject to the constraints:

$X_6 + X_1 \geq 70$ (nurse staffing requirement for period 1)
$X_1 + X_2 \geq 30$ (nurse staffing requirement for period 2)
$X_2 + X_3 \geq 60$ (nurse staffing requirement for period 3)
$X_3 + X_4 \geq 40$ (nurse staffing requirement for period 4)
$X_4 + X_5 \geq 20$ (nurse staffing requirement for period 5)
$X_5 + X_6 \geq 35$ (nurse staffing requirement for period 6)

$X_i \geq 0$ for i=1,2,3,...,6 (nonnegativity constraints)

The objective function coefficients are 1, 1, 1.5, 1.5, 2, and 2, and correspond to the decision variables X_1 to X_6, respectively. The constraint coefficients are all equal to one and were excluded. To illustrate, the constraint $1X_6 + 1X_1 \geq 70$ and the constraint $X_6 + X_1 \geq 70$ are equivalent.

Furthermore, the objective function coefficients are all dimensionless ratios of the amount nurses are paid for working in a given period relative to the base amount. Therefore, since each decision variable in the objective function has the same dimension (i.e., number of nurses), all six terms in the object function have the same dimension. Also, all the terms in each constraint pass the dimension check.

A spreadsheet that could be used to analyze this problem is given in Figure 4-1. The formulas used in this spreadsheet are shown in Figure 4-2. The top portion of Figure 4-1 contains the model inputs. In the middle of Figure 4-1 alternate values can be entered for the six decision variables. Finally, the bottom of Figure 4-1 contains the model outputs. The model output section is organized in a similar fashion to the model output sections of the models discussed in the previous chapter. As was done in the previous chapter, the Lotus 1-2-3 **/RangeNameLabelRight** command was used for the range A15..A20. Thus, the cells in the range B15..B20 have the range names of the labels entered in cells A15. .A20, respectively. This allowed entering the formulas in the model outputs section in a form similar to the mathematical LP model developed above.

Figure 4-3 contains an example feasible solution and Figure 4-4 contains the optimal solution to this problem. The optimal solution was obtained with the **Solver** feature available in Lotus 1-2-3. Referring to the optimal solution, the only period that had extra nurses was period 2. Given that staffing costs associated with periods one and two are cheaper than the staffing costs for the other periods, it is not surprising that any extra staffing would occur in one or both of these two periods.

Example Problem 2: Representing LPs Symbolically

> Because symbols are a sort of shorthand for model development, the development of LP models is often facilitated by developing them symbolically first and then expanding them into the complete model. To get some additional practice in working with LP models symbolically, let's express the Production Planning Over Time (PPOT) Model as discussed in example 5 of the text symbolically.

Solution:

First, we must express the decision variables and parameters symbolically. We will begin with the decision variables. For the purpose of this example, we will use upper case letters for the decision variables and lower case letters for the parameters. In the PPOT Model we define the following two decision variables:

Figure 4-1

	A	B	C	D
1	**Nurse Scheduling Problem**			
2				
3	**Model Inputs**			
4			Nurses	
5	Period	Time	Needed	
6	1	8 AM - 12 PM	70	
7	2	12PM - 4 PM	30	
8	3	4 PM - 8 PM	60	
9	4	8 PM - 12 PM	40	
10	5	12 PM - 4 AM	20	
11	6	4 AM - 8 AM	35	
12				
13	**Decision Variables**			
14				
15	X_1			
16	X_2			
17	X_3			
18	X_4			
19	X_5			
20	X_6			
21				
22	**Model Outputs:**			
23		Value	Limit	Surplus
24	Cost	0		
25	Nurses Period 1	0	70	-70
26	Nurses Period 2	0	30	-30
27	Nurses Period 3	0	60	-60
28	Nurses Period 4	0	40	-40
29	Nurses Period 5	0	20	-20
30	Nurses Period 6	0	35	-35

Figure 4-2

	A	B	C	D
1	**Nurse Scheduling Problem**			
2				
3	**Model Inputs**			
4			Nurses	
5	Period	Time	Needed	
6	1	8 AM - 12 PM	70	
7	2	12PM - 4 PM	30	
8	3	4 PM - 8 PM	60	
9	4	8 PM - 12 PM	40	
10	5	12 PM - 4 AM	20	
11	6	4 AM - 8 AM	35	
12				
13	**Decision Variables**			
14				
15	X_1			
16	X_2			
17	X_3			
18	X_4			
19	X_5			
20	X_6			
21				
22	**Model Outputs:**			
23		Value	Limit	Surplus
24	Cost	+X_1*1+X_2*1+X_3*1.5+X_4*1.5+X_5*2+X_6*2		
25	Nurses Period 1	+X_1+X_6	+C6	+B25-C25
26	Nurses Period 2	+X_1+X_2	+C7	+B26-C26
27	Nurses Period 3	+X_2+X_3	+C8	+B27-C27
28	Nurses Period 4	+X_3+X_4	+C9	+B28-C28
29	Nurses Period 5	+X_4+X_5	+C10	+B29-C29
30	Nurses Period 6	+X_5+X_6	+C11	+B30-C30

Figure 4-3

A	A	B	C	D
1	**Nurse Scheduling Problem**			
2				
3	**Model Inputs**			
4			Nurses	
5	Period	Time	Needed	
6	1	8 AM - 12 PM	70	
7	2	12PM - 4 PM	30	
8	3	4 PM - 8 PM	60	
9	4	8 PM - 12 PM	40	
10	5	12 PM - 4 AM	20	
11	6	4 AM - 8 AM	35	
12				
13	**Decision Variables**			
14				
15	X_1	35		
16	X_2	30		
17	X_3	30		
18	X_4	10		
19	X_5	10		
20	X_6	35		
21				
22	**Model Outputs:**			
23		Value	Limit	Surplus
24	Cost	215		
25	Nurses Period 1	70	70	0
26	Nurses Period 2	65	30	35
27	Nurses Period 3	60	60	0
28	Nurses Period 4	40	40	0
29	Nurses Period 5	20	20	0
30	Nurses Period 6	45	35	10

Figure 4-4

A	A	B	C	D
1	**Nurse Scheduling Problem**			
2				
3	**Model Inputs**			
4			Nurses	
5	Period	Time	Needed	
6	1	8 AM - 12 PM	70	
7	2	12PM - 4 PM	30	
8	3	4 PM - 8 PM	60	
9	4	8 PM - 12 PM	40	
10	5	12 PM - 4 AM	20	
11	6	4 AM - 8 AM	35	
12				
13	**Decision Variables**			
14				
15	X_1	55		
16	X_2	20		
17	X_3	40		
18	X_4	0		
19	X_5	20		
20	X_6	15		
21				
22	**Model Outputs:**			
23		Value	Limit	Surplus
24	Cost	205		
25	Nurses Period 1	70	70	0
26	Nurses Period 2	75	30	45
27	Nurses Period 3	60	60	0
28	Nurses Period 4	40	40	0
29	Nurses Period 5	20	20	0
30	Nurses Period 6	35	35	0

P_i = the amount to produce in period i i=1,2,3,4
I_i = the amount of ending inventory in period i i=1,2,3,4

In addition to these decision variables, we can express the parameters for this problem symbolically as:

d_i = the demand in period i i=1,2,3,4
c_i = the unit production cost in period i i=1,2,3,4
h_i = the inventory holding cost in period i i=1,2,3,4

Using these definitions, the PPOT Model can be expressed symbolically as:

$$Min \ \sum_{i=1}^{4} c_i P_i + \sum_{i=1}^{4} h_i I_i$$

subject to the constraints:

$$I_i = I_{i-1} + P_i - d_i \quad \text{for } i = 1,2,3,4$$

$$P_i, I_i \geq 0 \quad \text{for } i = 1,2,3,4$$

The first term in the objective function represents the production costs over the four periods while the second term represents the inventory holding costs over the four periods. Recall that the first constraint is called an *inventory balance constraint*, while the second constraint is simply the familiar nonnegativity constraint. In English, the inventory balance constraint says that the ending inventory in a given period is equal to the ending inventory from the prior period plus what is produced in the given period less what is used to meet demand in the given period. The "for i=1,2,3,4" after this constraint tells us we need one constraint like this in our expanded model for each period i, where i takes on the values 1 through 4. If you refer back to the complete model in the text you will see that indeed four inventory balance constraints were needed.

TRUE/FALSE QUESTIONS

1. ___ All managerial decision problems can be expressed as mathematical programming problems.

2. ___ The term programming was coined because of the large amount of computer programming that was initially required to solve mathematical programming problems.

3. ___ Linear programming problems are examples of stochastic models.

4. ___ Strict inequalities (< or >) are not permitted as constraints in linear programming models.

5. ___ Integer programming models require a solution method that forces the variables to assume integer values.

6. ___ Sunk costs should not be included in linear programming models.

7. ___ Nonnegativity constraints are typically examples of explicit constraints.

8. ___ Inconsistencies in dimensions of terms within the objective function or with a particular constraint are an indication that an error was made.

9. ___ A model passing the dimensionality check can safely be assumed to be free from errors.

10. ___ With the trial-and-error approach it can be difficult to find a feasible solution must less an optimal solution.

Answers:

1. F, 2. F, 3. F, 4. T, 5. T, 6. T, 7. F, 8. T, 9. F, 10. T

CHAPTER 5

REVIEW

A set of values for the decision variables that satisfy all the constraints is called a *feasible solution* to the linear program. Linear programs generally have an infinite number of feasible solutions. The *feasible* region is the set of all feasible solutions to a linear program. When nonnegativity constraints are added to a LP model, the feasible region will be restricted to the first (upper right) quadrant.

LPs may contain three types of constraints: 1) less-than-or-equal-to (≤), greater-than-or-equal-to (≥), and equal-to (=). In two dimensions, an equality constraint is a line. In three dimensions an equality constraint forms a plane, and in higher dimensions an equality constraint forms a hyperplane. For inequality constrains, the line corresponding to the constraint, called the *constraint line*, is plotted. Then, the halfspace which satisfies the inequality is determined.

Another way to think about the feasible region is that it is the *intersection* of all halfspaces corresponding to the constraints, since by definition the feasible region is the set of points that satisfy all the constraints. *Corner points* of the feasible region occur at the intersection of two constraint lines. The constraints that intersect at a corner point are called *binding constraints* at that corner point. The coordinates for corner points can be found by solving simultaneously the constraint lines of the binding constraints at the corner point.

If an optimal solution to a linear program exists, it will occur at a corner point of the feasible region. This is the result of the linearity assumption which makes it impossible for a feasible region to have disjoint pieces or jagged edges that could hamper the search for an optimal solution.

Constant objective function lines are called *objective function contours.* These contour lines can be used to solve two-variable problems by first graphing the feasible region and then plotting the objective function contour lines in the direction of increase for maximization problems or decrease for minimization problems until the best feasible point is found. Because the objective function is linear, objective function contours are parallel to each other.

There are four possible outcomes associated with linear programming models:

1. The LP has a unique optimal solution.
2. The LP has alternate optimal solutions. Alternate optimal solutions occur when more than one corner point has the best objective function value. In these cases, an infinite number of optimal solutions exist.
3. The problem is unbounded meaning the objective can be maximized to infinity for maximization problems, or minimized to negative infinity for minimization problems.

A LP will be unbounded if it has an open feasible region, and the direction of improved objective function values for the objective function contours is in the direction of the opened side of the feasible region. It is important to note, however, that all problems with an open feasible region are not unbounded. Typically, an unbounded LP has not been modeled correctly with some constraint or set of constraints left out of the model.

4. The LP is infeasible because there is no way to simultaneously satisfy all constraints. In these cases some of the constraints may need to be relaxed in order to obtain a feasible solution.

The graphical LP solution procedure involves three steps:

1. Plot the feasible region. If it is empty the problem is infeasible and cannot be solved.
2. Plot objective function contour lines for two values of the objective function. Continue plotting contours parallel to the first two in the direction of increase for maximization problems or decrease in the case of minimization problems until they no longer intersect with the feasible region. If it is impossible to leave the feasible region as you continue to plot contours, the problem is unbounded.
3. If the best objective function contour intersects the feasible region at a single corner point, then that point is the unique optimal solution. If the best contour lies on a border, any point on that border is an optimal solution. In either case, the optimal solution can be found by solving the set of binding constraints that intersect at the corner point.

A linear program is in *standard form* when: 1) all the constraints (excluding the nonnegativity constraints) are expressed as equalities, 2) all the variables are restricted to be nonnegative, and 3) all the variables appear on the left-hand side of the constraints, and 4) all the constants appear on the right-hand side of the constraints. A *slack variable* is the amount that the left-hand side of a less-than-or-equal-to constraint is less than the right-hand side of the constraint. Converting a less-than-or-equal-to constraint to standard form requires moving all variables to the left-hand side (and changing the signs appropriately), adding a nonnegative slack variable to the left-side, and replacing the $\leq$ with an =. A *surplus variable* is the amount the left-hand-side of a greater-than-or-equal-to constraint exceeds the right-hand side of the constraint. Converting a greater-than-or-equal-to constraint to standard form requires moving all variables to the left-hand side (and changing the signs appropriately), subtracting a nonnegative slack variable from the left-side, and replacing the $\geq$ with an =. Slack and surplus variables have a value of zero for binding constraints.

SOLVED PROBLEMS

Example Problem 1: Solving a LP With the Graphical Method

Find the optimal solution to the following LP using the graphical method.

$\max 3X_1 + X_2$
s.t.
$X_1 + X_2 \leq 150$
$0.5X_1 + X_2 \leq 100$
$X_1 \geq 50$
$X_1, X_2 \geq 0$

Solution:

The first step in solving a LP graphically is to draw the feasible region. Recall that to plot inequality constraints, we first plot the line corresponding to the constraint as an equality. Then we determine which halfspace satisfies the inequality. To illustrate, the first constraint is converted to an equality as follows:

$$X_1 + X_2 = 150$$

Then we find two points that satisfy this equality and plot them on a graph. If we plug a zero in for X_1, X_2 equals 150. Likewise, if we plug a zero in for X_2, X_1 equals 150. Thus, two points that satisfy the above equation are (0, 150) and (150, 0). A plot of this constraint line is shown below.

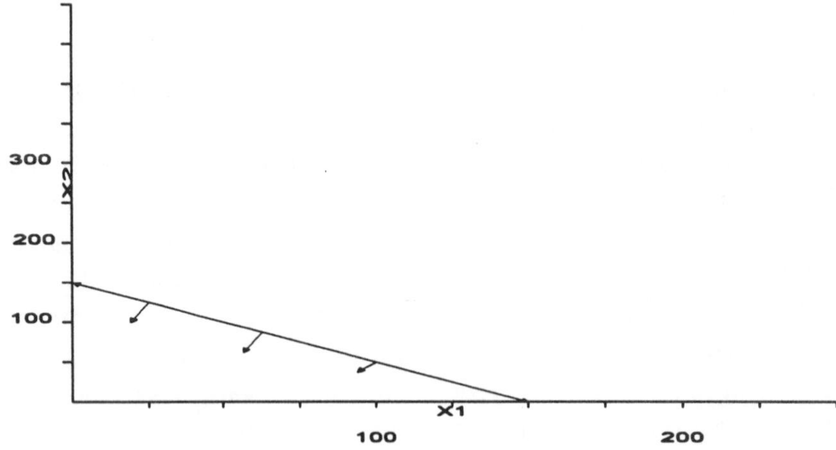

Once the constraint line has been plotted we can then determine which halfspace satisfies the constraint. Usually the easiest way to determine this is to see if the origin satisfies the constraint. Thus, we plug the point (0, 0) into the constraint and determine if this point satisfies the constraint. Since $0 + 0 \leq 150$, the origin satisfies the constraint and we conclude that all points below the constraint line also satisfy the constraint. This is indicated in the above graph by the downward arrows emanating from the constraint line.

The other two constraints are plotted in a similar fashion and shown below. Also, in the figure below, the location of the corner points of the feasible region are represented by the circles.

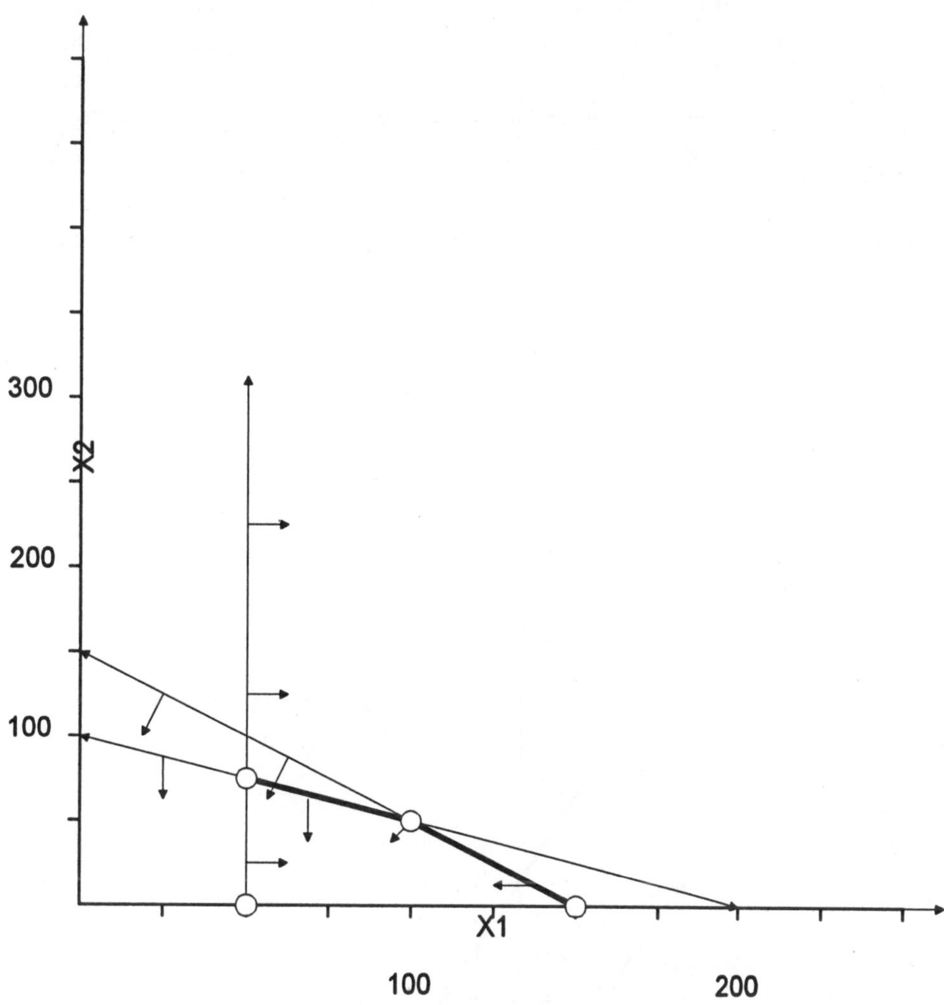

Since the feasible region is not empty a feasible solution exists. Therefore we next select two values for the objective function and plot their associated contours. To illustrate this, objective function values of 150 and 300 will be used. First, with an objective function value of 150 we have the following:

$$3X_1 + X_2 = 150$$

If a zero is plugged in for X_1, X_2 equals 150, and if a zero is plugged in for X_2, X_1 equals 50. Thus our two points are: (0, 150) and (50, 0). In a similar fashion we can obtain the points (0, 300) and (100, 0) for the contour line associated with an objective function value of 300. These two contour lines have been plotted in the following figure. Notice that as the contour lines are moved away from the origin, the value of the objective function increases. Given that this is a maximization problem, we want to find the contour line that is furthest from the origin but still intersects the feasible region. Since the objective function contour lines are parallel to one another, if we continued plotting lines further away from the origin it is easy to see that the last point of the feasible region that would intersect a contour line is the corner point (150, 0). This can be verified by actually plotting additional contour lines or by placing a straight edge on the figure, aligning it so it is parallel with the contour lines already plotted, and gradually moving it away from the origin until it no longer intersects the feasible region. The last point(s) intersected by the plotted contour lines or the straight edge is the optimal solution.

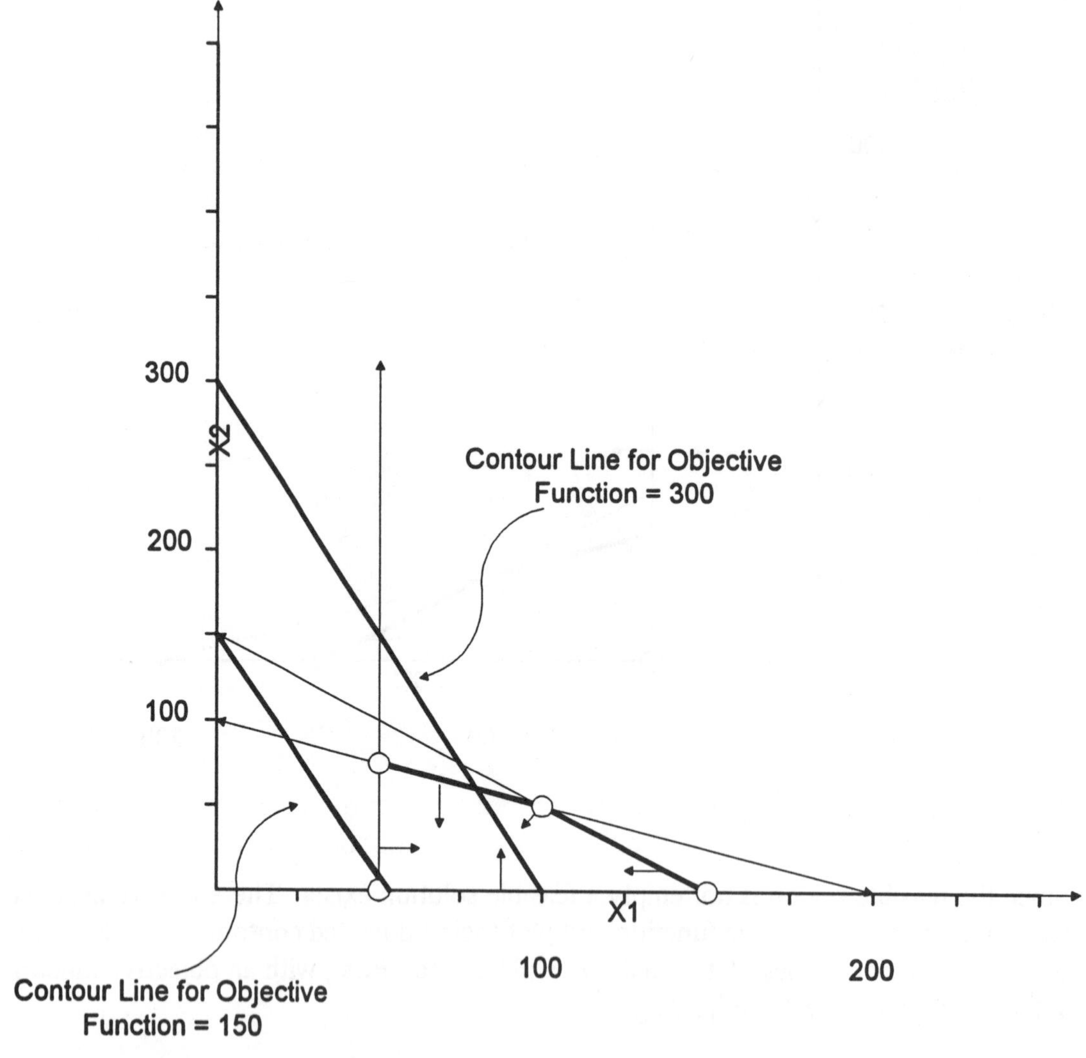

Thus, in this problem the optimal solution is $X_1 = 150$ and $X_2 = 0$. This results in an optimal solution of 450 (3*150 + 1*0).

Example Problem 2: Converting a LP Model to Standard Form

Convert the LP given in example problem 1 to standard form.

Solution:

The following LP was given in example problem 1:

$\max 3X_1 + X_2$
s.t.
$X_1 + X_2 \leq 150$
$0.5X_1 + X_2 \leq 100$
$X_1 \geq 50$
$X_1, X_2 \geq 0$

A linear program is in *standard form* when: 1) all the constraints (excluding the nonnegativity constraints) are expressed as equalities, 2) all the variables are restricted to be nonnegative, and 3) all the variables appear on the left-hand side of the constraints, and 4) all the constants appear on the right-hand side of the constraints. In the above problem, the last three requirements are already met. Thus, all that is required is that the constraints be expressed as equalities.

The first two constraint are of the less-than-or-equal type. Converting less-than-or-equal-to constraints to standard form requires moving all variables to the left-hand side (and changing the signs appropriately), adding a nonnegative slack variable to the left-side, and replacing the $\leq$ with an =. Thus, these two constraints can be modified as follows:

$$X_1 + X_2 + S_1 = 150$$
$$0.5X_1 + X_2 + S_2 = 100$$

The third constraint is of the greater-than-or-equal type. Converting a greater-than-or-equal-to constraint to standard form requires moving all variables to the left-hand side (and changing the signs appropriately), subtracting a nonnegative slack variable from the left-side, and replacing the $\geq$ with an =. Thus, the third constraint can be modified as:

$$X_1 - S_3 = 50$$

The complete LP model in standard form is:

$\max 3X_1 + X_2$
s.t
$X_1 + X_2 + S_1 = 150$
$0.5X_1 + X_2 + S_2 = 100$
$X_1 - S_3 = 50$
$X_1, X_2, S_1, S_2, S_3 \geq 0$

Example Problem 3: Using the Lotus 1-2-3 Solver

Verify the optimal solution obtained for example problem 1 with the graphical method by using the Lotus 1-2-3 Solver.

Solution:

The spreadsheet shown in Figure 5-1 was developed to find the optimal solution for this problem. The actual formulas entered into this spreadsheet are shown in Figure 5-2.

In the top part of Figure 5-1, the parameters and uncontrollable variables were entered. This information includes the objective function coefficients for X_1 and X_2, the constraint coefficients, and the right-hand side (RHS) constants.

The middle of Figure 5-1 contains cells where values for the two decision variables can be entered. To facilitate entering the formulas in the Model Outputs section, the **/R**ange**N**ame**L**abel**R**ight command was used on the range A14..A15. This gives cell B14 the range name X_1 and cell B15 the range name X_2.

The Model Outputs section contains formulas that correspond to the objective function and constraints, respectively. To enhance the flexibility of the spreadsheet, the formulas in this section refer to the information entered in the Parameters and Uncontrollable Variables section. In this way changing the value of a parameter requires only one modification to the spreadsheet, namely, entering the change over the old value. No changes to the formulas are required. Also note that a dollar sign ($) was placed in front of the range names that refer to the decision variables. Doing this permitted entering the formula for constraint 1 and then copying it for constraints 2 and 3. Also note that the complete constraints were entered including the mathematical operator and the right-hand sides.

After entering this information, the Lotus 1-2-3 Solver can be used to solve the problem. First, because an initial solution is needed, zeros were entered in cells B14 and B15. Next, from the Tools menu option, Range - Analyze - Solver were selected. In the dialog box that is displayed on the screen, the following information was entered. For adjustable cells, the range B14..B15 was specified. For constraint cells, the range B22..B26 was specified. Remember, when using the Lotus 1-2-3 Solver that the nonnegativity constraints must be included. Cell B20 was specified for the optimal cell. Finally, the max option and solve option were selected.

The optimal values for the decision variables are automatically placed in cells B14 and B15 after Lotus solves the problem. As is shown in Figure 5-3, the optimal solution of $X_1 = 150$ and $X_2 = 0$ found by the Lotus 1-2-3 Solver agrees with the solution we obtained using the graphical method.

Figure 5-1

A	A	B	C	D	E
1	**Example Problem 3**				
2					
3	**Parameters and Uncontrollable Variables:**				
4					
5		X1	X2	RHS	
6	Objective	3	2		
7					
8	Constraint 1	1	1	150	
9	Constraint 2	0.5	1	100	
10	Constraint 3	1	0	50	
11					
12	**Decision Variables:**				
13					
14	X_1	0			
15	X_2	0			
16					
17	**Model Outputs:**				
18					
19		Equation			
20	Objective	0			
21					
22	Constraint 1	1			
23	Constraint 2	1			
24	Constraint 3	0			
25	X1 >= 0	1			
26	X2 >= 0	1			

Figure 5-2

A	A	B	C	D	E
1	**Example Problem 3**				
2					
3	**Parameters and Uncontrollable Variables:**				
4					
5		X1	X2	RHS	
6	Objective	3	2		
7					
8	Constraint 1	1	1	150	
9	Constraint 2	0.5	1	100	
10	Constraint 3	1	0	50	
11					
12	**Decision Variables:**				
13					
14	X_1	0			
15	X_2	0			
16					
17	**Model Outputs:**				
18					
19		Equation			
20	Objective	+X_1*B6+X_2*C6			
21					
22	Constraint 1	+X_1*B8+X_2*C8<=D8			
23	Constraint 2	+X_1*B9+X_2*C9<=D9			
24	Constraint 3	+X_1*B10+X_2*C10>=D10			
25	X1 >= 0	+X_1>=0			
26	X2 >= 0	+X_2>=0			

Figure 5-3

A	A	B	C	D	E
1	**Example Problem 3**				
2					
3	**Parameters and Uncontrollable Variables:**				
4					
5		X1	X2	RHS	
6	Objective	3	2		
7					
8	Constraint 1	1	1	150	
9	Constraint 2	0.5	1	100	
10	Constraint 3	1	0	50	
11					
12	**Decision Variables:**				
13					
14	X_1	150			
15	X_2	0			
16					
17	**Model Outputs:**				
18					
19		Equation			
20	Objective	450			
21					
22	Constraint 1	1			
23	Constraint 2	1			
24	Constraint 3	1			
25	X1 >= 0	1			
26	X2 >= 0	1			

Example Problem 4: Using the Microsoft EXCEL Solver

Verify the optimal solution obtained for example problem 1 with the graphical method by using the Microsoft EXCEL Solver.

Solution:

The spreadsheet shown in Figure 5-4 was developed to find the optimal solution for this problem. The actual formulas entered into this spreadsheet are shown in Figure 5-5.

In the top part of Figure 5-4, the parameters and uncontrollable variables were entered. This information includes the objective function coefficients for X_1 and X_2, the constraint coefficients, and the right-hand side (RHS) constants.

The middle of Figure 5-4 contains cells where values for the two decision variables can be entered. To facilitate entering the formulas in the Model Outputs section, cell B14 was assigned the range name X_1 and cell B15 the range name X_2. This was accomplished by first highlighting cells A14..B15. Then, from the Insert menu, the options Names and Create were selected. Finally, the box associated with Left Column was selected.

The Model Outputs section contains formulas that correspond to the objective function and constraints, respectively. To enhance the flexibility of the spreadsheet, the formulas in this section refer to the information entered in the Parameters and Uncontrollable Variables section. In this way changing the value of a parameter requires only one modification to the spreadsheet, namely, entering the change over the old value. No changes to the formulas are required.

After entering this information, the Microsoft Excel Solver can be used to solve the problem. To begin, from the Tool menu option, Solver was selected. In the dialog box that is displayed on the screen, the following information was entered. For Set Target Cell, $B$20 was entered. Note that EXCEL refers to the objective as a target. Next, for the Equal To options, Max was selected since this is a maximization problem. For the By Changing Cells, the range $B$14..$B$15 was specified. In EXCEL, the changing cells refer to the cells that the decision maker can control or in our terminology, the decision variables. In the Subject to Constraints box the following formulas were entered:

$B$22 <= $C$22
$B$23 <= $C$23
$B$24 >= $C$24
X_1 >= 0
x_2 >= 0

Entering the constraints this way took advantage of the fact that cells B22, B23, and B24 contained the left-hand sides of the constraints, and cells C22, C23, and C24 contained the

Figure 5-4

	A	B	C	D
1	**Example Problem 4**			
2				
3	**Parameters and Uncontrollable Variables:**			
4				
5		X1	X2	RHS
6	Objective	3	2	
7				
8	Constraint 1	1	1	150
9	Constraint 2	0.5	1	100
10	Constraint 3	1	0	50
11				
12	**Decision Variables:**			
13				
14	X_1			
15	X_2			
16				
17	**Model Outputs:**			
18				Slack/
19		Value	Limit	Surplus
20	Objective	0		
21				
22	Constraint 1	0	150	150
23	Constraint 2	0	100	100
24	Constraint 3	0	50	-50

Figure 5-5

	A	B	C	D
1	**Example Problem 4**			
2				
3	**Parameters and Uncont**			
4				
5		X1	X2	RHS
6	Objective	3	2	
7				
8	Constraint 1	1	1	150
9	Constraint 2	0.5	1	100
10	Constraint 3	1	0	50
11				
12	**Decision Variables:**			
13				
14	X_1			
15	X_2			
16				
17	**Model Outputs:**			
18				Slack/
19		Value	Limit	Surplus
20	Objective	=X_1*B6+X_2*C6		
21				
22	Constraint 1	=X_1*B8+X_2*C8	=D8	=C22-B22
23	Constraint 2	=X_1*B9+X_2*C9	=D9	=C23-B23
24	Constraint 3	=X_1	=D10	=B24-C24

right-hand sides of the constraints. Alternatively, the actual constraints could have been entered in the Subject to Constraints box as follows:

X_1*B8+X_2*C8 <= D8
X_1*B9+X_2*C9 <= D9
X_1 >= D10
X_1 >= 0
X_2 >= 0

Remember when using the Microsoft EXCEL Solver that the nonnegativity constraints must be explicitly stated. Finally, the Solve option was selected and when the optimal solution was found OK was selected.

The optimal values for the decision variables are automatically placed in cells B14 and B15 after selecting OK. As is shown in Figure 5-6, the optimal solution of $X_1 = 150$ and $X_2 = 0$ found by the Microsoft EXCEL Solver agrees with the solution we obtained using the graphical method.

Figure 5-6

	A	B	C	D
1	**Example Problem 4**			
2				
3	**Parameters and Uncontrollable Variables:**			
4				
5		X1	X2	RHS
6	Objective	3	2	
7				
8	Constraint 1	1	1	150
9	Constraint 2	0.5	1	100
10	Constraint 3	1	0	50
11				
12	**Decision Variables:**			
13				
14	X_1	150		
15	X_2	0		
16				
17	**Model Outputs:**			
18				Slack/
19		Value	Limit	Surplus
20	Objective	450		
21				
22	Constraint 1	150	150	0
23	Constraint 2	75	100	25
24	Constraint 3	150	50	100

TRUE/FALSE QUESTIONS

1. ___ Because of the complexity of the solution procedure, LPs are almost always solved by computes.

2. ___ Linear programs generally have an infinite number of feasible solutions.

3. ___ A feasible solution is a set of values that satisfies at least one of the constraints.

4. ___ The nonnegativity constraints imply that a feasible solution is restricted to the upper right and left quadrants.

5. ___ In two dimensions, an equality constraint is simple a line.

6. ___ The line corresponding to an inequality constraint is referred to as the halfspace of the constraint.

7. ___ One way to think of the feasible region for a LP is as the intersection of all halfspaces corresponding to the constraints.

8. ___ If a given LP has an equality constraint, then its feasible region is the line segment of the equality constraint that intersects with the region defined by the inequality constraints.

9. ___ Generally, equality constraints have no effect on the size of the feasible region.

10. ___ Corner points of the feasible region correspond to the intersection of two constraint lines.

11. ___ If an optimal solution to a LP exists, it will occur at a corner point of the feasible region.

12. ___ Constant objective function value lines are known as objective function contours.

13. ___ If an LP has alternate optimal solutions it is referred to as unbounded.

14. ___ A LP with alternate optimal solutions suggests that the real system has not been modeled correctly.

15. ___ An infeasible solution occurs when more than one corner point has the best objective function value.

16. ___ While all alternate optimal solutions are as good as any of the others, there may be qualitative factors that make one solution more attractive than the others.

17. ___ Any LP with an open feasible region is unbounded.

18. ___ It is possible for an LP with an open feasible region to have alternate optimal solutions.

19. ___ An LP whose feasible region is empty is called infeasible.

20. ___ Infeasible problems cannot occur in practice.

21. ___ A slack variable represents the amount which must be added to the left-hand side of a constraint to make it equal to the right-hand side.

22. ___ The solution for a problem in standard form indicates which constraints are binding - those with positive slack or surplus.

Answers:

1. T, 2. T, 3. F, 4. F, 5. T, 6. F, 7. T, 8. T, 9. F, 10. T, 11. T, 12. T, 13. F, 14, F, 15. F, 16. T, 17. F, 18. T, 19. T, 20. F, 21. T, 22. F

CHAPTER 6

REVIEW

Parameters of LP models include the objective function coefficients, constraint coefficients, and the right-hand side constants. These parameters are assumed to be known and constant since LP models are deterministic. However, in reality the parameters in a LP model could be based on estimates. Thus, the optimal solution obtained to the model may not be the optimal solution to the real problem.

In cases where the parameters of a model are based on estimates, *sensitivity analysis* can be used to obtain information about how sensitive a LP solution is to changes in the input parameters. Typically, sensitivity analysis addresses how the current optimal solution or objective function value are affected by: 1) changes in the objective function coefficients, and 2) changes in the values of the right-hand sides. Changes in the parameters that result in a new optimal objective function value are referred to as a change in the LP's *value*. Changes in the parameters that result in new optimal values for the decision variables are referred to as a change in the *solution* of the LP. Changing the parameters to LP models can result in a change in the LP's value, a change in the LP's solution, or to changes in both the LP's value and solution.

Changes made to an objective function coefficient change the slope of the objective function contour. Since the feasible region is not affected by changes in objective function coefficients, whether or not an objective function coefficient change results in a new solution depends on whether or not a different corner point becomes the optimal solution because of the changed slope of the objective function contour. The slope of an objective function contour for a model with two decision variables X_1 and X_2, with X_1 corresponding to the horizontal axis and X_2 corresponding the vertical axis, is the coefficient of X_1 when the equation has been solved for X_2.

Changes in the right-hand side values of an inequality constraint may or may not have an impact on the optimal solution or value. Changing the right-hand side of an inequality constraint shifts the constraint parallel to itself. Depending on the direction of the shift, the feasible region may become larger, smaller, or possibly unchanged if the constraint is redundant.

Constraints are said to have been *tightened* if a new value for the right-hand side makes the constraint more difficult to satisfy. Increasing the right-hand side of a $\geq$ constraint and decreasing the right-hand side of a $\leq$ constraint are both examples of tightening a constraint. Constrains are said to have been *relaxed* if a new value for the right-hand allows more points to satisfy the constraint. Decreasing the right-hand side of a $\geq$ constraint and increasing the right-hand side of a $\leq$ constraint are both examples of relaxing a constraint.

Adding constraints to a model can potentially reduce the size of the feasible region. Therefore, adding a constraint to a LP model will either not affect the optimal objective function value or make it worse. Since constraints serve to restrict the number of feasible solutions, adding a constraint can never improve the optimal objective function value. If the current optimal solution satisfies a new constraint that is added, that solution will remain optimal. If the current optimal solution does not satisfy the new constraint, the model must be resolved with the new constraint.

Deleting non-redundant constraints from a LP model expands the feasible region and may result in a new corner point with a better objective function value. Deleting a constraint will either not affect the optimal objective function value or make it better. Removing a nonbinding constraint does not change the optimal solution or value. However, eliminating a binding constraint may change the optimal solution and value, and thus the model must be resolved.

When using the output from LINDO for sensitivity analysis the *reduced costs* in the variable section indicate how much the objective function coefficient of a variable would have to change for the variable to have a positive value in the solution. *Dual prices* provide the improvement that would be obtained in the value of the objective function corresponding to a one unit increase in the right-hand side of a constraint, holding all other parameters in the model constant. The range for which the dual prices are valid are given in the *RIGHT HAND SIDE RANGES* section of the LINDO output. These dual prices are symmetric and a *decrease* in the right-hand side will result in a change opposite in sign to the dual price. Nonbinding constraints have zero dual prices. The *objective function coefficient ranges* provide the allowable changes in the objective function coefficients such that the current solution remains optimal. The information provided for the objective function coefficient ranges assumes that only one coefficient is changed at a time and all other parameter are held constant.

The sensitivity report available with the EXCEL Solver provides the same sensitivity information as is available with LINDO. For each decision variable (or changing cell in EXCEL terminology) the optimal value, reduced cost and allowable increase and decrease are generated. Also, the EXCEL solver reports for each constraint the dual price (shadow price in EXCEL terminology) and the allowable range of right-hand sides for which the dual price is valid. One important difference between LINDO's output and EXCEL's output is that in LINDO a negative dual price means the objective function is "hurt" while a positive dual price means the objective function is "helped." In EXCEL, the sign of the dual price (shadow price) is exactly the change in the objective function with a positive dual price implying an increase in the objective function and a negative dual price implying a decrease in the objective function. Whether these changes help or hurt the objective function depends on whether the objective function is to be maximized or minimized.

Mathematically equivalent LP models may not provide the same sensitivity information. Thus, two important modeling principles are: 1) define a separate variable for every parameter you want sensitivity information on, and 2) if a group of variables have a common parameter, place a variable which is the sum of these variables in the objective function.

SOLVED PROBLEMS

Example Problem 1: Sensitivity Analysis on Objective Function Coefficients

To illustrate sensitivity analysis for the coefficients in the objective function, the LP model presented in example problem 1 of Chapter 5 will be used. Specifically the following model was given:

max $3X_1 + X_2$
s.t.
$X_1 + X_2 \leq 150$
$0.5X_1 + X_2 \leq 100$
$X_1 \geq 50$
$X_1, X_2 \geq 0$

The constraints for this LP, representative objective function contour lines, and the feasible region are shown in Figure 6-1. Also, the four corner points of the feasible region are labeled with the letters A-D. Given that this is a maximization problem and the two contour lines plotted in Figure 6-1, it is clear that corner point D is the optimal solution. Thus, the *optimal solution* is $X_1 = 150$ and $X_2 = 0$, and the *optimal value* is 450. Based on this solution, the first constraint is a binding constraint since it intersects corner point D. The second and third constraints do not intersect corner point D and are therefore nonbinding.

A contour line with a smaller slope (i.e., a larger negative slope) than the original contour lines has been added and is shown in Figure 6-2. Although we will not verify it here, larger values for the objective function can be attained by moving this new contour line to the right (i.e., away from the origin). Thus, based on visual inspection of Figure 6-2, we see that corner point D would remain the optimal solution. In fact we can verify based on visual inspection of Figure 6-2 that corner point D will be the optimal solution for any contour line with a smaller slope than the original contour lines.

We next consider the effect of increasing the slope of the contour line. In Figure 6-3 a new contour line is added with a larger slope than the original contour lines. Again, we will not verify it, but larger values of the objective function are achieved by moving the new contour in an upward direction away from the origin. As is shown in Figure 6-3, the new contour line results in corner point B becoming the optimal solution. Corner point B occurs at the intersection of constraints 2 and 3. Thus constraints 2 and 3 would become binding constraints and constraint 1 would become nonbinding. To determine the optimal solution, we could solve simultaneously the constraint lines for constraints 2 and 3. Since the constraint line for constraint 3 is: $X_1 = 50$, we know that X_1 equals 50 at point B.

Plugging 50 in for X_1 in constraint 2 yields: $0.5(50) + X_2 = 100$ or $X_2 = 75$. Thus the optimal solution with the new contour line is $X_1 = 50$ and $X_2 = 75$.

Figure 6-1

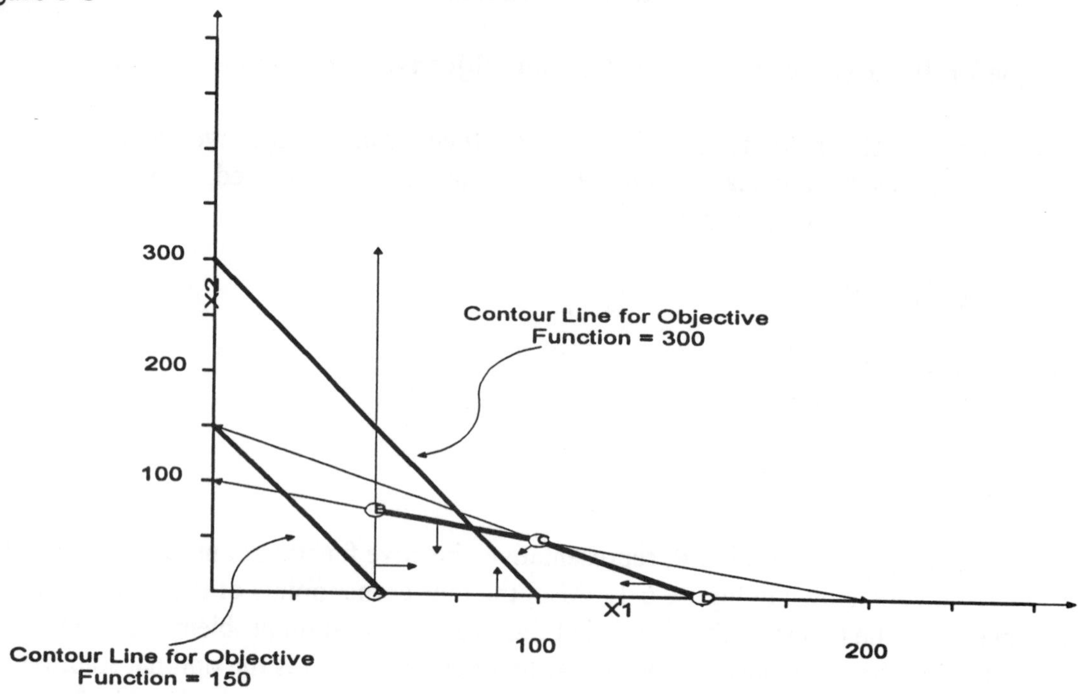

Figure 6-2

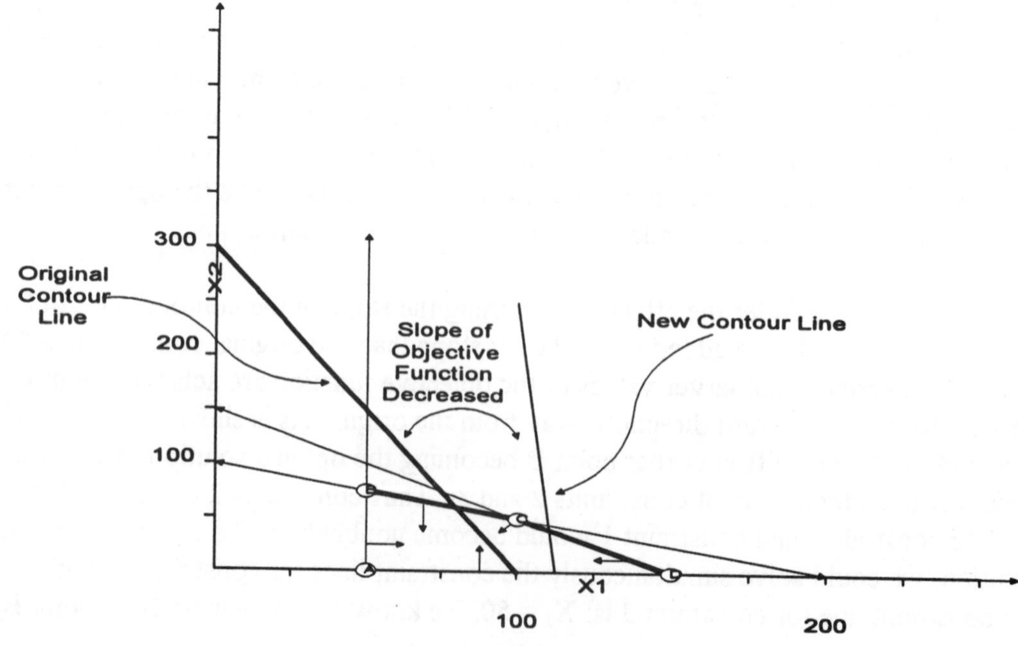

Figure 6-3

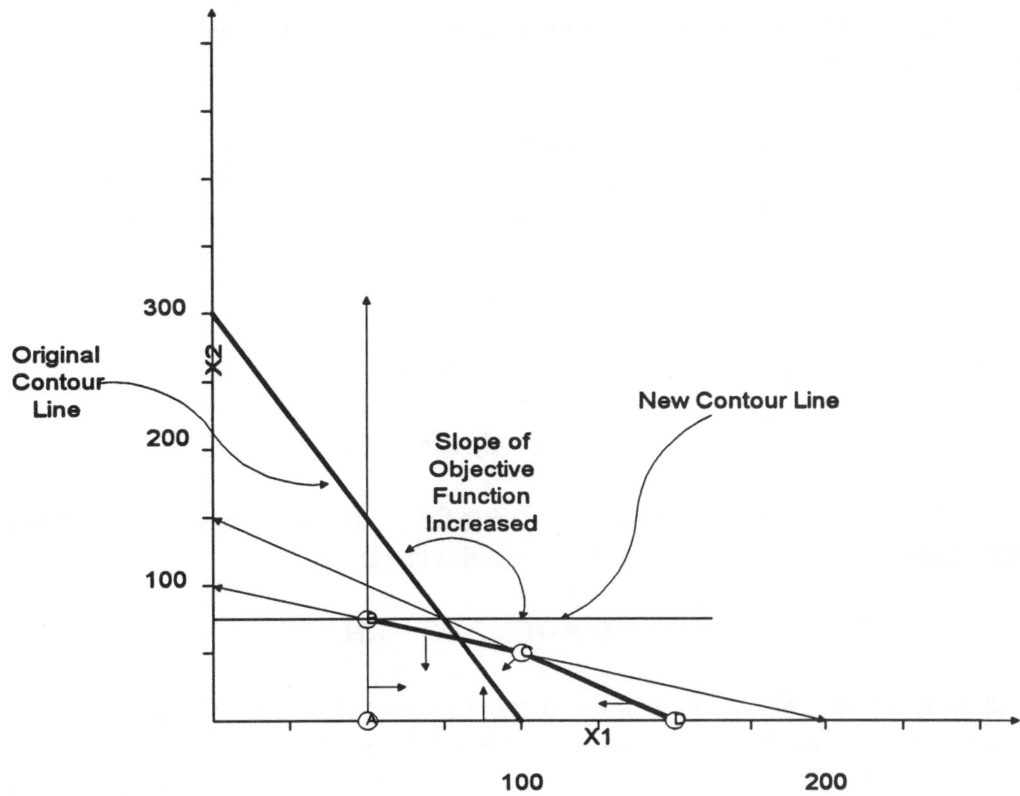

In this example, we have seen that we can decrease the slope of the objective function without causing a change in the optimal solution, however large enough increases in the slope of the objective function would cause a change in the optimal solution. The question that now arises is how do we know how much we can change the slope of the objective function without causing a change in the optimal solution. We will first answer this question intuitively and then answer it more mathematically.

To address this issue intuitively, refer to the original problem as depicted in Figure 6-1. In the original problem we determined that corner point D would be the last point that the contour lines would intersect as they were moved in a direction that increases the objective function value. Visually, we can verify in Figure 6-1 that as long as the slope of the contour lines is less than the slope of constraint line 1 (the binding constraint) and the value of the objective function increases as we move away from the origin, corner point D will be the optimal solution. Note that constraint lines 1 and 2, and the contour lines have negative slopes, and that these lines get steeper as the negative numbers increase in magnitude. We can also verify visually for this problem that if the slope of the contour lines is greater (i.e., a smaller negative number) than the slope of constraint line 1 and if the value of the objective function increases as we move away from the origin, corner point B will be the optimal solution. If the slope of the contour lines were exactly equal to the slope of constraint line 1, then corner points C and D would be alternate optimal solutions, as would all the points on the line segment that connects corner points C and D. Likewise, if the slope of the contour lines were exactly equal to the slope of constraint line 2, then corner points B and C would be alternate optimal solutions, as would all the points on the line segment connecting points B and C.

We can express these generalizations more precisely using the language of mathematics. Recall that the slope of a constraint line is the coefficient of X_1 when the equation has been solved for X_2. In general, if a constraint is expressed as:

$$C_1X_1 + C_2X_2 \leq RHS$$

it can be converted into the following constraint line:

$$C_1X_1 + C_2X_2 = RHS$$

where C_1 and C_2 are the constraint coefficients for X_1 and X_2, respectively, and RHS is the right-hand side constant. Solving this constraint line for X_2 yields:

$$X_2 = -(C_1/C_2)X_1 + RHS$$

Therefore, in general, the slope of a constraint line with two variables is $-(C_1/C_2)$. Also, it can be easily shown that the slope of the objective function contour lines are $-(C_1/C_2)$, where C_1 and C_2 are the objective function coefficients for X_1 and X_2, respectively.

To illustrate this, in the current example the slope of the objective function contour lines are -3 (-3/1). Likewise, the slopes for constraint lines 1 and 2 are -1 (-1/1) and -0.5 (-0.5/1), respectively.

Previously, we saw that corner point D would remain optimal as long as the slope for the contour lines was less than the slope of constraint line 1. We can now state this more precisely. Specifically, as long as the slope of the contour lines is less than -1, corner point D will be optimal. We can use this to quickly test alternative values of the objective function coefficients. For example, if we change C_1 in the objective function from 3 to 2 and hold C_2 constant at 1, the slope of the objective function contour lines would be -2 (-2/1). Since $-2 < -1$, corner point D would remain optimal. On the other hand, if we change C_2 to 6 holding C_1 constant at 3, the slope of the objective function contour lines would be -0.5 (-3/6). Since -0.5 is not less than -1, corner point D would not remain the optimal solution.

Regardless of whether a change in the objective function coefficients results in a new optimal solution or not, the value of the objective function must be recalculated. Previously, we investigated the effect of changing C_1 in the objective function from 3 to 2 while holding C_2 constant at 1. We noted that this change would not change the optimal solution. However, this change does change the value of the objective function. Specifically, the value of the objective function would decrease from 450 (3*150 + 1*0) to

300 (2*150 + 1*0). It is not always the case that a change in the objective function coefficients will lead to a change in the value of the objective function. To illustrate, if we changed the coefficient for X_2 in the objective function such that the optimal solution did not move from corner point D, the optimal solution value would still be 450 since the value of X_2 is zero and zero multiplied by the new value of C_2 is still zero.

Example Problem 2: Sensitivity Analysis on Right-Hand Side Constraint Constants

We will use the same model from the previous example to illustrate sensitivity analysis for the right-hand side constraint constants. The model was given as:

$\max 3X_1 + X_2$
s.t.
$X_1 + X_2 \leq 150$
$0.5X_1 + X_2 \leq 100$
$X_1 \geq 50$
$X_1, X_2 \geq 0$

We will illustrate sensitivity analysis for right-hand constants for both binding and nonbinding constraints, beginning with nonbinding constraints. Recall from the previous example that constraint 1 was a binding constraint while constraints 2 and 3 were nonbinding constraints.

When we plug the optimal values of the decision variable into constraint 2, we obtain the following:

$$.5(150) + 1(0) = 75.$$

Since the right-hand constant for constraint 2 is 100, the slack for this constraint is 25. This indicates there is more of this resource available than is needed. Thus, making additional quantities of this resource available should be of no value and should not improve the optimal solution. Let's check this intuition more rigorously. To do this assume that 50 additional units of this resource are made available. Constraint 2 is now expressed as:

$$0.5X_1 + X_2 \leq 150$$

and its corresponding constraint line is:

$$0.5X_1 + X_2 = 150$$

The new constraint line with the added resources is parallel to the original constraint line and is shown in Figure 6-4. The added resources now make constraint 2 redundant - it does not restrict the feasible region and therefore could now be eliminated without affecting the problem. Corner point B has also shifted upward. Previously corner point B was at the intersection of constraints 2 and 3. After shifting constraint 2, corner point B is now at the intersection of constraints 1 and 3. Furthermore, if you plot additional contour lines or use a straight edge, you will see that corner point D is still the optimal solution with $X_1 = 150$ and $X_2 = 0$. Also, since the coefficients in the objective function have not been changed, the optimal solution value is still 450. Thus, as our intuition suggested, adding extra resources to a nonbinding constraint did not improve the value of our optimal solution.

Figure 6-4

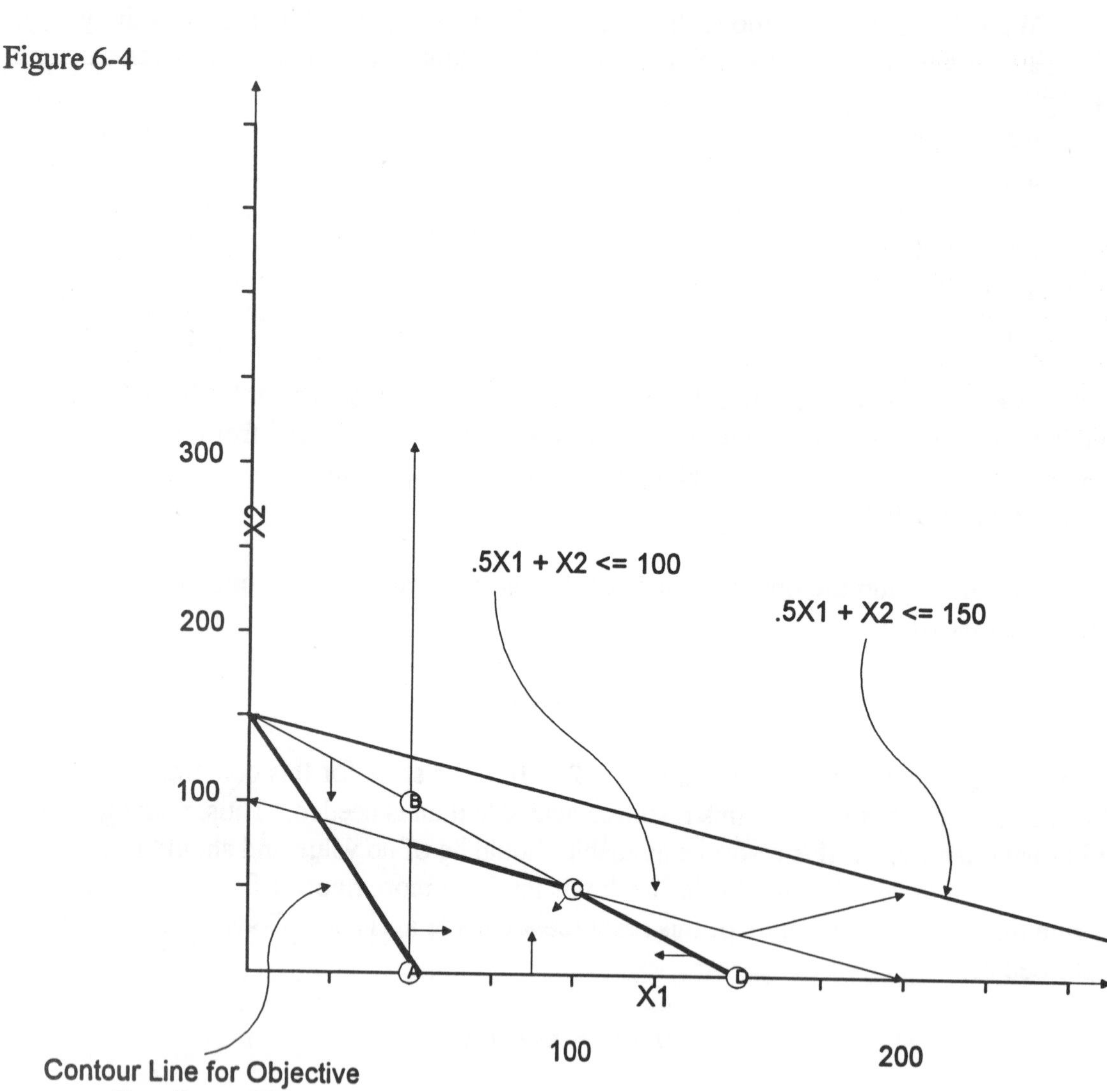

Referring to constrain 1, let's investigate what happens when we add resources to a binding constraint. When we plug the optimal values of the decision variables into constraint 1, we obtain the following:

$$1(150) + 1(0) = 150.$$

Since the right-hand constant for constraint 1 is 150, there is no slack for this constraint. This indicates that all of this resource is needed. Therefore, making additional quantities of this resource available should improve the optimal solution. Once again, let's check our intuition. To do this assume that 50 additional units of this resource are made available. Constraint 1 is now expressed as:

$$X_1 + X_2 \leq 200$$

and its corresponding constraint line is:

$$X_1 + X_2 = 200$$

As was just demonstrated, changing the right-hand side of a constraint results in a new constraint line that is parallel to the original constraint line. The new constraint line for constraint 2 with a right-hand side of 200 is shown in Figure 6-5. Adding resources to constraint 1 increases the size of the feasible region and corner point D shifts from (150, 0) to (200,0). Plotting the contour lines indicates that corner point D is the optimal solution and yields an improved solution value of 600 (3*200 + 1*0). Again, as our intuition suggested, adding extra resources to a binding constraint improved the value of the optimal solution.

Figure 6-5

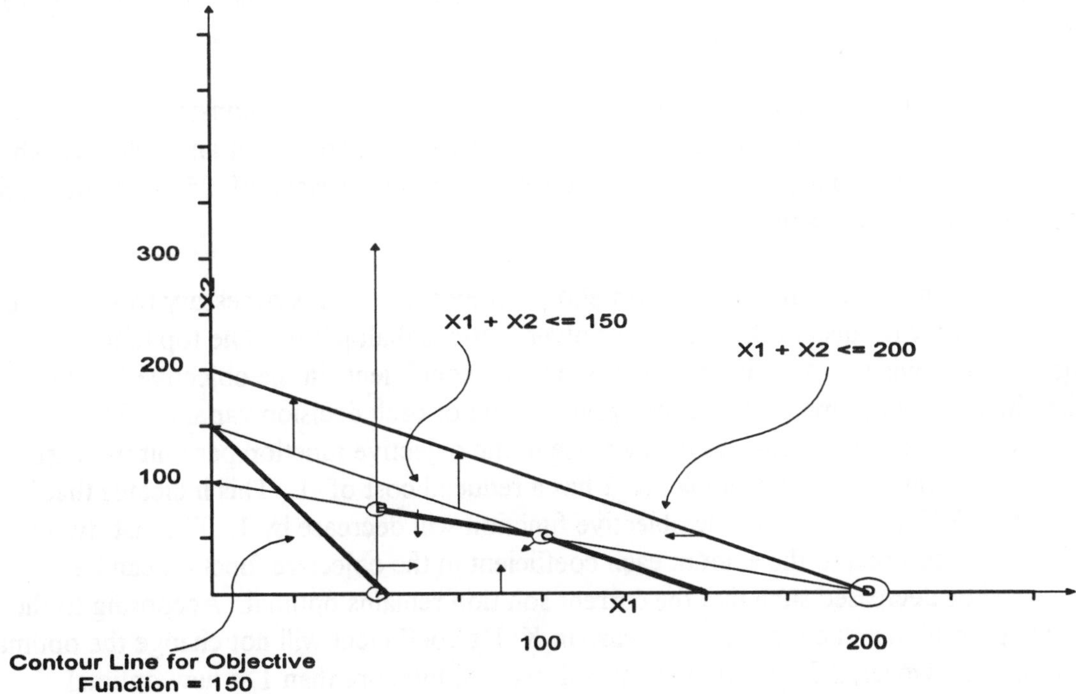

Example Problem 3: Sensitivity Analysis with EXCEL Solver

As the textbook noted, EXCEL can generate three reports when solving an LP. These reports are an Answer Report, a Limits Report, and a Sensitivity Report. Develop a spreadsheet to solve the problem presented in Example Problem 1 of this chapter. Then generate and interpret the information contained in each of the three reports.

Solution:

An EXCEL spreadsheet was developed to solve this problem in Example Problem 4 of Chapter 5. The spreadsheet with the optimal solution is shown in Figure 6-6. The formulas entered into this spreadsheet are shown in Figure 5-5. Since the steps to solve this LP were previously detailed in Example Problem 4 of Chapter 5 they will not be repeated here.

After obtaining a solution using the EXCEL Solver, the user is given a choice of selecting three reports. Figure 6-7 corresponds to the Answer Report. Likewise, Figures 6-8 and 6-9 correspond to the Sensitivity Report and Limits Report, respectively.

Referring to the Answer Report in Figure 6-7, the first table indicates that the objective function had an initial value of zero and a final or optimal value of 450. The initial value of the objective function was based on the initial or original values of the decision variables (or adjustable cells) shown in the second table in Figure 6-7. Specifically, both decision variables (X_1 and X_2) had initial values of zero. Also shown in the second table in Figure 6-7 is the final values for the decision variables. These final values correspond to the optimal solution to the LP.

The third table in Figure 6-7 provides information about the constraints. Specifically, this table provides the slack or surplus for each constraint and indicates which constraints were binding. Note that the second constraint has slack of 25, while the third constraint has a surplus of 100.

To obtain the Sensitivity Report shown in Figure 6-8, it is necessary to select the Assume Linear Model check box in the Solver Options dialog box. The top table in Figure 6-8 provides sensitivity information for the coefficients in the objective function. The Final Value column provides the optimal value of each decision variable. The Reduced Cost column measures the increase in the objective function per unit increase in the decision variable. For example, X_2 has a reduced cost of -1. This indicates that if we increase X_2 by one unit, the objective function will decrease by 1. The last two columns correspond to the amount each coefficient in the objective function can be increased or decreased such that the current solution remains optimal. According to the results presented in the table, any increase in X_1's coefficient will not change the optimal solution. However, if X_1's coefficient is decreased by more than 1, a new optimal

Figure 6-6

	A	B	C	D
1	**Example Problem 4**			
2				
3	**Parameters and Uncontrollable Variables:**			
4				
5		X1	X2	RHS
6	Objective	3	2	
7				
8	Constraint 1	1	1	150
9	Constraint 2	0.5	1	100
10	Constraint 3	1	0	50
11				
12	**Decision Variables:**			
13				
14	X_1	150		
15	X_2	0		
16				
17	**Model Outputs:**			
18				Slack/
19		Value	Limit	Surplus
20	Objective	450		
21				
22	Constraint 1	150	150	0
23	Constraint 2	75	100	25
24	Constraint 3	150	50	100

Figure 6-7

Microsoft Excel 5.0 Answer Report
Worksheet: [C5EX4.XLS]Sheet1
Report Created: 4/2/95 10:42

Target Cell (Max)

Cell	Name	Original Value	Final Value
$B$20	Objective Value	0	450

Adjustable Cells

Cell	Name	Original Value	Final Value
$B$14	X_1 X1	0	150
$B$15	X_2 X1	0	0

Constraints

Cell	Name	Cell Value	Formula	Status	Slack
$B$22	Constraint 1 Value	150	$B$22<=$C$22	Binding	0
$B$23	Constraint 2 Value	75	$B$23<=$C$23	Not Binding	25
$B$24	Constraint 3 Value	150	$B$24>=$C$24	Not Binding	100
$B$14	X_1 X1	150	$B$14>=0	Not Binding	150
$B$15	X_2 X1	0	$B$15>=0	Binding	0

Figure 6-8

Microsoft Excel 5.0 Sensitivity Report
Worksheet: [C5EX4.XLS]Sheet1
Report Created: 4/2/95 11:49

Changing Cells

Cell	Name	Final Value	Reduced Cost	Objective Coefficient	Allowable Increase	Allowable Decrease
$B$14	X_1 X1	150	0	3	1E+30	1
$B$15	X_2 X1	0	-1	2	1	1E+30

Constraints

Cell	Name	Final Value	Shadow Price	Constraint R.H. Side	Allowable Increase	Allowable Decrease
$B$22	Constraint 1 Value	150	3	150	50	100
$B$23	Constraint 2 Value	75	0	100	1E+30	25
$B$24	Constraint 3 Value	150	0	50	100	1E+30

Figure 6-9

Microsoft Excel 5.0 Limits Report
Worksheet: [C5EX4.XLS]Sheet1
Report Created: 4/2/95 10:47

Cell	Target Name	Value
$B$20	Objective Value	450

Cell	Adjustable Name	Value
$B$14	X_1 X1	150
$B$15	X_2 X1	0

Lower Limit	Target Result
50	150
0	450

Upper Limit	Target Result
150	450
0	450

solution will result. Thus, as long as X_1's coefficient in the objective function is between 2 and infinity, the solution of X_1 = 150 and X_2 = 0 will remain optimal. Recall that the sensitivity analysis information presented in these reports assumes that only one parameter is changed at a time and all the other parameters are held constant at their original levels.

The bottom table in Figure 6-8 contains sensitivity information for the constraints. To illustrate, the first constraint is binding and has a shadow price of 3. This means that the objective function will increase by 3 for each additional unit the right-hand side of this constraint is increased. The shadow price of 3 holds as long as the right-hand side is within the range given in the Allowable Increase and Allowable Decrease columns. Thus, the shadow price of 3 holds for the first constraint as long as the right-hand side for this constraint is between 50 and 200. Since the second constraint has slack, its shadow price is zero. In other words, since we already have more of this resource than is needed, obtaining more of this resource would not allow us to improve the optimal solution.

Figure 6-9 contains the Limit Report generated for this example. The top table simply reports the optimal value of the objective function. The bottom table indicates how much the changing cells (decision variables) can vary holding all the other parameters constant. Also reported in the bottom table is the objective function value (or target cell value) for the change.

TRUE/FALSE QUESTIONS

1. ___ While the objective function coefficients and constraint coefficients are considered parameters of a LP model, the right-hand side constants are not.

2. ___ Because LP models are deterministic, all the parameters are assumed known and constant.

3. ___ An optimal solution to a model is equivalent to an optimal solution to the real problem.

4. ___ Sensitivity analysis investigates about how people will react to the results of a LP solution.

5. ___ Changing the objective function coefficients changes the feasible region.

6. ___ Changes in the right-hand side values of an inequality constraint may or may not have an impact on the optimal LP solution and value.

7. ___ A constraint has been relaxed if the new value of the right-hand side makes the constraint more difficult to solve.

8. ___ Increasing the right-hand side of a ≥ constraint tightens the constraint.

9. ___ If the current optimal solution satisfies a newly added constraint, the current solution remains optimal.

10. ___ Deleting a nonbinding constraint at the current optimal solution does not affect the optimal solution.

11. ___ Deleting a redundant constraint changes the feasible region.

12. ___ Adding a constraint to a LP model will either leave the optimal objective function value the same or improve it.

13. ___ Dual prices are only valid within a certain range.

14. ___ The dual price for nonbinding constraints is always zero.

15. ___ Models that are mathematically equivalent will also provide equivalent sensitivity information.

16. ___ Linear programming should be viewed as a means of providing alternatives rather than providing the answer.

17. ___ If the cost of a resource is included in the objective function, the dual price indicates the maximum premium we should pay over the cost included in the objective function for an additional unit of this resource.

Answers:

1. F, 2. T, 3. F, 4. F, 5. F, 6. T, 7. F, 8. T, 9. T, 10. T, 11. F, 12. F, 13. T, 14. T, 15. F, 16. T, 17. T

CHAPTER 7

REVIEW

Multiobjective linear programming addresses the practical consideration that real-life problems often have multiple and perhaps conflicting objectives. Such multiobjective LPs have the same assumptions as ordinary LPs: 1) the objective function and constraints are linear functions of the decision variables, 2) the constraints are of the =, ≤, or ≥ type, and 3) fractional values for the decision variables are permitted.

Two approaches for dealing with the tradeoffs among multiple objectives are weighted objectives and absolute priorities. With the *weighted objectives* approach a combined objective function is created by applying weights to the alternative objectives based on their importance. Then the linear program is solved with this combined objective function. In order to use the weighted objectives approach, the coefficients in the objective function must have the same magnitude. If the coefficients associated with the different objectives vary considerably, then it will be required to scale one or more of the objectives by dividing its associated coefficients by a constant. Because different objectives are combined into a single objective function with the weighted objectives approach, the objective function has no direct meaning. Thus, we must evaluate each objective based on the optimal solution.

With the *absolute priorities* approach, the alternative objectives are ranked in terms of their priority. Then a series of linear programs are solved. In the first LP solved, the objective function corresponds to the highest ranked priority. In the second LP, the objective function for the highest priority goal becomes a constraint based on the first LP solution and the objective function corresponds to second highest priority. In the third LP, the objective functions for the first two LPs are constraints and the objective function corresponds to the third highest priority, and so on. With this procedure, anytime a higher priority objective leads to a unique optimal solution (i.e., a single corner point), the feasible region for the lower priority goals will be a single point and no change will occur to the optimal solution as lower priority objectives are introduced. However, if alternate optimal solutions exists, this procedure finds the alternative that best satisfies the next lower objective.

Another approach for dealing with multiobjective problems is goal programming. *Goal programming* can be used when each objective has a target or goal. Goal programming is distinguished from the other two approaches in that it attempts to *minimize deviations from prespecified goals.* With goal programming, goals are expressed mathematically with *soft constraints* (or *goal constraints*). In LPs, *hard constraints* represent the limitations or requirements that must be met and are not under the control of the decision maker. *Soft constraints* are used for situations where we have a desired target level, however this target can be violated if for example other important objectives can be improved. To create *goal constraints* (a type of soft constraint), we express the constraint as an equality with both slack and surplus variables. The slack and surplus variables associated with a goal are referred to as *deviational variables* since they are a measure of how far the solution deviates from the specified target.

Both the weighted objective approach and the absolute priority approach can be used in conjunction with goal programming. The weighted objective approach in goal programming uses linear weighted combinations of the deviational variables for the objective function of the linear program. Again, it is important to ensure that each constraint is of roughly the same magnitude. With the absolute priority approach, the highest priority goal is used as the objective function in the first LP. Then, based on the solution to the first LP, the objective function in the first LP becomes a constraint in the second LP and the second highest priority is used as the objective function. This process is repeated until all the objectives have been optimized.

SOLVED PROBLEMS

In this section the absolute priorities approach and the weighted objective approach will be illustrated for both multiobjective LPs and goal programming formulations.

Description of the Problem:

Color Watch Inc. makes watches for both men and women. Each week a particular assembly line produces only one model. However, while only one watch model is made on a given line in a given week, the model is made in both men's and women's sizes. Furthermore, the men's model can be made in up to six different colors while the women's model can be made in up to eight different colors. Production mangers prefer to limit the number of different color watches produced each week because switching colors requires shutting down the assembly line to prepare it for the new color and while the assembly line is being prepared for the new color, no watches are being produced. Manufacturing records indicate that it takes 1.5 times as long to change the line to accommodate the men's watch as it does to setup the line for women's watches. Also, manufacturing has determined that it is not practical to change the line more than 10 times in a given week. On the other hand, because a larger variety of color watches appeals to more customers, marketing prefers that the watches be produced in the maximum number of colors. In fact market research indicates that each color watch produced in a given week generates $1000 in revenue. Finally, note that manufacturing setups the line one time for a given color and produces a single batch of all of the watches in that color before setting up the line for the next color.

Mathematical Model

Based on the problem description, we can define the following two decision variables:

X_1 = number of different color men's watches to make this week, and

X_2 = number of different color women's watches to make this week.

In this problem, two different objectives are implied. The first objective is that manufacturing wishes to minimize the time associated with preparing the line to produce a new color watch. Since each time a new color watch is produced the line must be shut down, and since it takes 1.5 times longer to setup the line for men's watches, we can express this objective as follows:

$$\min 1.5X_1 + X_2$$

The other objective is associated with marketing's desire to produce watches with as many color options as possible. Since each color option generates $1000 in revenue per week, we can express this objective in the following manner:

$$\max 1000X_1 + 1000X_2$$

Next, we can express the constraints mathematically:

$X_1 \leq 6$ (men's watches have maximum of six color options)

$X_2 \leq 8$ (women's' watches have maximum of eight color options)

$X_1 + X_2 \leq 10$ (assembly line should not be shut down more than 10 times/week)

$X_1, X_2 \geq 0$ (nonnegativity constraints)

Example 1: Absolute Priorities Approach to Multiobjective LP

The feasible region and objective function contours for this example are shown in Figure 7-1. The small arrows emanating from the constraints indicate the halfspace that satisfies the constraint while the larger arrows emanating from the objective function contour lines indicate the direction in which the respective objective function values would be improved. Thus, the objective of minimizing color changeovers is improved by moving this contour line toward the origin, whereas the objective of maximizing revenues is improved by moving this contour line away from the origin.

Because of the large difference in magnitudes of the objective function coefficients between the two objectives, the second objective function corresponding to revenues was scaled by dividing its objective function coefficients by 1000. Thus, our two objective functions are:

$$\min 1.5X_1 + X_2$$
$$\max X_1 + X_2$$

To plot the contour line associated with minimizing the number of color changes, the objective function $1.5X_1 + X_2$ was set equal to 3. Plugging a zero in for X_1 and solving for X_2, and then plugging a zero in for X_2 and solving for X_1 yielded the points (0, 3) and (2, 0), respectively. Likewise, the second constraint was set equal to four and the points (0, 4) and (4, 0) were identified.

Visual inspection of Figure 7-1 indicates that the objective associated with minimizing assembly line changeovers is optimized at corner point A, while the objective associated with maximizing revenues has alternate optimal solutions corresponding to corner points C and D and all points on the line segment connecting points C and D. We note that there are alternate optimal solutions in this case because the slope for the contour line associated with revenues is equal to the slope of the binding constraint.

Figure 7-1

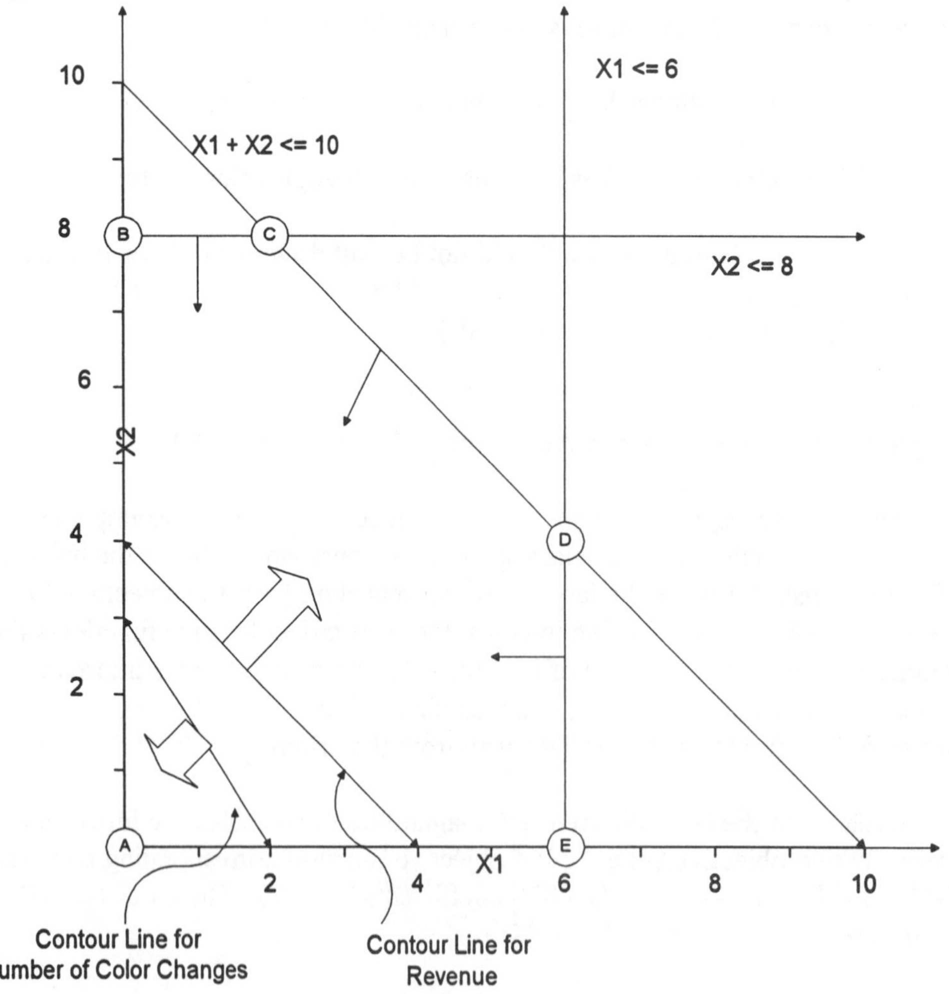

To illustrate solving this problem with the absolute priorities approach, assume that maximizing revenue is given higher priority than minimizing the number of times the assembly line is shut down. Then to apply the absolute priorities approach, we first solve the following LP:

max $1X_1 + 1X_2$
s.t.
$X_1 \leq 6$
$X_2 \leq 8$
$X_1 + X_2 \leq 10$
$X_1, X_2 \geq 0$

Referring to Figure 7-1 and as we previously observed, there are alternate optimal solutions to this problem. Specifically corner points C and D are both optimal solutions as are all the points on the line segment connecting points C and D. To verify this, point C's coordinates are (2, 8) while point D's coordinates are (6, 4). Plugging the coordinates of both of these points into the objective function yields an objective function value of 10.

Next we solve the following LP with the previous objective function entered as a constraint and the second objective added for the objective function:

min $1.5X_1 + 1X_2$
s.t.
$1X_1 + 1X_2 = 10$ (optimal solution of previous objective function)
$X_1 \leq 6$
$X_2 \leq 8$
$X_1 + X_2 \leq 10$
$X_1, X_2 \geq 0$

As is shown in Figure 7-2, adding the new constraint reduces the feasible region to the line segment connection points C and D. Also shown in Figure 7-2 are three contour lines corresponding to three values for the number of line changeovers. As can be seen from Figure 7-2, the last point that these contour lines would intersect in the feasible region (i.e., the line segment connecting points C and D) is point C. As we saw previously, the coordinates for point C are (2, 8). The objective function value corresponding to point C is 11. To verify that this is the optimal solution, recall that point D's coordinates are (6, 4) yielding an objective function value of 13 which is greater than 11. Thus, we found in this example that while there where alternate optimal solutions when only the first objective was considered, these alternate optimal solution were not equal when the second objective was considered.

Figure 7-2

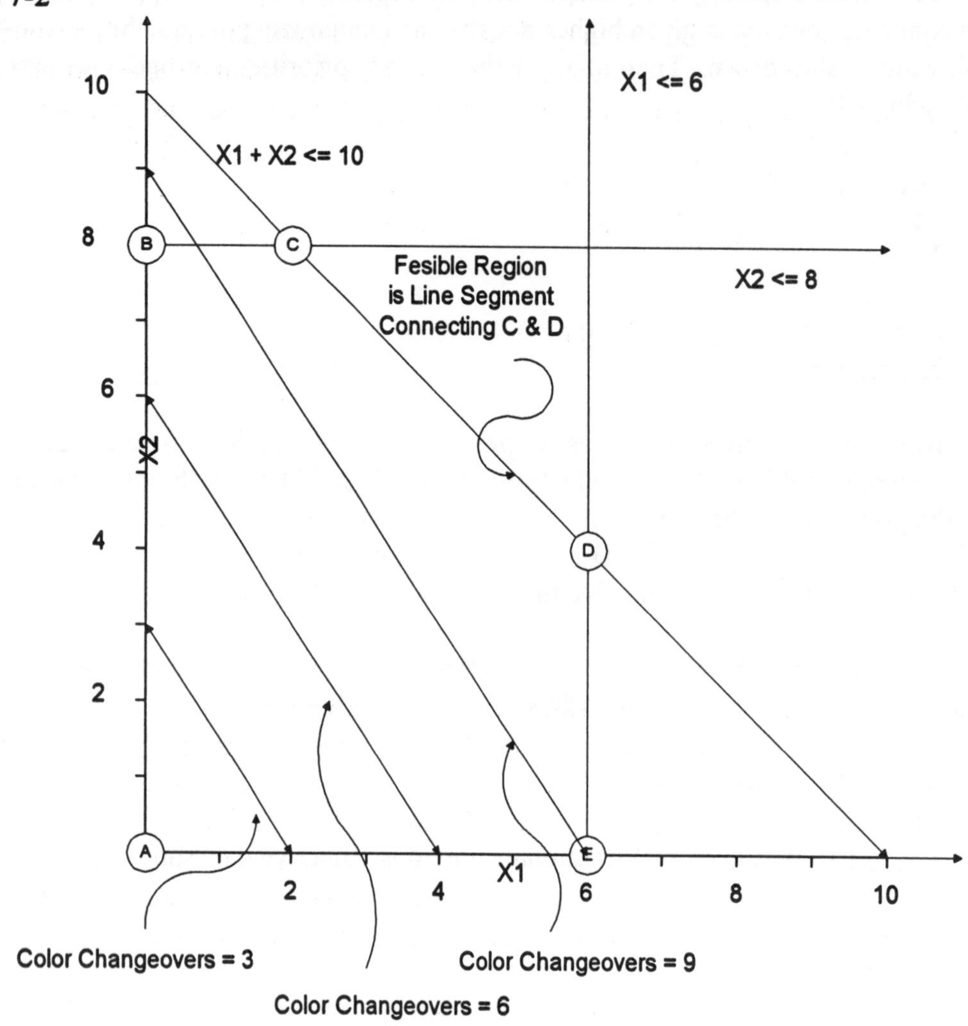

Example 2: Weighted Objective Approach to Multiobjective LP

To illustrate the weighted objective approach, assume that management gives four times as much weight to the revenue objective as it does to the color changeover objective. Thus, the coefficients of the revenue objective would be weighted by .8 (4/4+1) and the coefficients of the color changeover objective would be weighted by .2 (1/4+1). Recall that these objectives were expressed as:

max $1X_1 + 1X_2$, and
min $1.5X_1 + 1X_2$

Applying the respective weights to the objective functions yields:

max $.8(1X_1 + 1X_2) = .8X_1 + .8X_2$
min $.2(1.5X_1 + 1X_2) = .3X_1 + .2X_2$

Next, so that we can combine these two objectives functions we will convert the second objective function to a maximization type function by changing the signs of its coefficients. Thus, min $.3X_1 + .2X_2$ is equivalent to min $-.3X_1 - .2X_2$. Combining these two objective functions after changing the signs of the coefficients yields the following combined objective function:

$$\max .8X_1 + .8X_2 - .3X_1 - .2X_2 = .5X_1 + .6X_2$$

Thus, the complete model can be expressed as follows:

$\max .5X_1 + .6X_2$
s.t.
$X_1 \leq 6$
$X_2 \leq 8$
$X_1 + X_2 \leq 10$
$X_1, X_2 \geq 0$

If we set this objective function equal to 6 and plug in a zero for X_1, we get $X_2 = 5$. Similarly, if we plug in a zero for X_2, we get $X_1 = 6$. The corresponding contour line based on these two points is shown in Figure 7-3. Based on visual inspection of Figure 7-3 we can determine that the optimal solution is corner point C. However, because the objective function in this example is a combination of two different objectives that are each measured in different units, the value of the combined objective function has no direct meaning. Thus, we must go back and evaluate each objective independently based on the optimal solution obtained.

Figure 7-3

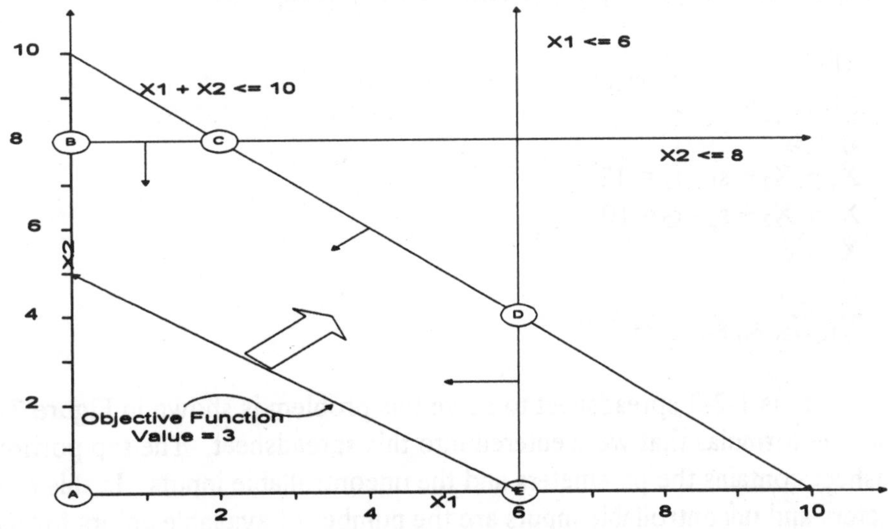

Example 3: Absolute Priorities Approach to Goal Programming

For the purpose of illustrating the absolute priorities approach to a goal program we assume that management now has set targets of $12,000 for weekly revenue and 10 for the number of color changeovers per week. Since each different color watch generates $1,000 in revenue per week, we can express the revenue goal as follows:

$$X_1 + X_2 + s_1 - r_1 = 12$$

Similarly, we can express the color changeover goal as:

$$X_1 + X_2 + s_2 - r_2 = 10$$

Further, if we assume that the maximizing revenue is ranked first and minimizing color changeovers is ranked second, then we have:

Priority 1 Goal: Min s_1
Priority 2 Goal: Min r_2

Thus, we would first solve the following LP corresponding to the priority 1 goal:

Min s_1
s.t.
$X_1 + X_2 + s_1 - r_1 = 12$
$X_1 + X_2 + s_2 - r_2 = 10$
$X_1 \leq 6$
$X_2 \leq 8$
$X_1, X_2, s_1, s_2, r_1, r_2 \geq 0$

Then, after obtaining the optimal solution and letting s_1^* represent the optimal value of s_1, we solve the following LP corresponding to the priority 2 goal:

Min r_2
s.t.
$s_1 = s_1^*$
$X_1 + X_2 + s_1 - r_1 = 12$
$X_1 + X_2 + s_2 - r_2 = 10$
$X_1 \leq 6$
$X_2 \leq 8$
$X_1, X_2, s_1, s_2, r_1, r_2 \geq 0$

A Lotus 1-2-3 spreadsheet to solve this problem is shown in Figure 7-4. Figure 7-5 shows the formulas that were entered into this spreadsheet. The top portion of the spreadsheet contains the parameters and the uncontrollable inputs. In this example the parameters and uncontrollable inputs are the number of available colors for men's and women's watches, respectively, and the target values for the two goals. The middle of the spreadsheet contains the decision variables, namely, X_1, X_2, s_1, s_2, r_1, and r_2. Note that the cells that contain the actual values of the decision variables were given range names corresponding to the decision variables. Thus, cell B23 was given the range name X_2 and cell E24 was given the name R_2. Doing this permitted entering the formulas for the constraints with the range names and not the actual cell addresses. Thus, the formulas entered into the spreadsheet more closely resemble the format of the constraints in mathematical models developed above.

The bottom of the spreadsheet contains the model outputs. The first two rows correspond to the constraints associated with the two goals. The next two rows correspond to the maximum number of colors available. The next rows contain nonnegativity constraints for each decision variable. Finally, the last two rows correspond to the priority goals.

The solution to the first LP is shown in Figure 7-6. Before solving LP problems with the Lotus Solver, initial values have to be entered for all decision variables. To accommodate this requirement, a zero was arbitrarily entered in all six cells that corresponded to the decision variables. Next, to solve the problem, the menu items Range-Analyze-Solver were selected. For the adjustable cells: B22..B23, D23..E23 was specified. For the constraint cells B29..B38 was entered. Finally, B40 was entered for the optimal cell, the min option was selected, and the solve menu button was selected.

As can be seen from Figure 7-6, the optimal solution is to make men's watches in six colors and to make women's watches in six colors. This results in no deviation from the revenue goal, however it requires two color changeovers over and above the target value of ten changeovers.

Next, the spreadsheet in Figure 7-6 can be modified to consider the second priority as follows.

1. In cell B39 add the constraint: S_1=0
2. Update the constraint cells range: B29..B39
3. Change the optimal cell from B40 to B41.

Making these changes and solving the problem does not change the optimal solution obtained after solving the first LP. Thus, in this case, alternate optimal solutions do not exist to the first LP.

Example Problem 4: Weighted Objective Approach to Goal Programming

Finally, to illustrate the weighted objective approach we assume that management places 4 times as much weight on the revenue goal as it does the color changeover goal. A LP model that combines the two objectives based on the specified weights is as follows:

Figure 7-4

	A	B	C	D	E	F	G
1	**Watch Production Planning Model**						
2							
3	***Parameters and uncontrollable inputs:***						
4							
5		Upper Bound					
6	Men's Watch						
7	Colors (X1)	6					
8							
9	Women's Watch						
10	Colors (X1)	8					
11							
12							
13		Color Changes	Revenues				
14	Target Values	10	12				
15							
16							
17							
18	***Decision Variables:***						
19							
20							
21		Colors		Deviations			
22	Men's	6		s	r		
23	Women's	6	1	0	0	Revenues	
24			2	0	2	Color Changes	
25							
26							
27	***Model Outputs:***						
28		Constraint	Value	Deviation	Total	Target	
29	Revenue	1	12	0	12	12	
30	Color Changes	1	12	-2	10	10	
31	Men's Colors	1	6				
32	Women's Colors	1	6				
33	Nonnegativity	1					
34	Constraints:	1					
35		1					
36		1					
37		1					
38		1					
39							
40	Priority 1	0	Minimize				
41	Priority 2	2	Minimize				

Figure 7-5

A	A	B	C	D	E	F	G
1	**Watch Production Planning Model**						
2							
3	***Parameters and uncontrollable inputs:***						
4							
5		Upper Bound					
6	Men's Watch						
7	Colors (X1)	6					
8							
9	Women's Watch						
10	Colors (X1)	8					
11							
12							
13		Color Changes	Revenues				
14	Target Values	10	12				
15							
16							
17							
18	***Decision Variables:***						
19							
20							
21		Colors		Deviations			
22	Men's	0		s	r		
23	Women's	0	1	0	0	Revenues	
24			2	0	0	Color Changes	
25							
26							
27	***Model Outputs:***						
28		Constraint	Value	Deviation	Total	Target	
29	Revenue	+X_1+X_2+S_1-R_1=C14	+X_1+X_2	+S_1-R_1	+C29+D29	+C14	
30	Color Changes	+X_1+X_2+S_2-R_2=B14	+X_1+X_2	+S_2-R_2	+C30+D30	+B14	
31	Men's Colors	+X_1<=B7	+X_1				
32	Women's Colors	+X_2<=B10	+X_2				
33	Nonnegativity	+X_1>=0					
34	Constraints:	+X_2>=0					
35		+S_1>=0					
36		+S_2>=0					
37		+R_1>=0					
38		+R_2>=0					
39							
40	Priority 1	+S_1	Minimize				
41	Priority 2	+R_2	Minimize				

Figure 7-6

A	A	B	C	D	E	F	G
1	**Watch Production Planning Model**						
2							
3	***Parameters and uncontrollable inputs:***						
4							
5		Upper Bound					
6	Men's Watch						
7	Colors (X1)	6					
8							
9	Women's Watch						
10	Colors (X1)	8					
11							
12							
13		Color Changes	Revenues				
14	Target Values	10	12				
15							
16							
17							
18	***Decision Variables:***						
19							
20							
21		Colors		Deviations			
22	Men's	0		s	r		
23	Women's	0	1	0	0	Revenues	
24			2	0	0	Color Changes	
25							
26							
27	***Model Outputs:***						
28		Constraint	Value	Deviation	Total	Target	
29	Revenue	0	0	0	0	12	
30	Color Changes	0	0	0	0	10	
31	Men's Colors	1	0				
32	Women's Colors	1	0				
33	Nonnegativity	1					
34	Constraints:	1					
35		1					
36		1					
37		1					
38		1					
39							
40	Priority 1	0	Minimize				
41	Priority 2	0	Minimize				

$\min .8s_1 + .2r_2$
s.t.
$X_1 + X_2 + s_1 - r_1 = 12$
$X_1 + X_2 + s_2 - r_2 = 10$
$X_1 \leq 6$
$X_2 \leq 8$
$X_1, X_2, s_1, s_2, r_1, r_2 \geq 0$

Figure 7-7 shows how the spreadsheet shown in Figure 7-4 can be modified to solve this problem. The only change required is that the two priority goals at the bottom of the spreadsheet shown in Figure 7-4 are replaced with the combined objective function. Thus, the formula (.8*S_1)+(.2*R_2) was entered in cell B40. After making this change; entering initial values for all decision variables; and specifying the appropriate ranges for the adjustable cells, constraint cells, and optimal cell, the problem was solved. Figure 7-7 shows the optimal solution obtained. Although not always the case, the same optimal solution was obtained using the weighted objective approach as was obtained with the absolute priorities approach. Figure 7-8 shows the formulas entered into the spreadsheet shown in Figure 7-7.

Figure 7-7

A	A	B	C	D	E	F	G
1	**Watch Production Planning Model**						
2							
3	***Parameters and uncontrollable inputs:***						
4							
5		Upper Bound					
6	Men's Watch						
7	Colors (X1)	6					
8							
9	Women's Watch						
10	Colors (X1)	8					
11							
12							
13		Color Changes	Revenues				
14	Target Values	10	12				
15							
16							
17							
18	***Decision Variables:***						
19							
20							
21		Colors		Deviations			
22	Men's	6		s	r		
23	Women's	6	1	0	0	Revenues	
24			2	0	2	Color Changes	
25							
26							
27	***Model Outputs:***						
28		Constraint	Value	Deviation	Total	Target	
29	Revenue	1	12	0	12	12	
30	Color Changes	1	12	-2	10	10	
31	Men's Colors	1	6				
32	Women's Colors	1	6				
33	Nonnegativity	1					
34	Constraints:	1					
35		1					
36		1					
37		1					
38		1					
39							
40	Obj. Function	0.4	Minimize				
41							

Figure 7-8

A	A	B	C	D	E	F	G
1	Watch Production Planning Model						
2							
3	***Parameters and uncontrollable inputs:***						
4							
5		Upper Bound					
6	Men's Watch						
7	Colors (X1)	6					
8							
9	Women's Watch						
10	Colors (X1)	8					
11							
12							
13		Color Changes	Revenues				
14	Target Values	10	12				
15							
16							
17							
18	***Decision Variables:***						
19							
20							
21		Colors		Deviations			
22	Men's	6		s	r		
23	Women's	6	1	0	0	Revenues	
24			2	0	2	Color Changes	
25							
26							
27	***Model Outputs:***						
28		Constraint	Value	Deviation	Total	Target	
29	Revenue	+X_1+X_2+S_1-R_1=C14	+X_1+X_2	+S_1-R_1	+C29+D29	+C14	
30	Color Changes	+X_1+X_2+S_2-R_2=B14	+X_1+X_2	+S_2-R_2	+C30+D30	+B14	
31	Men's Colors	+X_1<=B7	+X_1				
32	Women's Colors	+X_2<=B10	+X_2				
33	Nonnegativity	+X_1>=0					
34	Constraints:	+X_2>=0					
35		+S_1>=0					
36		+S_2>=0					
37		+R_1>=0					
38		+R_2>=0					
39							
40	Obj. Function	(+0.8*S_1)+(0.2*R_2)	Minimize				
41							

TRUE/FALSE QUESTIONS

1. ___ Multiobjective LPs have different assumptions than ordinary LPs.

2. ___ It is sometimes difficult to specify a single objective for a given planning scenario.

3. ___ One way to handle multiple conflicting objectives is to weight the different objectives and combine them into a single linear objective.

4. ___ When combining multiple objectives, the magnitudes of the coefficients corresponding to the different objectives is unimportant.

5. ___ It is possible to convert a minimization objective function to a maximization objective function simply by changing the signs of the coefficients in the objective function.

6. ___ A combined objective function has no direct meaning.

7. ___ In the weighted objective approach, the objectives are ranked from highest to lowest.

8. ___ In the absolute objective approach, anytime a higher priority solution leads to alternate optimal solutions, the feasible region for the lower priority goals will be a single point.

9. ___ The absolute priorities approach does not really tradeoff one objective with another.

10. ___ Multiobjective programming is an approach to multiple objective scenarios where each of the objectives has a target or goal.

11. ___ Both absolute priorities and the weighted objective approach can be used with goal programming.

12. ___ Soft constraints are not under the control of the decision maker.

13. ___ The solution to an ordinary LP does not allow a constraint to be violated.

14. ___ If two goal lines do not intersect in the original feasible region, alternate optimal solutions exist.

15. ___ The slack and surplus variables associated with each goal are referred to as deviational variables.

Answers:

1. F, 2. T, 3. T, 4. F, 5. T, 6. T, 7. F, 8. F, 9. T, 10. F, 11. T, 12. F, 13. T, 14. F, 15. T

CHAPTER 8

REVIEW

An *integer program* is a mathematical model where the decision variables are restricted to integer values. Decision variables that can take on any feasible integer value are referred to as *general integer variables*. Decision variables that can assume only a value of 0 or 1 are called *binary variables* or *zero-one variables*. Binary variables are particularly useful for modeling yes-or-no decisions in mathematical models. A *binary integer program* (BIP) is an integer program in which all the decision variables are binary variables. Often, planning models will have a combination of both integer and continuous variables. A *mixed integer program* (MIP) is a linear program that has integer (general and/or binary) decision variables and continuos decision variables.

A *linear programming relaxation* of an integer program is obtained by ignoring (or relaxing) the integer restrictions of the IP. Relaxing the integer restrictions is often used as the starting point in solving integer programs. If the optimal values of the decision variables to the LP relaxation are integers, then this is also the optimal solution to the original IP model. If on the other hand the optimal values of one or more of the decision variables to the LP relaxation are fractional, this solution is not a feasible solution to the IP.

The feasible region of an IP model is the set of integer points within the feasible region of the LP relaxation. While rounding or truncating the solution to the LP relaxation may result in a feasible integer solution, this solution may differ substantially from the optimal solution to the original IP model. In other words, feasible integer points close to the solution obtained from the LP relaxation may not be optimal. Furthermore, it is possible that none of the corner points of a feasible region are integer valued.

Two approaches for solving IP models are the branch and bound approach and the cutting plane approach. In the *branch and bound approach* the feasible region of the LP relaxation is divided into subregions so that only non-integer solutions are discarded. These subregions then become the feasible regions for a new LP. This process is repeated until integer-valued corner points of the subregions are found.

In the *cutting plane approach* constraints are added to the LP relaxation to force the optimal corner point to become integer valued. With the cutting plane approach, an added inequality constraint which does not eliminate any feasible integer solution is referred to as a *valid inequality*. A valid inequality that eliminates some fractional solutions is called a *cutting plane*. The cutting plane approach begins by adding a valid inequality of the solution to the LP relaxation that eliminates the non-integer solution. If the solution to the problem with the new valid inequality is integer this is the optimal solution to the IP. Otherwise another valid inequality is added to the model and the process is repeated until an integer solution is obtained.

Since standard sensitivity analysis assumes that fractional values for the decision variables are possible, it is not meaningful for integer programs. Thus, investigating the sensitivity of the parameters of an IP requires that the model be resolved for different parameter settings.

The amount of extra work required to solve an IP is related to how tight (or close) the solution of the LP relaxation is relative to the unknown IP optimal solution. Thus, a *tight* IP model is one whose LP relaxation provides an objective function value close to the IP's optimal objective function value. Because considerable amounts of computer time can be saved, it is desirable to develop tight IP models. For example, often the right-hand sides of the constraints can be adjusted based on the knowledge that the decision variables must assume integer values. Also, characteristics of a constraint can be used to adjust the right-hand side of a constraint (e.g., the left-hand side of a constraint will always be an even number). Finally, it is often possible to logically determine the optimal values of some of the decision variables prior to solving the model. *Variable pegging* locks in or assigns these variables their optimal value before solving the problem. This saves time by reducing the number of integer decision variables that must be considered by the IP solution procedure.

SOLVED PROBLEMS

Example Problem 1: Solving an IP Model with Excel

> Cash Register Incorporated (CRI) assembles three types of cash registers: a deluxe, regular, and economy model. Each deluxe model assembled and sold contributes \$10 to profits while the regular and economy models each contribute \$7.5 and \$13, respectively. The assembly times for the three cash registers are 4 hours, 5 hours, and 2 hours, respectively. In the upcoming week there will be 153 hours available in the assembly department. After finishing in assembly, each cash register is tested for one hour. There are three cash register testers, each specializing in a particular cash register model. The tester for the deluxe models will be available 10.75 hours in the upcoming week (he went home 45 minutes early in the prior week and will make up the time in the upcoming week). Likewise, the tester for the regular cash registers will be available 13 hours in the upcoming week, and the tester for the economy cash registers will be available 15 hours. Finally, the deluxe and economy cash registers share a common component of which there will only be 55 available in the week being planned. The deluxe model requires 2 of these components while the economy model requires four. How many cash registers of each model should CRI assemble in the upcoming week?

To solve this problem we first define the following decision variables:

X_1 = the number of deluxe cash registers to assemble in the upcoming week.

X_2 = the number of regular cash registers to assemble in the upcoming week.
X_3 = the number of economy cash registers to assemble in the upcoming week.

Next we can develop the objective function as follows:

$$\max 10X_1 + 7.5X_2 + 13X_3$$

Next, we can develop the constraints for the available assembly time and the limited supply of components that are shared by the deluxe and economy models as follows:

$$4X_1 + 5X_2 + 2X_3 \leq 153$$
$$2X_1 + 4X_3 \leq 55$$

Next, we consider the limited testing time available as follows:

$$1X_1 \leq 10.75$$
$$1X_2 \leq 13$$
$$1X_3 \leq 15$$

Since it is not possible to sell a partially assembled or negative number of cash registers, to complete the mathematical model we add the nonnegativity and integer constraints. The complete IP model is given below:

$$\max 10X_1 + 7.5X_2 + 13X_3$$
s.t.
$$4X_1 + 5X_2 + 2X_3 \leq 153$$
$$2X_1 + 4X_3 \leq 55$$
$$1X_1 \leq 10.75$$
$$1X_2 \leq 13$$
$$1X_3 \leq 15$$
$X_1, X_2, X_3 \geq 0$ and integer.

Figure 8-1 contains an Excel Spreadsheet to solve this problem. The formulas entered into this spreadsheet are shown in Figure 8-2. To solve this the Tools - Solver menu items were selected. For the target cell (objective function), **$E$28** was entered. Next, since this is a maximization problem, the max option was selected. For the changing cells (decision variables), the range **$B$19:$B$21** was specified. Finally, the following formulas corresponding to the constraints were entered:

$E$29 <= $B$13 (assembly time)
$E$30 <= $C$13 (common component)
$B$31 <= $D$13 (test time available for deluxe registers)
$C$31 <= $E$13 (test time available for regular registers)
$D$31 <= $F$13 (test time available for economy registers)
$B$19:$B$21 >= 0 (nonnegativity)

Figure 8-1

	A	B	C	D	E	F	G
1	**Cash Register Weekly Production Planning Model**						
2							
3							
4	***Parameters and uncontrollable inputs:***						
5							
6			Number				
7		Assembly	of	Hours to	Hours to	Hours to	
8		Time	Components	Test	Test	Test	Profit
9	Deluxe (X1)	4	2	1			10
10	Regular (X2)	5	0		1		7.5
11	Economy (X3)	2	4			1	13
12							
13	Available	153	55	10.75	13	15	
14							
15							
16	***Decision variables:***						
17							
18		Quantity					
19	Deluxe (X1)	0					
20	Regular (X2)	0					
21	Economy (X3)	0					
22							
23							
24	***Model outputs:***						
25							
26		X1	X2	X3	Total		
27	Quantity	0	0	0			
28	Profit	0	0	0	0		
29	Ass. Time	0	0	0	0		
30	Components	0	0	0	0		
31	Test Time	0	0	0			

Figure 8-2

	A	B	C	D	E	F	G
1	**Cash Register Weekly Production Planning Model**						
2							
3							
4	***Parameters and uncontrollable inputs:***						
5							
6			Number				
7		Assembly	of	Hours to	Hours to	Hours to	
8		Time	Components	Test	Test	Test	Profit
9	Deluxe (X1)	4	2	1			10
10	Regular (X2)	5	0		1		7.5
11	Economy (X3)	2	4			1	13
12							
13	Available	153	55	10.75	13	15	
14							
15							
16	***Decision variables:***						
17							
18		Quantity					
19	Deluxe (X1)	0					
20	Regular (X2)	0					
21	Economy (X3)	0					
22							
23							
24	***Model outputs:***						
25							
26		X1	X2	X3	Total		
27	Quantity	=B19	=B20	=B21			
28	Profit	=B27*G9	=C27*G10	=D27*G11	=B28+C28+D28		
29	Ass. Time	=B27*B9	=C27*B10	=D27*B11	=B29+C29+D29		
30	Components	=B27*C9	=C27*C10	=D27*C11	=B30+C30+D30		
31	Test Time	=B27*D9	=C27*E10	=D27*F11			

The solution obtained is shown in Figure 8-3. Since we did not specify that the decision variables should be integers, the solution shown in Figure 8-3 corresponds to the LP relaxation of the integer model. The optimal solution to the LP relaxation resulted in two decision variables with fractional values. Specifically the optimal solution obtained was $X_1 = 10.75$, $X_2 = 13$, and $X_3 = 8.375$. This solution provides a profit of $313.875. However, as was noted previously, it is not possible to sell a partial cash register. Therefore, we need to resolve this problem by adding the integer constraints. To accomplish this, the following constraint was added to the previously entered constraints:

$B$19:$B$21 INT

Adding this constraint adds the requirement that the decision variables in cells B19, B20, and B21 take on only integer values. The solution obtained to the IP model is shown in Figure 8-4. With the added integer constraints none of the decision variables takes on a fractional value. The optimal solution to the IP model is $X_1 = 10$, $X_2 = 13$, and $X_3 = 8$. Because adding the integer constraints serves to restrict or reduce the feasible region, we know that it is not possible to obtain an improved solution as a result of adding these constraints. In fact we would generally expect the solution to deteriorate as a result of adding these constraints. This is exactly what we observed in the case. Specifically the optimal solution decreased from a profit of $313.875 to a profit of $301.5.

Example Problem 2: Tightening an IP Model

Can anything be done to tighten the IP model presented in the previous example?

The IP model presented in the previous example was:

$$\max 10X_1 + 7.5X_2 + 13X_3$$
s.t.
$$4X_1 + 5X_2 + 2X_3 \leq 153$$
$$2X_1 + 4X_3 \leq 55$$
$$1X_1 \leq 10.75$$
$$1X_2 \leq 13$$
$$1X_3 \leq 15$$
$$X_1, X_2, X_3 \geq 0 \text{ and integer.}$$

First, notice that since X_1 must be an integer, the right-hand side of the third constraint must also be an integer. Therefore, since 10 is the largest integer that is less-than-or-equal-to 10.75, we can tighten the third constraint as follows:

$$1X_1 \leq 10$$

Next, if we plug in the maximum values of X_1 - X_3 based on constraints 3-5 into the first constraint we get 135 (4x10 + 5x13 + 2x15). Therefore, since the maximum possible value for the left-hand side of constraint 1 is 135, we can tighten it as follows:

Figure 8-3

	A	B	C	D	E	F	G
1	**Cash Register Weekly Production Planning Model**						
2							
3							
4	***Parameters and uncontrollable inputs:***						
5							
6			Number				
7		Assembly	of	Hours to	Hours to	Hours to	
8		Time	Components	Test	Test	Test	Profit
9	Deluxe (X1)	4	2	1			10
10	Regular (X2)	5	0		1		7.5
11	Economy (X3)	2	4			1	13
12							
13	Available	153	55	10.75	13	15	
14							
15							
16	***Decision variables:***						
17							
18		Quantity					
19	Deluxe (X1)	10.75					
20	Regular (X2)	13					
21	Economy (X3)	8.375					
22							
23							
24	***Model outputs:***						
25							
26		X1	X2	X3	Total		
27	Quantity	10.75	13	8.375			
28	Profit	107.5	97.5	108.875	313.875		
29	Ass. Time	43	65	16.75	124.75		
30	Components	21.5	0	33.5	55		
31	Test Time	10.75	13	8.375			

Figure 8-4

	A	B	C	D	E	F	G
1	**Cash Register Weekly Production Planning Model**						
2							
3							
4	***Parameters and uncontrollable inputs:***						
5							
6			Number				
7		Assembly	of	Hours to	Hours to	Hours to	
8		Time	Components	Test	Test	Test	Profit
9	Deluxe (X1)	4	2	1			10
10	Regular (X2)	5	0		1		7.5
11	Economy (X3)	2	4			1	13
12							
13	Available	153	55	10.75	13	15	
14							
15							
16	***Decision variables:***						
17							
18		Quantity					
19	Deluxe (X1)	10					
20	Regular (X2)	13					
21	Economy (X3)	8					
22							
23							
24	***Model outputs:***						
25							
26		X1	X2	X3	Total		
27	Quantity	10	13	8			
28	Profit	100	97.5	104	301.5		
29	Ass. Time	40	65	16	121		
30	Components	20	0	32	52		
31	Test Time	10	13	8			

$$4X_1 + 5X_2 + 2X_3 \leq 135$$

Finally, since any integer values for X_1 and X_3 plugged into the second constraint will yield an even number, this constraint can be tightened in the following way:

$$2X_1 + 4X_3 \leq 54$$

The IP model incorporating all these changes is:

$$\max\ 10X_1 + 7.5X_2 + 13X_3$$
s.t.
$$4X_1 + 5X_2 + 2X_3 \leq 135$$
$$2X_1 + 4X_3 \leq 54$$
$$1X_1 \leq 10$$
$$1X_2 \leq 13$$
$$1X_3 \leq 15$$
$$X_1, X_2, X_3 \geq 0 \text{ and integer.}$$

TRUE/FALSE QUESTIONS

1. ___ In general, integer programming models are no more difficult to solve than corresponding linear programs.

2. ___ A mathematical model where the coefficients in the objective function are restricted to integer values is called an integer program.

3. ___ General integer variables are decision variables which can take on any feasible integer value.

4. ___ General integer variables can be used to model yes-or-no decisions.

5. ___ Another name for binary variables is zero-one variables.

6. ___ A binary integer program is an integer program where some but not all of the decision variables are restricted to be either zero or one.

7. ___ A mixed integer program has both general integer and binary integer decision variables, but no continuos variables.

8. ___ A linear programming relaxation of the integer program is created by relaxing or ignoring the integer restrictions of the IP.

9. ___ If the optimal decision variables to the LP relaxation turn out to be integers, then that solution is also optimal to the IP.

10. ___ A feasible rounded or truncated solution to the LP relaxation may be far from the optimal solution of the original IP.

11. ___ It is not possible to have feasible regions such that none of the corner points are integer valued.

12. ___ The branch and bound approach attempts to add constraints to the LP relaxation to force the optimal corner point to become integer-valued.

13. ___ A valid inequality that eliminates some fractional solutions is known as a cutting plane.

14. ___ To determine the sensitivity of an integer program to its parameters, the model must be resolved with different parameter settings.

15. ___ Large amounts of computer time can be saved by developing loose IP models.

16. ___ A tight LP model is one whose LP relaxation provides an objective function value close to the IP's optimal objective function value.

17. ___ Because of the power offered by today's computers, the time to solve IP models is not noticeably different from the time to solve regular LP models.

18. ___ Variable pegging requires that the optimal value for one or more decision variables be determined logically prior to solving the IP model.

Answers:

1. F, 2. F, 3. T, 4. F, 5. T, 6. F, 7. F, 8. T, 9. T, 10. T, 11. F, 12. F, 13. T, 14. T, 15. F, 16. T, 17. F, 18. T

CHAPTER 9

REVIEW

A *network* is a set of *nodes* that are connected by undirected lines called *branches* or by arrows called *arcs*. *Undirected networks* use branches to indicate a connection between two nodes while *directed networks* use arcs to indicate a directional relationship among the nodes. Typically, branches and arcs are defined by the numbers of the nodes they connect. *Flow* represents the movement of objects through a network.

Network optimization is an important area of management science because: 1) networks can be used to model a wide variety of decision problems, 2) networks are understandable and accepted by managers because they provide a visual picture of the problem, and 3) the mathematical properties associated with networks permit the development of special algorithms to solve large problems.

A *path* in a network is a sequence of nodes that are connected to one another by branches or arcs. By definition, a path must begin at one node and end at another node, however, the path may include a node more than once. A network is said to be *connected* if a path between every pair of nodes exists. A *directed path* is a path where all the arcs are pointing in the same direction. A *cycle* is a path whose first and last nodes are the same. *A directed cycle* is a cycle with all the arcs pointing in the same direction.

A *tree* is a connected network with no cycles. A *spanning tree* is a tree that contains all the nodes of the original network.

Source nodes are nodes from which flow originate and *sink nodes* are nodes at which flows terminate. Source notes typically have some supply while sink nodes typically have a demand. The *conservation of flow* principle states that the total flow into a node must equal the flow out of the node. *Arc capacity* represents the total amount of flow that is allowed on a given arc.

A number of applications of network models were presented in the chapter including the transportation problem, the transshipment problem, transportation planning, equipment replacement, the maximum flow problem, network design, project scheduling, and investment planning.

A path in a project network from the beginning to ending nodes represents a sequence of activities that must be performed in sequential order. The time required to complete these activities is the *length of the path*. Since a project can be completed no earlier than the length of the longest path, the longest path is referred to as the *critical path*. Any delay in completing the activities on the critical path results in delay in completing the project. Activities on the critical path are referred to as *critical activities*.

In working with project networks the following quantities are typically calculated for each activity: 1) the earliest start time (ES), 2) the earliest finish time (EF), 3) the latest start time (LS), and 4) the latest finish time (LF). The earliest start time for any activity leaving a node is equal to the largest early finish time for all activities entering the node. The latest finish time for all activities that end at a node is equal to the smallest latest start time for all activities leaving the node. *Slack* represents the amount of time an individual activity can be delayed without delaying the entire project. Slack for an activity is computed as LS - ES or LF - EF. All activities on the critical path have zero slack.

Crashing an activity refers to shortening individual activity times by allocating additional resources to complete the activity.

A *dummy activity* is a fictitious arc that is added to a project network solely to show precedence relationships. Dummy activities have no meaning in terms of the actual set of project activities.

SOLVED PROBLEMS

Example Problem 1: Shortest Route Problem

A traveler from a small town wants to find the route that minimizes the bus fares she must pay. Since her town does not have a bus terminal, she must first take a bus to one of three adjacent towns that does have a bus terminal. Each of these bus terminals has service to the other bus terminals as well as service to the traveler's final destination. The traveler has obtained the following bus fare information:

Bus Fare to Travel	To City			
From City	1	2	3	Destination
Home Town	6	9	12	-
1	-	2	6	10
2	2	-	5	7
3	4	7	-	6

To illustrate, the bus fare to travel from city 3 from city 1 is \$4. Likewise, the bus fare to travel from the traveler's home town to city 2 is \$9, and the fare to travel from city 1 to the traveler's destination is \$10. Note that the bus fares are not symmetrical in the above table. In other words it costs different amounts to travel from city i to j than it does to travel from city j to i. These asymmetrical costs could be the result of travel patterns, different labor contracts in the different cities, the scale of operations of the different bus terminals, or various other factors. Develop a network diagram to help the traveler pick the lowest cost route.

Solution:

Figure 9-1 shows the network diagram developed for this problem. In Figure 9-1 each city is represented by node in the diagram and the bus routes between cities by directed arcs. The traveler's home town city is represented by node S while the destination city is represented by node T. Also, in Figure 9-1 each arc is labeled as Xij where i corresponds to the starting node of the arc and j corresponds to the ending node of the arc. Furthermore, the bus fare associated with each arc is shown in Figure 9-1. To illustrate, from the above table the bus fare to travel from city 3 to city 1 is $4. To reflect this, arc X31 in Figure 9-1 has a cost of $4. Likewise, it was given that if the traveler initially took a bus to city 1, the bus fare would be $6. Thus, in Figure 9-1, arc XS1 has a cost of $6.

The shortest route problem discussed in the text is used when the decision maker seeks to find a route that minimizes time or cost. Note that this problem is a variation of the shortest route problem discussed in the chapter. The difference being that in this problem the costs are asymmetrical as we discussed previously. Developing the network diagram for this problem is similar to the diagram developed in Example 3 in the text. A directed arc is used to represent each possible bus route between two cities and one unit of supply was assigned to node S and one unit of demand was assigned to node T.

Figure 9-1

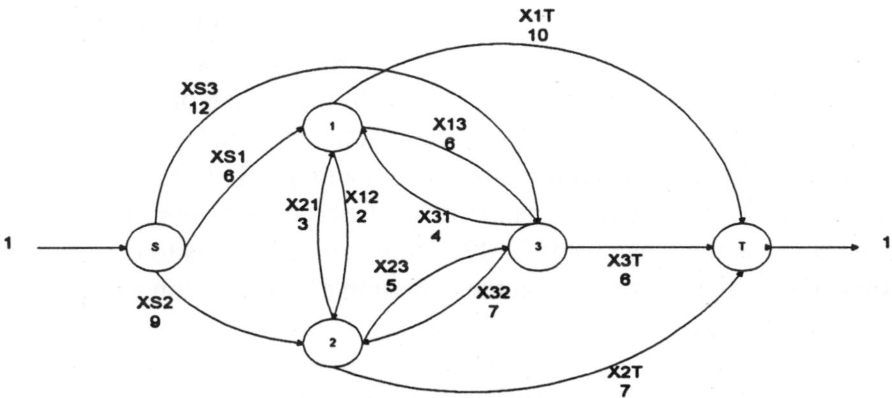

Next we can develop the corresponding LP model to this network diagram. Our objective is to minimize the traveler's total bus fare. The only restrictions are the conservation of flows for each node. Recall that the conservation of flow for a node requires that the flow out of the node equal the flow into the node. The complete LP model for this situation is as follows:

min $12X_{S1} + 2X_{12} + 6X_{13} + 3X_{21} + 9X_{S2} + 5X_{23} + 4X_{31} + 7X_{32} + 12X_{S3} + 10X_{1T} + 7X_{2T} + 6X_{3T}$

s.t.

$X_{S1} + X_{S2} + X_{S3} = 1$ (conservation of flow for node S)

$X_{1T} + X_{12} + X_{13} - X_{S1} - X_{21} - X_{31} = 0$ (conservation of flow for node 1)

$X_{2T} + X_{21} + X_{23} - X_{S2} - X_{12} - X_{32} = 0$ (conservation of flow for node 2)

$X_{3T} + X_{31} + X_{32} - X_{S3} - X_{13} - X_{23} = 0$ (conservation of flow for node 3)

$- X_{1T} - X_{2T} - X_{3T} = -1$ (conservation of flow for node T)

$X_{ij} \geq 0$, $i = S, 1, 2, 3; j = 1, 2, 3, T$ (nonnegativity)

The objective function minimizes the sum of the bus fares. To illustrate how the constraints were developed we will refer to the first constraint. Since the flow out of a node must equal the flow into the node, the flow out minus the flow in must equal zero. The flow into node S is 1. The flow out of node S is the sum X_{S1}, X_{S2}, and X_{S3}. Expressing this as flow out minus flow in yields:

$$X_{S1} + X_{S2} + X_{S3} - 1 = 0$$

To obtain an equation identical to constraint 1 requires moving the constants to the right-hand side as follows:

$$X_{S1} + X_{S2} + X_{S3} = 1$$

Figure 9-2 contains a Lotus spreadsheet that can be used to find the route that minimizes total bus fares. At the top of the spreadsheet, the fares between all pairs of cities that buses travel between have been entered. In the middle of Figure 9-2, the decision variables have been entered. As we have done previously, the Lotus command /RangeNameLablesRight (/RNLR) was used with the range A17..A28. This gave the cells in the range B17..B28 the range names of the labels entered in cells A17..A28. To illustrate, cell B21 has the range name X_13. Doing this allows us to use range names for the decision variables that closely match the definition of the decision variables in the mathematical model above.

The bottom of Figure 9-2 contains the model outputs. Figure 9-3 shows the formulas that were entered in the model output section. The first row of the model outputs (i.e., row 33) corresponds to the objective function to minimize total bus fare. The next five rows are the conservation of flow constraints for each node in the network. Finally, the last twelve constraints are the nonnegativity constraints for each decision variable. Recall, that Lotus does not assume that the decision variables are nonnegative

Figure 9-2

	A	B	C	D	E
1	**Bus Route Problem**				
2					
3	***Parameters and uncontrollable inputs:***				
4					
5					
6	Bus fares between cities:				
7					
8	From City	City 1	City 2	City 3	Destination
9	Home Town	6	9	12	
10	City 1		2	6	10
11	City 2	2		5	7
12	City 3	4	7		6
13					
14					
15	***Decision Variables:***				
16					
17	X_S1	0			
18	X_S2	0			
19	X_S3	0			
20	X_12	0			
21	X_13	0			
22	X_21	0			
23	X_23	0			
24	X_31	0			
25	X_32	0			
26	X_1T	0			
27	X_2T	0			
28	X_3T	0			
29					
30					
31	***Model outputs:***				
32					
33	Total Bus Fare	0			
34	Node S	0			
35	Node 1	1			
36	Node 2	1			
37	Node 3	1			
38	Node T	0			
39	nonnegativity	1			
40	"	1			
41	"	1			
42	"	1			
43	"	1			
44	"	1			
45	"	1			
46	"	1			
47	"	1			
48	"	1			
49	"	1			
50	"	1			

Figure 9-3

A	A	B
31	***Model outputs:***	
32		
33	Total Bus Fa	(X_S1*B9)+(X_S2*C9)+(X_S3*D9)+(X_12*C10)+(X_13*D10)+(X_21*B11)+(X_23*D11)+(X_31*B12)+(X_32*C12)+(X_1T*E10)+(X_2T*E11)+(X_3T*E12)
34	Node S	+X_S1+X_S2+X_S3=1
35	Node 1	+X_1T+X_12+X_13-X_S1-X_21-X_31=0
36	Node 2	+X_2T+X_21+X_32-X_S2-X_12-X_32=0
37	Node 3	+X_3T+X_31+X_32-X_S3-X_13-X_23=0
38	Node T	-X_1T-X_2T-X_3T=-1
39	nonnegativity	+X_S1>=0
40	"	+X_S2>=0
41	"	+X_S3>=0
42	"	+X_12>=0
43	"	+X_13>=0
44	"	+X_21>=0
45	"	+X_23>=0
46	"	+X_31>=0
47	"	+X_32>=0
48	"	+X_1T>=0
49	"	+X_2T>=0
50	"	+X_3T>=0

and therefore these constraints must be explicitly entered when solving mathematical programming models with Lotus.

To obtain the optimal solution to this problem, the Range-Analyze-Solver menu items were selected. For the adjustable cells the range B17..B28 was specified. Recall that the cells in the adjustable cell range cannot be empty. Thus, a zero was initially entered into each of these cells. For the constraint cells the range B34..B50 was entered. Next, B33 was entered for the optimal cell. Finally, min and solve were selected with the mouse and the optimal solution shown in Figure 9-4 was obtained. According to the optimal solution the traveler should take a bus from her home town to city 1. Then, she should take a bus from city 1 to city 2 and then from city 2 to her final destination. Such a route will cost her $15.

Example Problem 2: Project Scheduling

Project Management Inc. (PMI) has collected the following data on a project that is about to begin:

Activity	Immediate Predecessor	Completion Time (days)	Crash cost/day	Maximum Days Crashed
A	none	5	2	1
B	none	7	3	1
C	A	8	2	2
D	A	7	4	2
E	B,C	10	3	1
F	D,E	4	1	2

At a normal rate, how long will this project take to complete? If PMI desires to complete the project in 23 days what do you recommend?

Solution:

We begin by using the information provided in the table to construct the network diagram shown in Figure 9-5. In Figure 9-5 each arc is labeled by the letter of the activity it corresponds to and duration of the activity.

From Figure 9-5 we note that there are three paths through the network. One path consists of the activities A, C, E, and F (or alternatively, nodes 1, 2, 3, 4, and 5) with a duration or length of 27 days. A second path is activities A, D, and F with a length of 16 days. The last path has a length of 21 days and consists of activities B, E, and F. Path A, C, E, and F is the critical path since it is the longest path. Furthermore, activities A, C, E, and F are the critical activities and any delay in the completion of these activities would cause a delay in completing the project. Since all paths must be finished to complete the project, the time to complete this project is 27 days.

Figure 9-4

A	A	B	C	D	E
1	**Bus Route Problem**				
2					
3	***Parameters and uncontrollable inputs:***				
4					
5					
6	Bus fares between cities:				
7					
8	From City	City 1	City 2	City 3	Destination
9	Home Town	6	9	12	
10	City 1		2	6	10
11	City 2	2		5	7
12	City 3	4	7		6
13					
14					
15	***Decision Variables:***				
16					
17	X_S1	1			
18	X_S2	0			
19	X_S3	0			
20	X_12	1			
21	X_13	0			
22	X_21	0			
23	X_23	0			
24	X_31	0			
25	X_32	0			
26	X_1T	0			
27	X_2T	1			
28	X_3T	0			
29					
30					
31	***Model outputs:***				
32					
33	Total Bus Fare	15			
34	Node S	1			
35	Node 1	1			
36	Node 2	1			
37	Node 3	1			
38	Node T	1			
39	nonnegativity	1			
40	"	1			
41	"	1			
42	"	1			
43	"	1			
44	"	1			
45	"	1			
46	"	1			
47	"	1			
48	"	1			
49	"	1			
50	"	1			

Figure 9-5

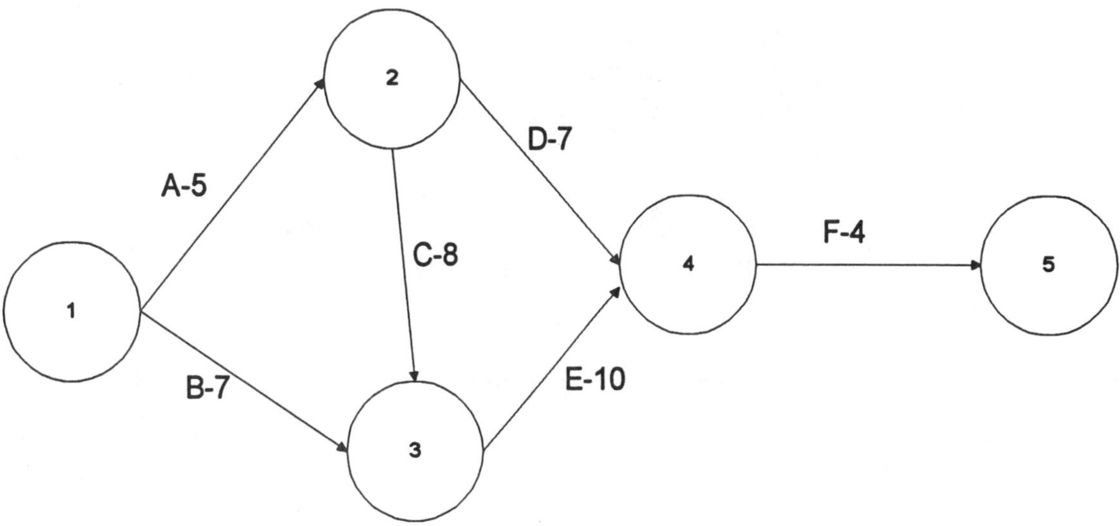

To develop schedules for the resources needed to complete a project, project mangers are often interested in determining the earliest start (ES) and finish (EF) time, and latest start (LS) and finish (LF) time for each activity. The earliest start and finish times for this project are shown in square brackets ([]) in Figure 9-6. To calculate the ES and EF times we start at the left of the network and work our way to the right. For all activities at the starting node, the earliest start time is set to zero. Thus, both activities A and B have ES times of 0. If activity A is started at its earliest start time of time zero, its earliest finish time would be 5 (0 + 5) since it takes 5 days to complete activity A. Recall that EF = ES + t. Likewise, if activity B is started at time zero, its earliest finish time is day 7 (0 + 7). Since there is only one arc leading in to node 2, both activities C and D would have an earliest start time of 5. In other words, since both activities C and D cannot be started until activity A is finished, the earliest start time for activities C and D is equal to the earliest finish time of activity A. Since activities C and D have durations of 7 and 8 respectively, their earliest finish time are 12 (5 + 7) and 13 (5 + 8), respectively. Moving on to activity E, we notice that both activities B and C must be finished before activity E can be started. Since activity E cannot be started until both activities B and C are completed, the earliest start time for activity E is the larger of the two earliest finish time for activities B and C. Recall that the early start time for any activity leaving a node is equal to the largest early finish time for all activities entering the node. In this case since activity C has the largest earliest finish time, the earliest start time for activity E is day 13. Given a duration of 10, activity E's early finish time is calculated to be 23 (13 + 10). The remaining early start and finish time can be calculated in a similar fashion.

The latest start times and latest finish times are shown in the curved brackets ({}) in Figure 9-7. To calculate the latest start and finish time we work our way from the right to the left. Also, recall that LS = LF - t and the latest finish times for all ending

Figure 9-6

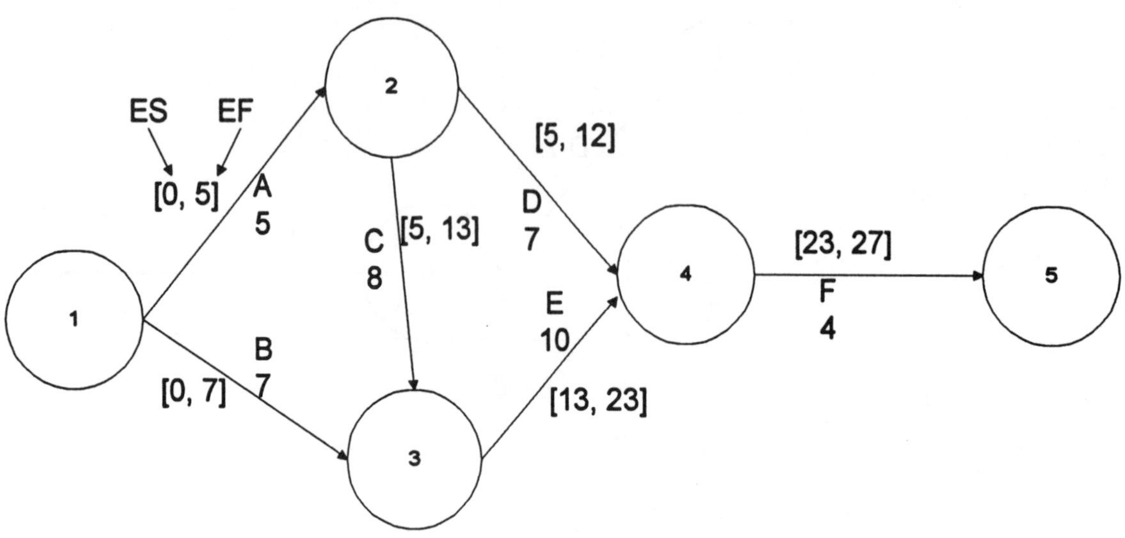

Figure 9-7

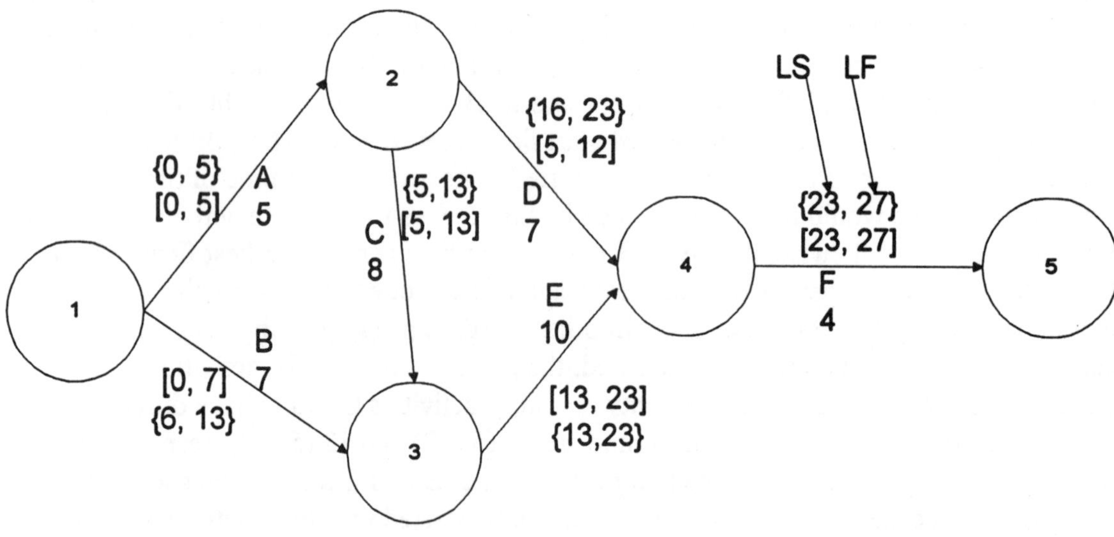

activities are equal to the minimum completion time. In this example, activity F is the only ending activity and the minimum completion time is 27 days. Thus, the latest finish time for activity F is set equal to 27 days. Then using the formula for LS, activity F's LS is calculated to be 23 (27 - 4). Working backwards, since activity F's latest start time is day 23, activities D and E must be finished no later than day 23. Therefore, activities D and E both have a latest finish time of 23. Since these activities have durations of 7 and 10 respectively, their latest start times are 16 (23 - 7) and 13 (23 - 10), respectively. Moving on to activity C, since activity E has a latest start time of 13, activity C can finish no later than 13. Also, since activity C has a duration of 8, to finish by time 13, it can start no later than 5. Hence activity C's LS and LF times are 5 and 13, respectively.

Turning to activity A, we observe that activity C can start as late as day 5 while activity D can start as late as day 16. Recall that the latest finish time for all activities that end at a node is equal to the smallest latest start time for all activities leaving the node. In this case the latest start times for the activities leaving node 2 are 5 and 16. In order not to delay the project, we must pick the smallest of these latest start times or 5 in this case. Thus, the latest finish time for activity A is 5. If we picked 16 as the latest finish time for activity A, then activity C would not be stared in time to complete the project since it has a latest start time of day 5. The latest start and finish times are calculated for the remaining activities in a similar fashion.

In addition to determining the earliest start and finish times, and the latest start and finish times for each activity, project managers are also interested in the slack for each activity. Recall that the slack is computed as LS - ES or LF - EF. In English, slack is the amount of time that an individual activity can be delayed without delaying the minimum project completion date. Clearly, all activities on the critical path will have zero slack. The table below summarizes the project scheduling results:

Activity	ES	EF	LS	LF	Slack
A	0	5	0	5	0
B	0	7	6	13	6
C	5	13	5	13	0
D	5	12	16	23	7
E	13	23	13	23	0
F	23	27	23	27	0

Finally, recall that management desired to complete this project within 23 days. Since the critical path is 27 days, some of the activities will need to be *crashed* to meet this objective. The help make this decision, we will use the information in the last two columns of the table that provided the data for this problem. In the second to last column we have the cost to crash or shorten each activity one day and in the last column we have the maximum number of days each activity can be crashed. To develop a mathematical model we define the following decision variables:

S_i = the earliest start time for activity i
F_i = the earliest finish time for activity i
X_i = the amount to crash or shorten activity i

We know that:

$F_i = S_i + t_i$ (where t_i is the regular duration of activity i), and
Activity Time for Activity i After Crashing = $t_i - X_i$

Our objective is to minimize the costs associated with crashing the activities such that we complete the project by day 23. Mathematically, we can state the objective function as:

$\min 2X_A + 3X_B + 2X_C + 4X_D + 3X_E + 1X_F$

Next, we develop the early start constraints as follows:

$S_A = 0$
$S_B = 0$
$S_C = F_A$
$S_D = F_A$
$S_E \geq F_C$
$S_E \geq F_C$
$S_F \geq F_D$
$S_F \geq F_E$

In a similar fashion, we can develop the early finish constraints in the following way:

$F_A = S_A + 5 - X_A$
$F_B = S_B + 7 - X_B$
$F_C = S_C + 8 - X_C$
$F_D = S_D + 7 - X_D$
$F_E = S_E + 10 - X_E$
$F_F = S_F + 4 - X_F$

Next, we add constraints for the maximum amount each activity can be crashed:

$X_A \leq 1$
$X_B \leq 1$
$X_C \leq 2$
$X_D \leq 2$
$X_E \leq 1$
$X_F \leq 2$

Finally, we add a constraint for the desired completion time of 23 days and the nonnegativity constraints:

$F_F \leq 23$
$X_i, S_i, F_i \geq 0$

Combining this yields the complete LP model as follows:

$\min 2X_A + 3X_B + 2X_C + 4X_D + 3X_E + 1X_F$
s.t.

$S_A = 0$
$S_B = 0$
$S_C = F_A$
$S_D = F_A$
$S_E \geq F_C$
$S_E \geq F_C$
$S_F \geq F_D$
$S_F \geq F_E$
$F_A = S_A + 5 - X_A$
$F_B = S_B + 7 - X_B$
$F_C = S_C + 8 - X_C$
$F_D = S_D + 7 - X_D$
$F_E = S_E + 10 - X_E$
$F_F = S_F + 4 - X_F$
$X_A \leq 1$
$X_B \leq 1$
$X_C \leq 2$
$X_D \leq 2$
$X_E \leq 1$
$X_F \leq 2$
$F_F \leq 23$
$X_i, S_i, F_i \geq 0$

Figure 9-8 contains a spreadsheet that was used to solve this LP and Figure 9-9 shows the formulas that were entered into Figure 9-8. The top of Figure 9-8 contains model inputs which include the activity times, the cost to crash each activity one day, and the maximum amount each activity can be crashed. The middle section of the Figure 9-8 contains the decision variables. Note for each activity there are three decision variables: the earliest start for the activity (column B), the earliest finish for the activity (column D), and the amount to crash the activity (column F). The Range-Name-Labels-Right command was used so that the cells in columns B, D, and F could be referred to by the labels entered in columns A, C, and E, respectively. To illustrate, cell B22 has the range name SD and cell F20 has the range name XB.

The bottom section of Figure 9-8 contains the model outputs. Row 29 corresponds to the objective function of minimizing the costs associated with crashing the project. Rows 30-37 correspond to the early start time constraints. Rows 38-43 correspond to the early finish time constraints. Rows 44-49 correspond to the maximum amount each activity can be crashed. Row 50 corresponds to a constraint that ensures that the project is completed by the specified time entered in the model inputs section. Finally, rows 61-68 contain the nonnegativity constraints. Note that because of the way the decision variables were organized, it was possible to use the copy command to enter many of these formulas for the constraints. For example, once the constraint for the amount activity A could be crashed was entered in cell B44, it was copied to cells B45-B49. Similarly, the nonnegativity constraint for SA entered in cell B51 was copied to cells

Figure 9-8

	A	B	C	D	E	F
1	Project Crashing Model					
2						
3	*Parameters and uncontrollable inputs:*					
4						
5			Daily	Max. Days		
6	Activity	Time	Crash Cost	Crashed		
7	A	5	2	1		
8	B	7	3	1		
9	C	8	2	2		
10	D	7	4	2		
11	E	10	3	1		
12	F	4	1	2		
13						
14	Target Completion Date		23			
15						
16						
17	*Decision Variables:*					
18						
19	SA	0	FA	5	XA	0
20	SB	0	FB	7	XB	0
21	SC	5	FC	11	XC	2
22	SD	5	FD	12	XD	0
23	SE	11	FE	21	XE	0
24	SF	21	FF	23	XF	2
25						
26						
27	*Model Outputs:*					
28						
29	Crash Cost	6				
30	ES A	1				
31	ES B	1				
32	ES C	1				
33	ES D	1				
34	ES E	1				
35	ES E	1				
36	ES F	1				
37	ES F	1				
38	EF A	1				
39	EF B	1				
40	EF C	1				
41	EF D	1				
42	EF E	1				
43	EF F	1				
44	Max Crash A	1				
45	Max Crash B	1				
46	Max Crash C	1				
47	Max Crash D	1				
48	Max Crash E	1				
49	Max Crash F	1				
50	Finish by Day 23	1				
51	nonnegativity	1				
52	nonnegativity	1				
53	nonnegativity	1				
54	nonnegativity	1				
55	nonnegativity	1				
56	nonnegativity	1				
57	nonnegativity	1				
58	nonnegativity	1				
59	nonnegativity	1				
60	nonnegativity	1				
61	nonnegativity	1				
62	nonnegativity	1				
63	nonnegativity	1				
64	nonnegativity	1				
65	nonnegativity	1				
66	nonnegativity	1				
67	nonnegativity	1				
68	nonnegativity	1				
69						

Figure 9-9

A	A	B	C	D	E	F
1	Project Crashing Model					
2						
3	***Parameters and uncontrollable inputs:***					
4						
5			Daily	Max. Days		
6	Activity	Time	Crash Cost	Crashed		
7	A	5	2	1		
8	B	7	3	1		
9	C	8	2	2		
10	D	7	4	2		
11	E	10	3	1		
12	F	4	1	2		
13						
14	Target Completion Date		23			
15						
16						
17	***Decision Variables:***					
18						
19	SA	0	FA	5	XA	0
20	SB	0	FB	7	XB	0
21	SC	5	FC	11	XC	2
22	SD	5	FD	12	XD	0
23	SE	11	FE	21	XE	0
24	SF	21	FF	23	XF	2
25						
26						
27	***Model Outputs:***					
28						
29	Crash Cost	(C7*XA)+(C8*XB)+(C9*XC)+(C10*XD)+(C11*XE)+(C12*XF)				
30	ES A	+SA=0				
31	ES B	+SB=0				
32	ES C	+SC=FA				
33	ES D	+SD=FA				
34	ES E	+SE>=FB				
35	ES E	+SE>=FC				
36	ES F	+SF>=FD				
37	ES F	+SF>=FE				
38	EF A	+FA-SA+XA=B7				
39	EF B	+FB-SB+XB=B8				
40	EF C	+FC-SC+XC=B9				
41	EF D	+FD-SD+XD=B10				
42	EF E	+FE-SE+XE=B11				
43	EF F	+FF-SF+XF=B12				
44	Max Crash A	+XA<=D7				
45	Max Crash B	+XB<=D8				
46	Max Crash C	+XC<=D9				
47	Max Crash D	+XD<=D10				
48	Max Crash E	+XE<=D11				
49	Max Crash F	+XF<=D12				
50	Finish by Day 23	+FF<=C14				
51	nonnegativity	+SA>=0				
52	nonnegativity	+SB>=0				
53	nonnegativity	+SC>=0				
54	nonnegativity	+SD>=0				
55	nonnegativity	+SE>=0				
56	nonnegativity	+SF>=0				
57	nonnegativity	+FA>=0				
58	nonnegativity	+FB>=0				
59	nonnegativity	+FC>=0				
60	nonnegativity	+FD>=0				
61	nonnegativity	+FE>=0				
62	nonnegativity	+FF>=0				
63	nonnegativity	+XA>=0				
64	nonnegativity	+XB>=0				
65	nonnegativity	+XC>=0				
66	nonnegativity	+XD>=0				
67	nonnegativity	+XE>=0				
68	nonnegativity	+XF>=0				
69						

B52-B56. The ability to copy formulas can save considerable amounts of time and can also reduce data entry errors.

To obtain the optimal solution to this problem, the Range-Analyze-Solver menu items were selected. For the adjustable cells the range B19..B24, D19..D24, F19..F24 was specified. Recall that the cells in the adjustable cell range cannot be empty. Thus, a zero was initially entered into each of these cells. For the constraint cells the range B30..B68 was entered. Next, B29 was entered for the optimal cell. Finally, min and solve were selected with the mouse and the optimal solution shown in Figure 9-8 was obtained.

Referring to Figure 9-8 we note that activities C and F were each crashed 2 days at total cost of $6. Based on this, the early start times for activities A-F are 0, 0, 5, 5, 11, and 21, respectively. Similarly, the early finish times of the activities are 5, 7, 11, 12, 21, and 23. Notice that activity F is now finished by the target completion date.

TRUE/FALSE QUESTIONS

1. ___ A network is a collection of nodes which are connected by branches or arcs.

2. ___ Branches indicate a specific direction and the resulting network is called a directed network.

3. ___ The movement of objects through a network is called a flow.

4. ___ Networks are often accepted more readily by managers because they provide a visual picture of the problem under study.

5. ___ A path may not include a given node more than once.

6. ___ If a path exists between every pair of nodes, the network is considered connected.

7. ___ If all arcs are pointed in the same direction, we call the path a cycle.

8. ___ A tree is a connected network with no cycles.

9. ___ A tree that contains only a subset of the nodes in the original network is called a spanning tree.

10. ___ Nodes from which flows originate are called sink nodes.

11. ___ The conservation of flow principle states that at any node, the total flow into the node must equal the total flow out.

12. ___ Arc capacity is the total amount of flow that is allowed on an arc.

13. ___ In the transshipment problem flows go directly from sources to sinks.

14. ___ The maximum flow problem is applicable to situations where the decision maker seeks to determine the maximum amount that can be transported form a source to a sink when the arcs of the network have limited capacity.

15. ___ In any network flow problem with integer data, the optimal solution will be integer.

16. ___ The shortest path in a project network is called the critical path.

17. ___ The early start time for any activity leaving a node is equal to the smallest early finish time for all activities entering the node.

18.___ The slack is the amount of time that an individual activity can be delayed without delaying the minimum project completion date.

19. ___ The critical path consists of all activities with non-zero slack.

20. ___ Shortening individual activity times by allocating additional resources is called crushing the activity.

21. ___ A dummy activity is a fictitious arc in a project network that is used to show precedence and has no meaning in the actual set of project activities.

Answers:

1. T, 2. F, 3. T, 4. T, 5. F, 6. T, 7. F, 8. T, 9. F, 10. F, 11. T, 12. T, 13. F, 14. T, 15. T, 16. F, 17. F, 18. T, 19. F, 20. F, 21. T

CHAPTER 10

REVIEW

A *heuristic* is a "rule of thumb" to guide decision making or for finding approximate solutions to optimizations problems. Heuristics are used in several ways. First, they can be used to provide good starting solutions for exact optimization algorithms. Second, heuristic rules can be used to intelligently direct the operation of an optimizing algorithm. Finally, heuristics can be used to reduce the computational requirements. For example, heuristic procedures are commonly used to solve large combinatorial optimization problems, i.e., problems that require the selection or arrangement of discrete objects.

Four reasons for using heuristics instead of exact optimization algorithms are: 1) exact optimization algorithms may require too much time or money to develop and run, 2) the software needed for exact optimization algorithms may not be available, 3) it may not be justified to invest the time and effort to solve a problem with an exact optimization algorithm when the inputs are based on imprecise estimates, and 4) mangers may prefer simple heuristic solutions that are understandable to the solutions provided by exact optimization algorithms that they do not understand. The major disadvantage of heuristic algorithms is that they do not produce guaranteed optimal solutions.

Heuristic algorithms can be classified as construction heuristics or improvement heuristics. *Construction heuristics* build a feasible solution by adding individual components one at a time and terminate when a feasible solution is obtained. *Greedy heuristics* that seek to maximize the improvement at each step are examples of construction heuristics. *Improvement heuristics* begin with a feasible solution and successively improve it by a series of exchanges or mergers. Often, heuristic algorithms will combine construction and improvement approaches. Typically, an initial solution is obtained with a construction heuristic and then an improvement heuristic is used to identify better solutions.

In addition to construction heuristics and improvement heuristics, there are several other generic heuristic approaches. For example, in m*athematical programming* a solution to an integer programming problem may be obtained by rounding the solution obtained from the LP relaxation. As another example, *decomposition* may be used where a problem is solved in stages. As a final example, a problem may be *partitioned* into smaller subproblems each of which is solved independently.

Heuristics are particularly applicable to integer programs because: 1) large integer programs are difficult to solve optimally, 2) good feasible solutions can be used to speed up the performance of optimization algorithms, and 3) good feasible solutions provide bounds on the optimal solution.

Neighborhood search approaches are often used to obtain heuristic solutions to integer programs and other complex problems. A *neighborhood* consists of solutions that are close together. For example, a neighborhood could be defined as the set of all solutions that differ from a given solution by exactly one variable. Likewise, a neighborhood could be defined as the set of all solutions that differ from a given solution by two or fewer decision variables. Note that increasing the size of the neighborhood increases the computational effort. Thus, there is a trade-off between the amount of computation required and the quality of the solution obtained. Using neighborhood search, all solutions in the neighborhood are examined, and if a better feasible solution is found it becomes the current solution. This process is continued until no solution in the neighborhood improves the value of the objective function.

Designing heuristics is currently much an art. In designing heuristics it is useful to begin with a comprehensive mathematical model of the problem, even if it cannot be solved. A good heuristic should have the following features: 1) simplicity, 2) computational efficiency, 3) accuracy, and 4) robustness.

As a decision maker it is useful to ask the following questions about a heuristic: Does the heuristic provide a guarantee on the quality of the solution? What is the average solution quality? Does the solution quality depend on problem characteristics such as problem size or structure? How does computation time increase as the problem size increases?

Most heuristics used in optimization problems employ search methods. When a search procedure terminates when it has found the best solution within a particular neighborhood, such a solution is called a *local optimum*. The best solution to the problem is called the *global optimum* solution. Depending on the search procedure and particular problem, it is likely that a local optimum is quite far away from the global optimum solution. Three popular heuristic search procedures are *tabu search*, *simulated annealing*, and *genetic algorithms*.

Because solving problems with nonlinear relationships are much more difficult to solve than problems with linear relationships, nonlinear relationships are frequently approximated with linear relationships. By approximating nonlinear relationships with linear relationships, linear programming solvers can be used to obtain reasonably good solutions with much less computational effort. When using linear approximations remember these rules:

1. When approximating a nonlinear profit function with linear segments in a maximization LP model, it must be that the slopes of the line segments do not increase as you move from left to right.

2. When approximating a nonlinear cost function with linear segments in a minimization LP model, it must be that the slopes of the line segments do not decrease as you move from left to right.

3. When approximating a nonlinear function, more segments result in a better approximation, but the number of variables included in the LP model increases since one decision variable is needed for each segment.

SOLVED PROBLEMS

Example Problem 1: Plant Layout Problem

A manufacturer has completed the production of its new plant and now must decide where to locate its six departments on the shop floor. The shop floor has been divided into six equal areas and each location has been labeled with a number from 1 - 6 as shown below:

1	2	3
4	5	6

Material flows between the locations are limited to rectangular movements and thus diagonal movements are not permitted. Thus, to move material from location 1 to location 6 would require traveling through locations 2 and 3 or through locations 4 and 5. Material cannot be transferred diagonally from location 1 to location 5. The travel distance between adjacent locations is 10 feet.

Management has collected data on the amount of material that moves between its six departments on a daily basis as follows:

	A	B	C	D	E	F
A	-	100	120	75	50	110
B	-	-	45	110	35	80
C	-	-	-	90	55	85
D	-	-	-	-	75	130
E	-	-	-	-	-	65

To illustrate, the amount of material that moves between departments B and D is 110 units each day. Management wishes to assign the six departments to the six locations so that the total distance traveled moving materials between the departments is minimized.

Solution:

We will use a construction heuristic to develop an initial layout solution and then illustrate how an improvement heuristic can be used to identify better solutions. For the construction heuristic we will employ a greedy approach. Specifically, we will develop an initial solution by identifying the two departments that the most material moves between and locate them together. Then, the next highest material flow between two departments will be identified and these two departments assigned adjacent location. This process is repeated until all departments have be assigned a location.

Referring to the material flows table, we observe that the largest material flow of 130 corresponds to flows between departments D and F. Thus we arbitrarily assign departments D and F to locations so that they are adjacent. One possible assignment is to assign department D to location 1 and department F to location 2 as is shown below:

D	F	

The next largest material flow is 120 corresponding to departments A and C. Again, we will choose a location for these two departments so that they are adjacent to one another. One possible assignment is to assign department A to location 3 and department C to location 6 as shown below:

D	F	A
		C

Continuing, we observe that the next largest flow is 110 which corresponds to flows between departments A and F, and departments B and D. Departments A and F have already been assigned and are adjacent to one another. Also, since department D has already been assigned to location 1, we assign department B to location 4 so that it is adjacent to department D.

D	F	A
B		C

Now there is only one department and one location left, so we assign department E to location 5. The complete initial shop layout is shown below:

D	F	A
B	E	C

Before investigating ways of improving the initial layout, we have to have a measure for the quality of the solution. Since the objective is to minimize the travel distances associated with moving parts between the departments, one measure is the total distance traveled by all parts which can be calculated as follows:

$$\text{Total Travel Distance} = \sum_{i=1}^{N-1} \sum_{j=i+1}^{N} D_{ij} F_{ij}$$

where:

D_{ij} = the distance between departments i and j
F_{ij} = the material flow between departments i and j
N = the number of departments

To illustrate this formula, we first will calculate the travel distances for all material that travels to or from department A. From our initial layout solution we can determine that the travel distances from department A to departments B, C, D, E and F are 30, 10, 20, 20, and 10 respectively. Furthermore, the amount of materials moved between department A and departments B, C, D, E, and F are 100, 120, 75, 50, and 110, respectively. The total distance materials travel between department A and the other five departments given the initial layout is:

$$30(100) + 10(120) + 20(75) + 20(50) + 10(110) = 7800$$

In a similar fashion, the total distance material travels between department B and the other departments can be calculated. Note that in the previous calculation we already included the material flows between departments A and B. Since we do not want to double count these material flows, we only consider the material flows between department B and departments C, D, E, and F as follows:

$$20(45) + 10(110) + 10(35) + 20(80) = 3950$$

To complete the analysis, we calculate the material travel distances for departments C, D, and E as follows:

Department C: $30(90) + 10(55) + 20(85) = 4950$
Department D: $20(75) + 10(130) = 2800$
Department E: $10(65) = 650$

Summing these distances yields a total travel distance of 20,150 (7800 + 3950 + 4950 + 2800 + 650) for the initial shop layout developed. In other words, using the above formula to compute total travel distance yields 20,150 feet for the initial shop layout.

Now that we have an initial layout and a performance measure to evaluate layouts, we can focus our attention on finding better layouts. In this case there are 720 (6!) ways to assign the six departments to the six locations so it is not practical to enumerate and evaluate all possible layouts. Therefore, we will use a neighborhood search algorithm to generate alternative solutions. In this example we will define the neighborhood for a given layout as all layouts where the position of only two departments is different from the given layout. Thus, alternative layouts are created by switching the location of two departments. The set of neighborhood layouts for the initial layout would be generated by switching the location of departments A & B, A & C, A & D, A & E, A& F, B & C, B & D, B & E, B& F, C& D, C & E, C & F, D & E, D & F, and E & F.

For example, the first alternative layout listed above is obtained by switching the location of departments A and B as follows:

D	F	B
A	E	C

Notice that making this change only changes the distance of material movements that involve either or both departments A and B. The distance traveled by material that does not move between either of these departments is unchanged. Thus, to determine the effect of this change requires that we only consider the flows that involve departments A and B. In the initial layout developed, we determined that the material flows involving departments A and B traveled 11,750 (7800 + 3950) feet. After switching these two departments, the travel distance of all parts that travel to or from department A and B is 13,000 (8850 + 4150) feet and is calculated as follows:

Department A: 30(100) + 20(120) + 10(75) + 10(50) + 20(110) = 8850
Department B: 10(45) + 20(110) + 20(35) + 10(80) = 4150

Since 13,000 is greater than 11,750, switching departments A and B is not advantageous.

Next consider switching departments A and C in the original layout as shown below:

D	F	C
B	E	A

Now we only have to recalculate the distance traveled for material that travels directly between departments A and C:

Department A: 20(100) + 10(120) + 30(75) + 10(50) + 20(110) = 8150
Department C: 20(90) + 20(55) + 10(85) = 3750.

In the original layout the total distance for the materials that traveled directly between departments A and C was 12,750 (7800 + 4950) feet. In the new layout with departments A and C switched the total distance is 11,900 (8150 + 3750) feet. Thus, the new layout does offer an improvement over the original solution since 11,900 is less than 12,750. This procedure would be repeated for the other 13 possible two-way switches. After each of these layouts is evaluated the one that offers the most improvement would be selected and then all the neighborhood layouts of it could be investigated. This process is continued until none of the neighborhood layouts offers an improvement over the existing layout.

Example Problem 2: Heuristic Procedure for Rearranging 0-1 Matrices

In manufacturing it is often desirable to identify subsets of parts that have similar processing requirements so that they can be processed together. Parts with similar processing requirements are called part families. Many organizations have found that dividing parts into part families and processing these parts together provides substantial benefits such as reduced work-in-process levels, shorter lead times, less scrap, and less material handling. One way parts can be divided into part families is based on the machines or equipment the parts require in their processing. According to this approach, the more equipment two parts have in common in their processing, the more important it is that they be placed into the same part family. One way to represent the relationship between parts and machines is with a part-machine matrix. In this matrix the rows correspond to parts and the columns correspond to machines. A "1" is placed in the matrix if a particular part is processed on a given machine, otherwise a "0" is placed in the matrix. In the matrix shown below there are five parts labeled 1-5 and five machines labeled A-E.

	A	B	C	D	E
1	1	0	1	0	1
2	0	1	0	1	0
3	1	0	1	0	1
4	0	1	0	1	0
5	1	0	1	0	0

To illustrate, the part-machine matrix above indicates that part 1 requires machines A, C, and E while part 2 requires machines B and D. One way to identify part families is to rearrange the rows and columns of the matrix so that blocks of 1s are formed along the diagonal of the matrix. Indeed, a large amount of research has been devoted to developing heuristic algorithms that rearrange the rows and columns of the part-machine matrix to obtain this block diagonal form. One such algorithm is called the Direct Clustering Algorithm[1] and consists of the following five steps:

1. Count the number of ones in each row and column. Rearrange the matrix with columns in decreasing order and rows in increasing order of the number of ones.
2. Start with the first column of the matrix and move all rows with ones in this column to the top of the matrix. Repeat this for all other columns until all rows have been rearranged.
3. If the matrix has changed go to step 4. Otherwise stop.
4. Starting with the first row of the matrix, move columns which have a ones in this row to the left-most position in the matrix. Repeat this for all other rows until all columns have been rearranged.
5. If the matrix has changed go back to step 2. Otherwise stop.

---

[1] Chan, H.M., and Milner, D.A., "Direct Clustering Algorithm for Group Formation in Cellular Manufacture," *Journal of Manufacturing Systems*, volume 1, 1982, 65-75.

The Direct Clustering Algorithm will be used to rearrange the part-machine matrix shown above. In step 1 the number of ones in each column and row are counted:

	A	B	C	D	E	Total Ones in Row
1	1	0	1	0	1	3
2	0	1	0	1	0	2
3	1	0	1	0	1	3
4	0	1	0	1	0	2
5	1	0	1	0	0	2
Ones in Column	3	2	3	2	2	

Next, the matrix is rearranged with the columns in decreasing order of ones. Columns A and C have 3 ones while columns B, D, and E have 2 ones. Thus one way to rearrange the columns in decreasing order is columns A, C, B, D, and E as shown below.

	A	C	B	D	E	Total Ones in Row
1	1	1	0	0	1	3
2	0	0	1	1	0	2
3	1	1	0	0	1	3
4	0	0	1	1	0	2
5	1	1	0	0	0	2
Ones in Column	3	3	2	2	2	

Next, the matrix is rearranged with the rows in increasing order of ones. Rows 2, 4, and 5 have 2 ones and are moved to the top. Rows 1 and 3 have 3 ones and are moved to the bottom as shown below.

	A	C	B	D	E	Total Ones in Row
2	0	0	1	1	0	2
4	0	0	1	1	0	2
5	1	1	0	0	0	2
1	1	1	0	0	1	3
3	1	1	0	0	1	3
Ones in Column	3	3	2	2	2	

Moving on to step 2, we start with the first column of the matrix and transfer rows with ones in this column to the top of the matrix. Rows 5, 1, and 3 have ones in the first column and are transferred to the top. Since rows 2 and 4 have not been moved yet, we move on to the second column. Again, rows 5, 1, and 3 have ones in the second column, but these rows have already been moved to the top so we move on to the third column.

Rows 2 and 4 both have ones in the third column so they would be moved next to the top. Now all rows have been moved and the sequence of the rows is 5, 1, 3, 2, and 4:

	A	C	B	D	E
5	1	1	0	0	0
1	1	1	0	0	1
3	1	1	0	0	1
2	0	0	1	1	0
4	0	0	1	1	0

Since the matrix has changed, step 3 tells us to move on to step 4. In step 4 we start with the first row of the new matrix and transfer columns which have ones in this row to the left-most position. Both columns A and C have ones in the first row, but they are already in the left-most position so no change is needed. Since all the columns have not been checked yet, we move on to the second row. Columns A, C, and E have ones in the second row. Columns A and C have already been assigned to the first two columns, but column E can be moved over to the third column. Now only columns B and D need to be assigned. Moving to the third row, columns A, C, and E have ones in this row, however, these columns have already been considered so we move to the fourth row. Columns B and D have ones in the fourth row so they are assigned the next left-most positions. Now all columns have been considered with the sequence being A, C, E, B, and D as follows:

	A	C	E	B	D
5	1	1	0	0	0
1	1	1	1	0	0
3	1	1	1	0	0
2	0	0	0	1	1
4	0	0	0	1	1

Again, since the matrix has changed step five tells us to return to step 2. Starting with the first column we transfer rows with ones in this column to the top of the matrix. rows 5, 1, and 3 have ones in the first column but they are already at the top of the matrix so no change is needed. Moving on to the second column, rows 5, 1, and 3 again are the only rows with ones. Thus, we move on to the third column. In the third column rows 1 and 3 have ones so still no change is required. Moving to the fourth column, rows 2 and 4 both have ones and are next transferred to the top of the matrix. Now all rows have been considered and no change was required. Therefore according to step 3, we terminate the procedure.

The above solution indicates that parts 5, 1, and 3 be grouped together to form one part family and that parts 2 and 4 be grouped together to form another part family. Ideally, machines A, C, and E could be grouped together to form a department that is dedicated to the production of parts 5, 1, and 3, and machines B and D could be grouped together to process parts 2 and 4.

Numerous other procedures exist to rearrange part-machine matrices and most of these are easily implemented on computers. Additionally, rearranging matrices to discover clusters of similar entities is applicable to a variety of other situations. For example, a matrix with rows corresponding to customers and columns corresponding to product attributes could be constructed. Rearranging such a matrix into a block diagonal form would generate product specifications for serving specific target markets. As another example, a warehouse manager could develop a matrix with rows corresponding to customer invoices and columns corresponding to inventory items. Thus a one would indicate that a particular customer ordered a given inventory item. Rearranging this matrix into a block diagonal form would indicate which inventory items tend to be ordered together. Based on this knowledge, the warehouse manager could place inventory items that tend to be ordered together next to each other so that the order picking time is minimized.

TRUE/FALSE QUESTIONS

1. ___ A heuristic is a rule of thumb used to find an exact solution to an optimization problem.

2. ___ Using an old golf ball when hitting over water is an example of a heuristic.

3. ___ Heuristics can be used to provide good starting solutions for exact optimization algorithms.

4. ___ Because of the iterative nature of heuristics, it is generally difficult to use spreadsheets to implement the actual computational processes associated with heuristics.

5. ___ A disadvantage of heuristics is that they often increase the computational requirements.

6. ___ Heuristics can be used as the basis for rules that intelligently direct the operations of an optimizing algorithm.

7. ___ In cases where the inputs to the optimization model are based on rough estimates, it may be pointless to spend the time and money to solve the problem with an exact optimization procedure.

8. ___ One advantage of heuristic algorithms is their ability to produce guaranteed optimal solutions.

9. ___ Improvement heuristics build a feasible solution by adding individual components one at a time.
10. ___ Greedy heuristics seek to maximize the improvement at each step.

11. ___ It is not possible to develop a heuristic algorithm that combines construction and improvement approaches.

12. ___ Partitioning refers to solving a problem in stages.

13. ___ Referring to solving integer programming models, a good feasible solution can speed up the performance of optimizing algorithms.

14. ___ Increasing the size of the neighborhood when using a neighborhood search procedure results in more computational effort.

15. ___ Designing heuristics is more of a science than an art.

16. ___ In designing heuristics, it is good practice to start with a comprehensive mathematical model of the problem, even if it cannot be solved.

17. ___ Simplicity, computational efficiency, robustness, and accuracy are all desired characteristics of heuristics.

18. ___ Most heuristics in optimization problems are search methods.

19. ___ A local optimum is another name for the best solution to the problem.

20. ___ Because of the power available in today's computers, problems involving nonlinearities are no more difficult to solve than problems with linear relationships.

Answers:

1. F, 2. T, 3. T, 4. T, 5. F, 6. T, 7. T, 8. F, 9. F, 10. T, 11. F, 12. F, 13. T, 14. T, 15. F, 16. T, 17. T, 18. T, 19. F, 20. F

CHAPTER 11

REVIEW

In many practical situations the future is uncertain and therefore probabilistic models and statistical methods are useful tools for analyzing and solving decision making problems. Almost every business decision is subject to *risk* i.e., the chance of an undesirable consequence.

As was the case with deterministic models, probabilistic models can be descriptive or prescriptive. *Descriptive probabilistic* models provide an evaluation of decision alternatives to assess the effects of uncertainty and the ability to predict future outcomes. *Prescriptive probabilistic* models seek the best solution, typically in terms of expected value.

Risk analysis is the study of the effects of uncertainty in decision making. In modeling uncertainty we can assume the parameters come from a continuous distribution or a discrete distribution. When modeling parameters that can assume continuous values, a continuous probability distribution is used in the analyses. Continuous distributions are often difficult to work with since analytical solutions often require calculus. To simplify the calculations, a discrete distribution can often be used to approximate the continuous distribution over the range of possible values.

Discrete probability distributions have a finite range of values. While this can greatly simplify the calculations required, it can also result in less accuracy and realism.

Selecting an appropriate probability distribution for the probabilistic components of the model is often one of the most difficult tasks associated with probabilistic modeling. Two ways to select a probability distribution are to: 1) collect and analyze data, and 2) estimate the probabilities judgmentally.

The collecting and analyzing approach is appropriate when sufficient historical data are available. Using this approach, a frequency distribution and histogram are first developed. Then, estimates of key parameters such as the mean and standard deviation can be calculated. The purpose of data analysis is to make generalizations about the nature of random variables that we are modeling. If we assume that the data represent some underlying population, we may be able to fit one of the well-studied theoretical distributions to the data. A theoretical distribution allows for extreme events that may not be present in the empirical data. Also, using a theoretical distribution can smooth out irregularities that exist in the empirical data. The most common continuous distributions are the uniform, exponential, triangular, and normal distributions. Common discrete distributions include the discrete uniform and Poisson distributions.

The first step in selecting a distribution to model probabilistic parameters is to decide what general type of distribution is appropriate. One way to do this is to compare the shape of histogram of the data to the shape of various theoretical distributions. Also knowledge of the variable's role in the model and calculating the parameters of the distribution can be used help select a distribution.

After selecting a distribution we need to decide how well the chosen distribution fits the data. One frequently used approach to assess the quality of fit between the data and the chosen distribution is the *Chi-square goodness of fit test*. To apply the Chi-square test, the data are first grouped into k cells such that each of the k cells have at least five observations. Then we compute the expected number of observations in each of the cells based on the chosen distribution. Finally, we compare the difference between the actual number of observations in each cell to the expected number in each cell.

If historical data is not available or the historical data that is available is no longer representative of the situation, then probability estimates can be estimated judgmentally. One simple approach to estimating a probability distribution is by carefully asking questions. Caution should be exercised with this approach. For example, many people will underestimate the probability of rare events.

In dealing with projects where the activity times are not deterministic, the expected project completion time is the sum of the expected activity times for those activities on the critical path. Furthermore, assuming the activity times are independent, the variance of the project completion time is the sum of the variances of the activity completion times for those activities on the critical path. The fact that the project completion time is the sum of independent activity times allows us to assume that the project completion time is normally distributed.

Uncertainty makes optimization problems considerably more difficult to solve. A *stochastic optimization model* is one in which some of the model input information is not known with certainty and is therefore described probabilistically. Although we may solve these models for an optimal solution, it is more valuable to evaluate the risk associated with that solution. A simpler deterministic model is often first developed and then modified to develop a stochastic optimization model.

When using probabilistic models, the expected value criterion is often used for making decisions. The *expected value* of a decision is found by summing the product of the payoff associated with a state of nature and the probability that that state of nature will occur. The expected value approach is based on the fact that the average outcome for a large number of independent decisions will converge to the expected value of the decision that was selected. Since this average only holds over the long run when the decision is made numerous times, in a one-time decision we cannot rely on this average.

Linear regression analysis is used to estimate the expected value of some unknown quantity as a function of other variables. The variable we attempt to estimate is called the *dependent variable* and the variables we use to predict the dependent variable are called the *independent variables*. In linear regression, we assume that the relationship between the dependent variable and the independent variables is linear. A *simple linear regression model* is a regression model with a single independent variable while a *multiple linear regression model* is a regression model with more than one independent variable. The *coefficient of determination* is a statistic used to measure how well the regression line fits the data. Specifically, the coefficient of determination indicates what fraction of the total variation in the dependent variable about its mean is explained by the regression line.

Forecasting involves the estimation of quantities for some future time based on historical data. The stream of historical data is called a *time series*. A time series generally consists of four components: trend, cyclical, seasonal, and irregular. *Trend* is the long-term gradual shifting of the time series. The *cyclical component* is a regular sequence above or below the trend line. The *seasonal component* is a repeating pattern from one year to the next. The *irregular component* is the remaining variation in the time series after the trend, cyclical, and seasonal components are accounted for. Thus, the irregular component are fluctuations due to random variability which are short-term and nonrepetitive.

A *moving average* is a forecasting technique that uses the average of the last k periods as the forecast for the next period. *Exponential* smoothing is another forecasting technique and uses a weighted average of the data values in the time series to develop a forecast for the next period. With exponential smoothing a value between 0 and 1 for a parameter called the *smoothing constant* must be selected. As the smoothing constant is increased from 0 to 1, more weight is placed on the last period's data value. The *Mean Absolute Deviation (MAD)* is the average absolute value of all forecast errors over all data points and can be used to measure the fit of a forecasting technique to the actual data. Thus, the MAD can be used to help determine k when using moving averages and/or the value for the smoothing constant when exponential smoothing is used.

SOLVED PROBLEMS

Example Problem 1: Project Management with Uncertain Activity Times

The optimistic, most likely, and pessimistic times for the activities of a project are shown in Figure 11-1. What is the probability that the project will be finished by time 30?

Solution:

To begin, we will calculate the expected time and the variance for each activity. Recall that the expected activity time, t, is calculated as follows:

$$t = (o + 4m + p)/6$$

Figure 11-1

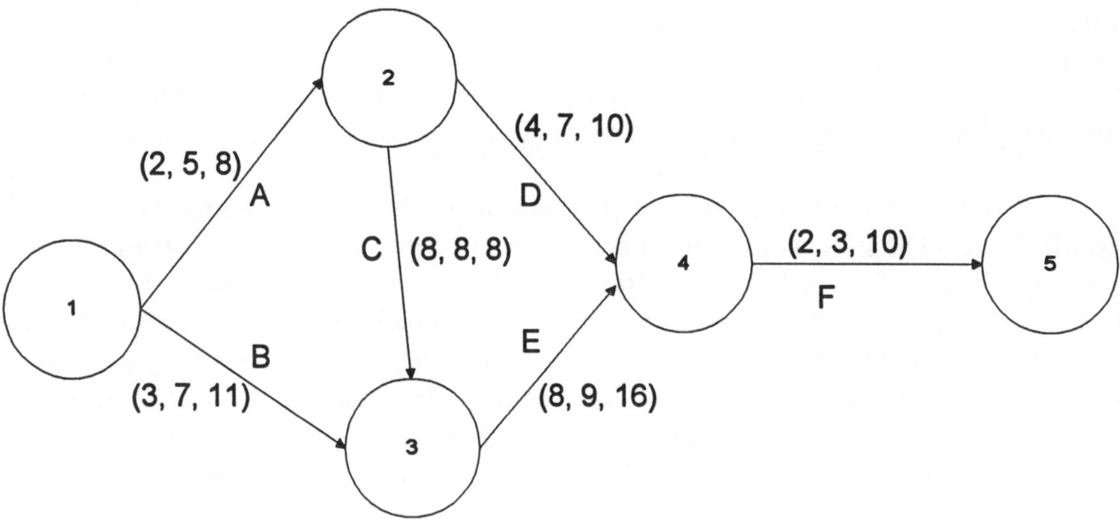

Likewise, the variance of each activity time is calculated as:

$$\sigma^2 = ((p - o)/6)^2$$

To calculate the expected activity times and the variances, these formulas were entered into the spreadsheet shown in Figure 11-3. Figure 11-4 shows the actual formulas that were entered into spreadsheet shown in Figure 11-3. The expected activity times and variances have been added to the network diagram shown in Figure 11-2 using the convention (t, σ^2).

Figure 11-2

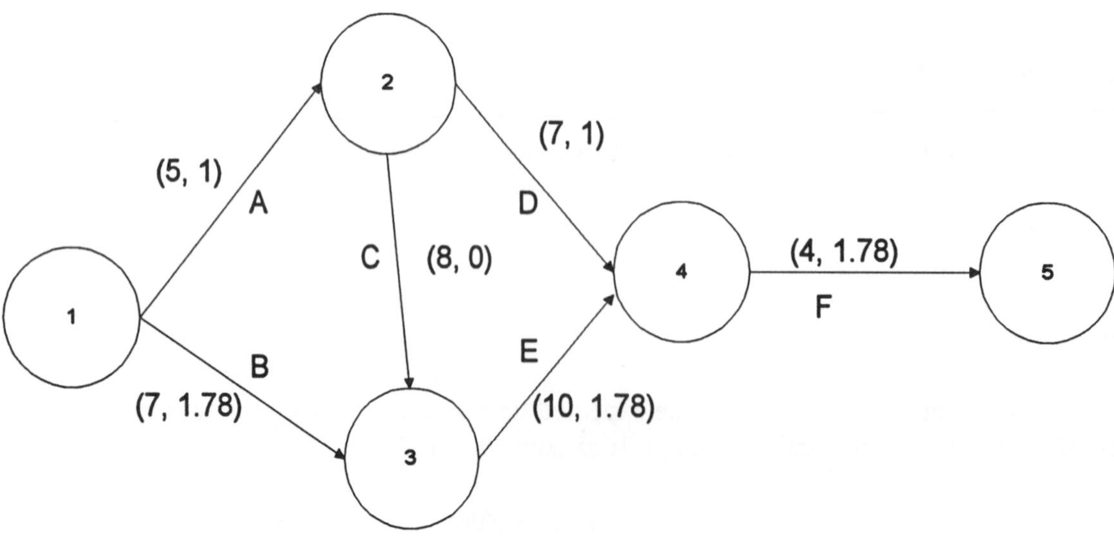

Figure 11-3

A	A	B	C	D	E	F
1	**Project Management with Uncertain Activity Times**					
2						
3			**Time Estimates**			
4	**Activity**	Optimistic	Most Likely	Pessimistic	**Expected**	**Variance**
5	A	2	5	8	5	1.00
6	B	3	7	11	7	1.78
7	C	8	8	8	8	0.00
8	D	4	7	10	7	1.00
9	E	8	9	16	10	1.78
10	F	2	3	10	4	1.78

Figure 11-4

	A	B	C	D	E	F
1	Project Management with Uncertain Activity Times					
2						
3			Time Estimates			
4	Activity	Optimistic	Most Likely	Pessimistic	**Expected**	**Variance**
5	A	2	5	8	(+B5+(4*C5)+D5)/6	((+D5-B5)/6)^2
6	B	3	7	11	(+B6+(4*C6)+D6)/6	((+D6-B6)/6)^2
7	C	8	8	8	(+B7+(4*C7)+D7)/6	((+D7-B7)/6)^2
8	D	4	7	10	(+B8+(4*C8)+D8)/6	((+D8-B8)/6)^2
9	E	8	9	16	(+B9+(4*C9)+D9)/6	((+D9-B9)/6)^2
10	F	2	3	10	(+B10+(4*C10)+D10)/6	((+D10-B10)/6)^2

From Figure 11-2 we note that there are three paths through the network: 1) A, C, E, and F; 2) A, D, and F; and 3) B, E, and F. The expected path completion time, E(T), is the sum of the expected activity times for those activities on the path. Likewise, the variance of completion time for a path is the sum of activity variances for those activities on the path assuming that the activity times are independent. Thus, we can compute the following:

Path	Expected Time E(T)	Variance	Standard Deviation
A-C-E-F	27	4.56	2.14
A-D-F	16	3.78	1.94
B-E-F	21	5.34	2.31

To illustrate, the E(T) of 16 for path A-D-F was calculated as (5 + 7 + 4). Likewise the variance of 3.78 for this path was calculated as (1 + 1 + 1.78). Finally, the standard deviation for each path was calculated by taking the square root of the path's variance.

Having determined the previous information, we are now in a position to determine the probability that the project will be finished by time 30. Note that for all practical purposes only path A-C-E-F has a chance of exceeding the specified time of 30. Given the other two paths have expected completion times of 16 and 21, respectively, and given their respective standard deviations, it is almost certain that these paths will finish by time 30. Thus, we only need to consider the probability that path A-C-E-F finishes by time 30 since the other two paths will finish by time 30 with almost a 100% certainty.

Drawing a picture similar to the one shown in Figure 11-5 is very helpful for solving these types of problems. Since the expected time for completing a path is the sum of several independent activity times, we can assume that the path completion time is normally distributed. Thus, in Figure 11-5 we show the completion time of path A-C-E-F as being normally distributed with a mean or expected completion time of 27. The area under the normal curve that we are interested in has been cross-hatched. More specifically, since we are interested in finding the probability that this path is completed by time 30 we have cross-hatched the area under the normal curve that is to the left of time 30. To find the area under normal curve that is cross-hatched we calculate the z-value as follows:

$$z = (T - E(T))/\sigma = (30 - 27)/2.14 = 1.40$$

Using the z-table in the Appendix of your text, we find that the area from negative infinity to 1.40 is .9192. Thus, the probability that this project is finished by time 30 is 91.92%.

Figure 11-5

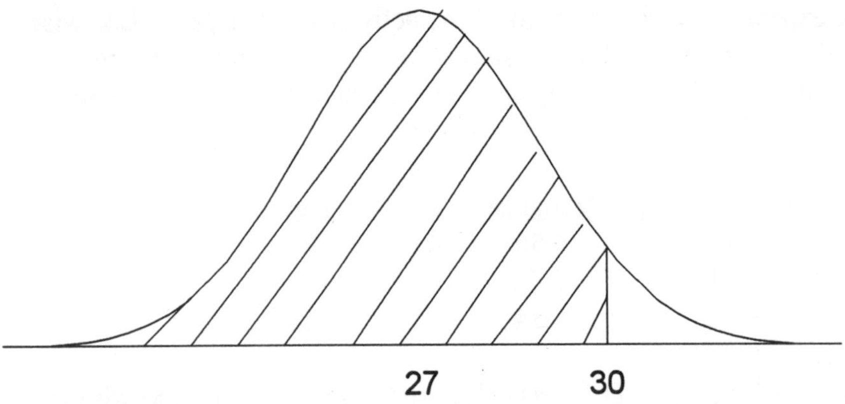

Example Problem 2: Regression Analysis with Spreadsheets

Reseller Inc. is a value added reseller of software products. Company management has decided to investigate whether linear regression can be used to forecast the sales of its products. To begin this investigation, the company has collected the sales figures for one of its database software packages for the last eight years as shown below. Develop a regression model for this software program.

Year:	1	2	3	4	5	6	7	8
Sales:	1500	4000	5000	6000	9500	12500	14000	13000

Solution:

In this situation we will investigate whether sales can be predicted as a function of the time period. Thus, time period is our independent variable and unit sales is our dependent variable.

The data provide above were entered into a Lotus 1-2-3 spreadsheet as shown in Figure 11-6. The values for the independent variable (time period) were entered in cells A5 - A12 and the values for the dependent variable (unit sales) were entered in cells B5-B12.

Since linear regression assumes that there is a linear relationship between the independent and dependent variables, a plot was developed to visually inspect this relationship. This plot is shown in Figure 11-6 in the range D3..H19. To construct this plot the range A5..A12 was specified for the x-range, B5..B12 was specified for the A-range, and the command Options-Format-A-Symbols was specified so that only the points

Figure 11-6

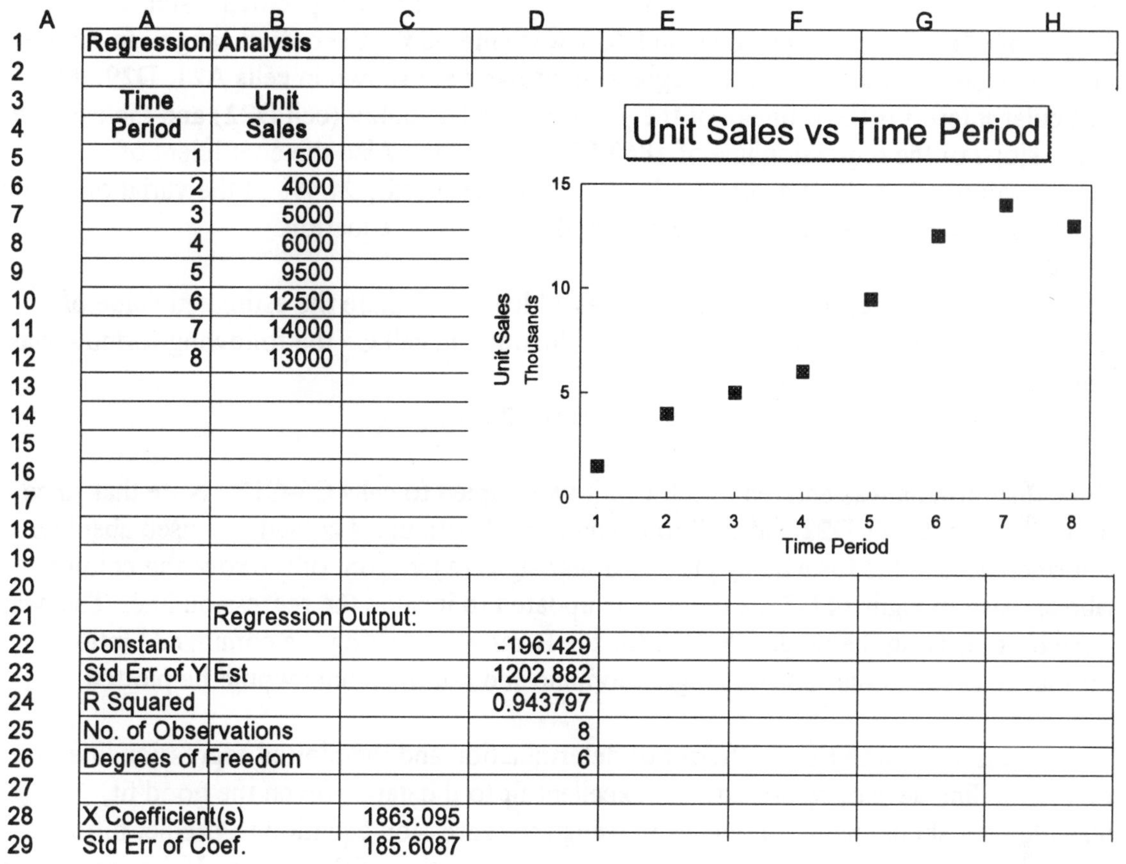

	A	B	C	D
1	**Regression**	**Analysis**		
2				
3	**Time**	**Unit**		
4	**Period**	**Sales**		
5	1	1500		
6	2	4000		
7	3	5000		
8	4	6000		
9	5	9500		
10	6	12500		
11	7	14000		
12	8	13000		
13				
14				
15				
16				
17				
18				
19				
20				
21		Regression	Output:	
22	Constant			-196.429
23	Std Err of Y	Est		1202.882
24	R Squared			0.943797
25	No. of Observations			8
26	Degrees of Freedom			6
27				
28	X Coefficient(s)		1863.095	
29	Std Err of Coef.		185.6087	

would be shown in the graph and not the line connecting the points. The plot indicates that using a line to estimate the relationship between these variables is appropriate

Next, Lotus's built in regression analysis routine was used by selecting the Range-Analyze-Regression menu items. For the x-range A5..A12 was specified. Similarly, for the y-range B5..B12 was specified, and A21 was entered for the output range. In Figure 11-7 the results obtained from the regression analysis are shown in cells A21..D29. Of particular interest is the estimate of the y intercept of -196.429 (cell D22) and the estimate of the slope of the regression line of 1863.095 (cell C28). Also the coefficient of determination of 94.4% is given in cell D24. In other words, 94.4% of the variation of the data points around the mean is explained by the regression equation.

Finally, in Figure 11-7 a column was added to calculate the estimated value of sales based on the regression equation. To illustrate, in cell C5 the following formula was entered:

+$D$22+($C$28*A5)

Once this formula was entered in cell C5, it was copied to cells C6-C12. Note that since we do not want cells D22 and C28 to change as the formula is copied, we used absolute cell references in the formula by placing dollar signs ($) in front of the row and column labels. Also in Figure 11-7 the graph was updated to include the regression line. This was done by specifying the range C5..C12 for the B-range and using the command Options-Format-B-Lines so that only the regression line and not the points would be plotted.

Based on both the coefficient of determination and the plotted regression line, the regression line developed provides an excellent fit to the data. Given the good fit, management should have confidence in using the regression equation to predict future demand assuming that the past data remains representative of the future. If for example, a new competitor emerged, the past data may no longer be representative of the future and new model might be needed. To predict the demand for any period in the future, we simply substitute the corresponding period number into the regression equation. To illustrate the forecast for period 9 would be calculated as follows:

$$F_9 = -196.429 + 1863.095(9) = 16571.426$$

Example Problem 3: Forecasting with Exponential Smoothing and Moving Averages

A pizza delivery business has tracked the number of pizzas ordered each week for the last six weeks. To help in scheduling workers, the manager is interested in developing a simple forecasting technique that she can use to predict demand for the upcoming week. Develop spreadsheets that forecast pizza demand for the upcoming week based on a three-week moving average and exponential smoothing with a smoothing constant of 0.1.

Week	1	2	3	4	5	6
Sales	600	400	500	600	700	600

Figure 11-7

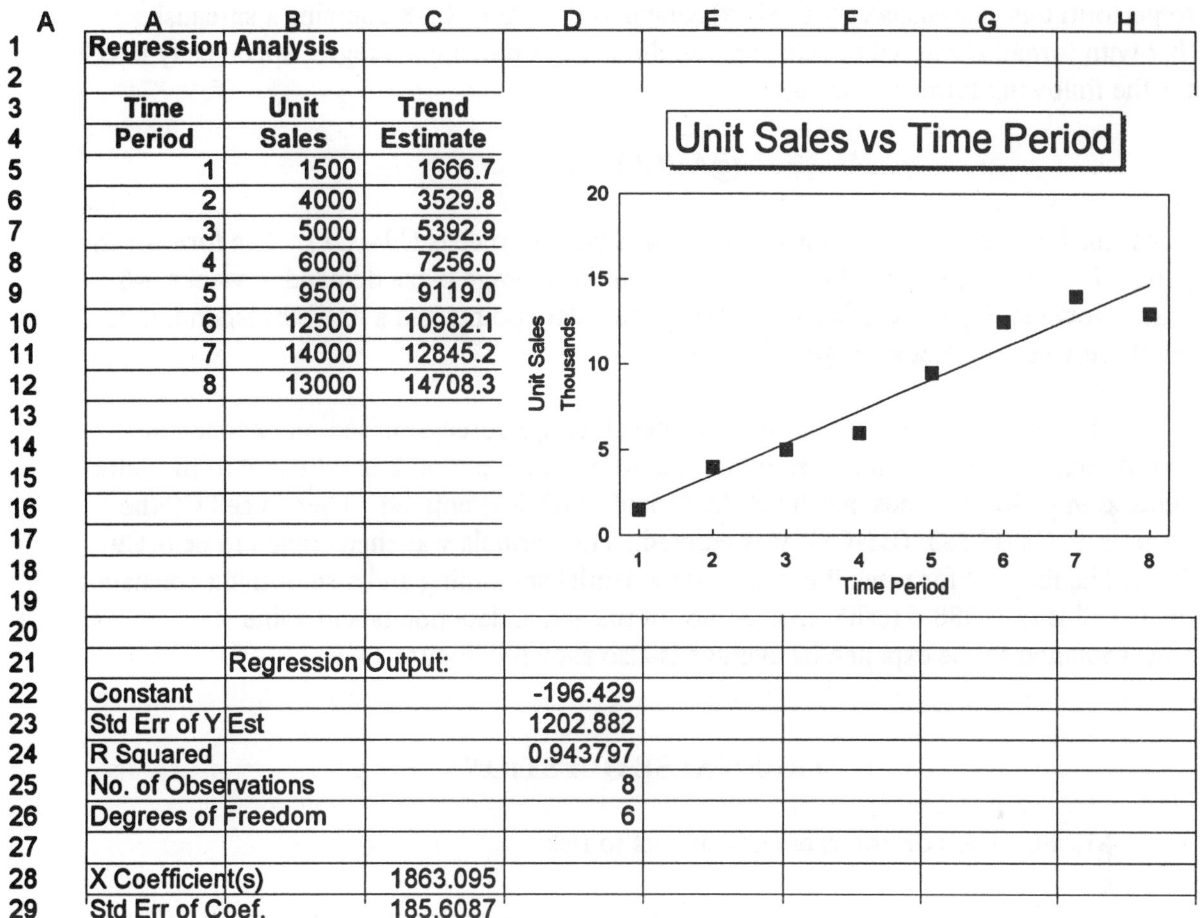

	A	B	C	D
1	Regression Analysis			
2				
3	Time	Unit	Trend	
4	Period	Sales	Estimate	
5	1	1500	1666.7	
6	2	4000	3529.8	
7	3	5000	5392.9	
8	4	6000	7256.0	
9	5	9500	9119.0	
10	6	12500	10982.1	
11	7	14000	12845.2	
12	8	13000	14708.3	
13				
14				
15				
16				
17				
18				
19				
20				
21		Regression Output:		
22	Constant			-196.429
23	Std Err of Y Est			1202.882
24	R Squared			0.943797
25	No. of Observations			8
26	Degrees of Freedom			6
27				
28	X Coefficient(s)		1863.095	
29	Std Err of Coef.		185.6087	

Solution:

Although Lotus 1-2-3 does not contain built-in procedures to perform moving averages or exponential smoothing (as of version 4.0 for windows), entering the formulas to perform this analysis is very easily accomplished. Figure 11-8 contains a spreadsheet that with formulas entered to calculate the three-week moving average. Specifically in cell C8 the following formula was entered:

@AVG(B5..B7)

Once this formula was entered in cell C8 it was copied to cells C9 - C11. The forecast for period 7 is 633.3 (see cell C11) and is based on the average pizza demand in weeks 4-6. Also, shown in Figure 11-8 is a plot of the actual data points and a line corresponding to the three-week moving average.

In Figure 11-9 is a spreadsheet for developing a forecast based on exponential smoothing. With exponential smoothing the forecast for period 2 is set equal to the actual demand in period 1. Thus in cell C8 the formula +B7 was entered. Then in cell C9 the formula: +C8+($B$3*(B8-C8)) was entered. This formula was then copied to cells C9-C13. The forecast for week 7 based on exponential smoothing and a smoothing constant of .1 (cell B3) is 588.6 (cell C13). A plot of the actual data points and a line corresponding to the exponential average is also shown in Figure 11-9.

TRUE/FALSE QUESTIONS

1. ___ Most business decisions are not subject to risk.

2. ___ Probabilistic models can only be prescriptive and cannot be descriptive.

3. ___ In modeling uncertainty, we may assume either a continuous distribution or a discrete distribution.

4. ___ When variables are independent, the correlation coefficient is zero resulting in considerable simplification.

5. ___ Discrete distributions are often difficult to work with since analytical solutions require calculus.

6. ___ One difficult tasks associated with probabilistic modeling is selecting an appropriate probability distribution for the probabilistic components of a model.

7. ___Outliers are observations that do not seem to coincide with the rest of distribution.

Figure 11-8

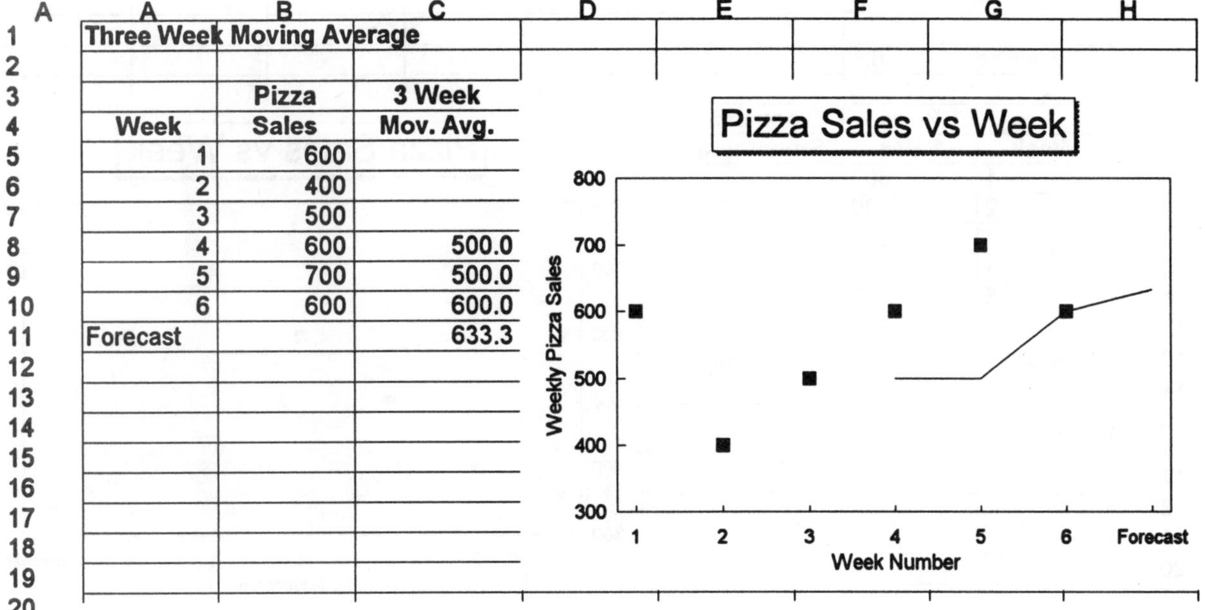
A
A
B
C
D
E
F
G
H
1
2
3
4
5
6
7
8
9
10
11
12
13
14
15
16
17
18
19
20
Three Week Moving Average
Week
Pizza
Sales
3 Week
Mov. Avg.
1
2
3
4
5
6
600
400
500
600
700
600
500.0
500.0
600.0
Forecast
633.3
Pizza Sales vs Week
800
700
600
500
400
300
Weekly Pizza Sales
1
2
3
4
5
6
Forecast
Week Number

Figure 11-9

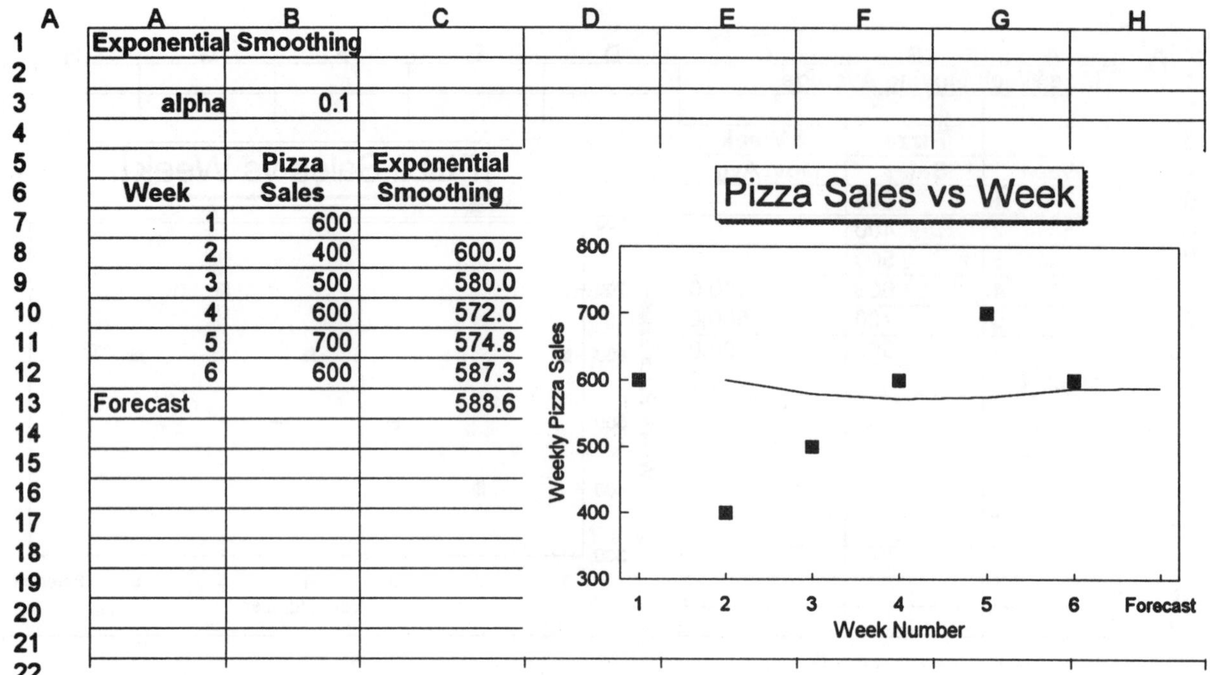

A	B	C
Exponential	Smoothing	
alpha	0.1	
	Pizza	Exponential
Week	Sales	Smoothing
1	600	
2	400	600.0
3	500	580.0
4	600	572.0
5	700	574.8
6	600	587.3
Forecast		588.6

8. ___ If there is reason to believe that outliers are due to chance, they should be excluded from the data.

9. ___ A drawback associated with using an empirical probability distribution is that it may have certain irregularities.

10. ___A problem with using theoretical distributions is that they typically do not allow for extreme events.

11. ___ A theoretical distribution can be used to smooth out irregularities that may exist in empirical data.

12. ___ The uniform distribution is often used when a quantity is known to vary between two extremes but little else is known about it.

13. ___ The first step in selecting a distribution to fit observed data is to decide what general type of distribution may be appropriate.

14. ___ The Chi-square goodness of fit test is a statistical test used to assess whether the observed data are a sample form a particular distribution.

15.___ In using the judgment approach to estimate probabilities, the analyst should be aware that people often underestimate the probability of rare events.

16. ___The expected project completion time is the sum of all activity times in the network diagram.

17. ___ Because the activity times are assumed not to be independent, the variance of the project completion time is the sum of the variances of the activity completion times for those activities on the critical path.

18. ___ Uncertainty makes optimization problems considerably more difficult to solve.

19. ___ A stochastic optimization model is one where all of the model input information is not known with certainty.

20. ___ In developing stochastic optimization models, it is often helpful to first construct a simpler deterministic model and then change the deterministic variables into probabilistic variables.

21. ___ The expected value approach is based on the fact that the average outcome for a large number of independent decisions will converge to the expected value of the decision that was selected.

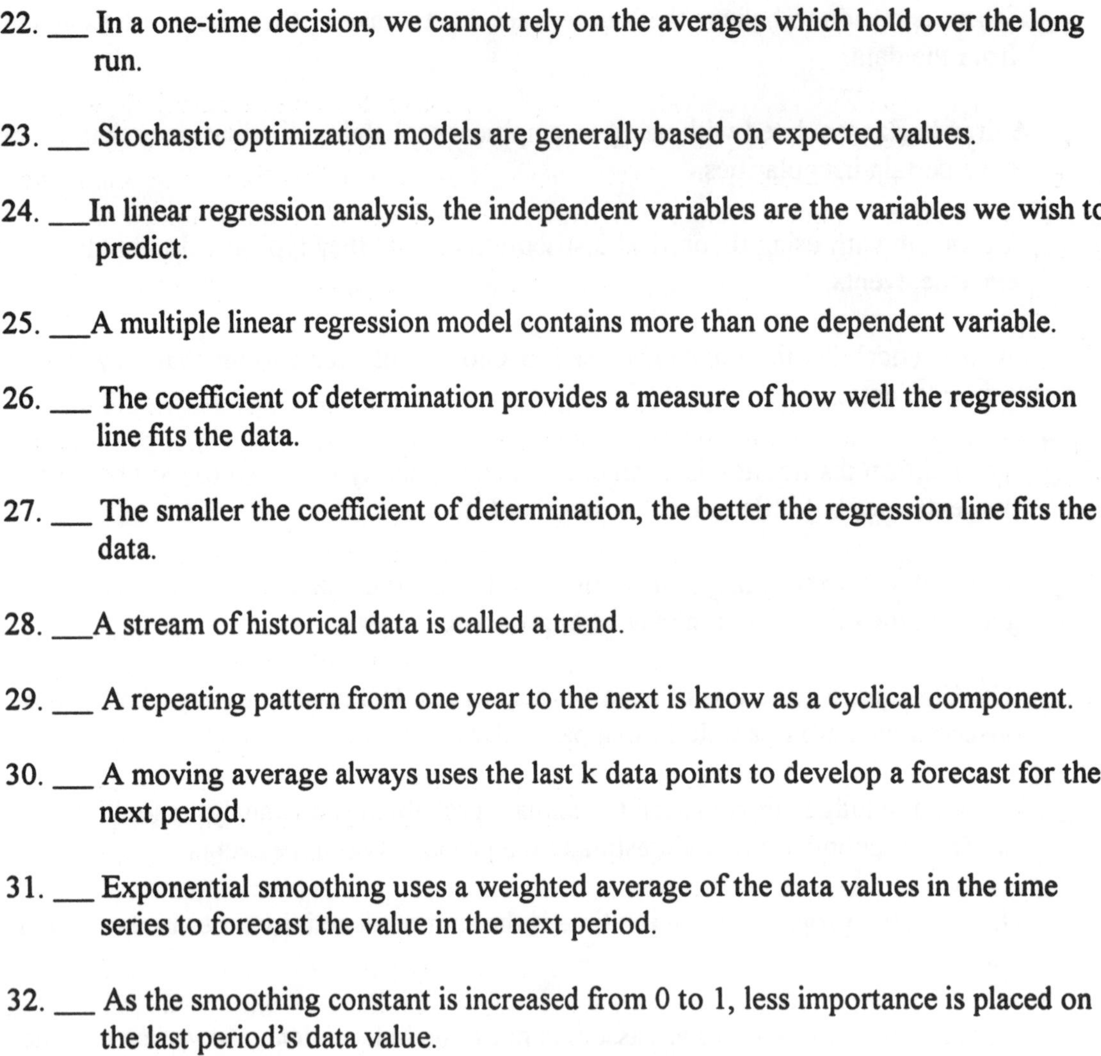

22. ___ In a one-time decision, we cannot rely on the averages which hold over the long run.

23. ___ Stochastic optimization models are generally based on expected values.

24. ___In linear regression analysis, the independent variables are the variables we wish to predict.

25. ___A multiple linear regression model contains more than one dependent variable.

26. ___ The coefficient of determination provides a measure of how well the regression line fits the data.

27. ___ The smaller the coefficient of determination, the better the regression line fits the data.

28. ___A stream of historical data is called a trend.

29. ___ A repeating pattern from one year to the next is know as a cyclical component.

30. ___ A moving average always uses the last k data points to develop a forecast for the next period.

31. ___ Exponential smoothing uses a weighted average of the data values in the time series to forecast the value in the next period.

32. ___ As the smoothing constant is increased from 0 to 1, less importance is placed on the last period's data value.

Answers:

1. F, T. F, 3. T, 4. T, 5. F, 6. T, 7. T, 8. F, 9. T, 10. F, 11. T, 12. T, 13. T, 14. T, 15. T, 16. F, 17. F, 18. T, 19. F, 20. T, 21. T, 22. T, 23. T, 24. F, 25. F, 26. T, 27. F, 28. F, 29. F, 30. T, 31. T, 32. F

CHAPTER 12

REVIEW

Decision analysis is the study of how people make decisions, particularly when faced with imperfect or uncertain information, as well as a collection of techniques to support the analysis of decision problems. Decision analysis differs from other modeling approaches in that it explicitly considers preferences and attitudes, and it models the decision process itself. Also, in contrast to optimization models such as linear programming, decision analysis problems typically deal with a much smaller set of alternatives.

Decision theory techniques are applicable to decision situations that: 1) are important, 2) are probably unique, 3) allow time for study, 4) are complex, and 5) involve uncertainty.

Generating alternatives corresponding to the choices a decision maker can make is the first step in structuring a decision problem. Once the alternatives are generated, the next task is to define the outcomes that may occur once a decision is made. Outcomes associated with decisions are often called *states of nature*. Finally, decision makers must define the criteria that will be used to evaluate the alternatives. One criteria often used is the *payoff* associated with a given state of nature occurring and the selection of a particular decision alternative. The payoff of making decision D and having state of nature S occur is expressed as V(D, S). Payoffs are usually summarized in a *payoff table* where the rows of the table correspond to the decision alternatives and the columns correspond to the possible states of nature.

Decision problems can be represented graphically with a *decision tree*. Decision tress consist of: 1) square decision nodes, 2) decision branches stemming from the decision nodes, 3) circular state of nature nodes, and 4) state of nature branches stemming from the state of nature nodes. Decision trees are read from left to right but are solved from right to left.

Decision problems where probabilities for the states of nature are available are called *decisions under risk. Decisions under uncertainty* refer to situations where we are unable to quantify the probabilities associated with the states of nature.

There are a number of approaches for dealing with decisions under uncertainty. With the *Laplace approach* an equal probability is assigned to each state of nature. Aggressive decision makers can use the *maximax criterion* which attempts to maximize the maximum gain. The *maximin* criterion is more appropriate for conservative decision makers who would choose to maximize the minimum return. One final approach is the criterion *minimax regret* which seeks to minimize the maximum opportunity loss that might occur. *Opportunity loss* or *regret* for any decision and state of nature is the difference between the best decision for a given state of nature and the payoff for that decision and state of nature.

Decisions under risk involve probabilistic information about the likelihood of the states of nature. Probabilities for the states of nature can be developed objectively or subjectively. In either case, with probabilities assigned to the states of nature, the expected value can be calculated for each decision alternative and the decision alternative with the highest expected payoff selected as the optimal solution.

Decision trees can be used to perform the expected value calculations. When working with decision trees, we always work from right to left. At each state of nature branch the expected payoff is computed by multiplying the values at the end of the state of nature branches by their associated probabilities and summing. At decision nodes, the decision branch with the highest payoff is selected. Performing these operations is called *folding back* the tree.

Perfect information refers to knowing in advance what state of nature will occur. The *expected value of perfect information* or *EVPI* is the difference between the expected payoff under perfect information and the optimal decision without perfect information. Alternatively, EVPI can be computed as the *expected opportunity loss* or *expected regret* for the best decision using the expected value criterion. Since EVPI represents the maximum amount we can improve our outcome by having better information, it also represents an upper limit on the maximum amount we should be willing to pay for better information. Sensitivity analysis can be used to assess the amount the probabilities can change without affecting the optimal decision.

Multistage decision trees can be used to model complex sequences of decisions. To illustrate, multistage decision trees can be used in situations where a decision maker considers acquiring additional information before making a decision.

Prior probabilities, denoted $P(S_j)$ are the initial probabilities assigned to the states of nature. Revised probabilities obtained by acquiring additional information or indicator information are called *posterior probabilities.* In statistical terminology, the states of nature are *conditional* upon the indicators where the probability of state of nature S_j given an indicator I_k is denoted as $P(S_j|I_k)$. If S_j is the true state of nature, $P(I_k|S_j)$ is the *indicator reliability* and represents the probability that the acquisition of new information results in I_k.

The *expected value of sample information* (*EVSI*) is the expected value of the optimal decision strategy with sample information minus the expected value of the optimal decision without sample information. When the EVSI is greater than the costs for the added information, then the strategy that included obtaining sample information is optimal. Since sample information is at best perfect, EVSI $\leq$ EVPI.

Utility theory provides an approach for quantifying a decision maker's relative preferences for particular outcomes. One way to determine an individual's utility function is to pose to the individual a series of decision scenarios. Furthermore, a decision maker's utility function can be used in place of payoffs to compute expected values that reflect the decision maker's preferences toward risk. Doing this requires that we replace the payoffs in the payoff table with their equivalent utilities, and then compute the expected utility for each decision.

The *analytic hierarchy process* (*AHP*) is a technique for incorporating multiple criteria into decision making. AHP consists of the following four steps: 1) breaking the decision problem into a hierarchy of interrelated decision criteria and decision alternatives, 2) developing judgmental preferences for the decision criteria and decision alternatives, 3) computing relative priorities for each of the decision elements, and 4) aggregating the relative priorities to arrive at a priority ranking of the decision alternatives.

SOLVED PROBLEMS

Example Problem 1: Decision Making Under Uncertainty

A company is considering three capacity expansion options: 1) using subcontractors to meet demand, 2) expand the existing facility, and 3) build a new plant. The company has determined that three states of nature are possible although it has no information for the probabilities that these states of nature will occur. The three possible states of nature are: 1) low demand, 2) medium demand, and 3) high demand. The profits for each capacity expansion option under each state of nature are provided in the payoff matrix shown below. Analyze this situation using the Laplace, maximax, maximin, and minimax regret approaches.

	Low Demand	Medium Demand	High Demand
Subcontract	100	125	150
Expand	75	140	155
New Plant	-25	10	175

Solution:

With the Laplace approach we treat each state of nature as equally likely and evaluate the decision by simply averaging the payoffs as follows:

Subcontract: (100 + 125 + 150)/3 = 125

Expand: (75 + 140 + 155)/3 = 123.3
New Plant: (-25 + 10 + 175)/3 = 53.3

Subcontracting has the highest average and therefore would be the chosen alternative if the Laplace method were used.

The maximax approach is an optimistic approach because we first identify the maximum payoff associated with each option and then pick the decision that has the maximum payoff. Using the maximax approach, the maximum payoff for each option is:

Subcontract: 150
Expand: 155
New Plant: 175

Building a new plant has the largest maximum payoff so it would be selected. Note that the maximax procedure will always select the decision with the largest payoff in the payoff table.

The maximin approach is a conservative approach because we first identify the worst or lowest payoff for each option and then pick the biggest minimum payoff. Using the maximin approach, the minimum payoff for each option is:

Subcontract: 100
Expand: 75
New Plant: -25

With the maximin approach, subcontracting would be the chosen decision since it has the largest minimum payoff.

Finally, the minimax regret approach requires that we convert the payoffs to opportunity losses. The opportunity loss for any decision and state of nature is calculated as the difference between the best decision for that particular state of nature and the payoff for that decision and state of nature. To illustrate, in the payoff table given above, the highest payoff associated with the low demand state of nature is 100. Therefore, if the decision to subcontract was made and demand turned out to be low, there would be no opportunity loss since subcontracting has the highest payoff under the low demand state of nature. On the other hand, if it was decided to expand and demand turned out to be low there would be an opportunity loss of 25 (100-75) because the payoff would be 75 when it could have been 100 if the subcontracting option had been selected. The table below contains all the opportunity loss information for this problem.

	Low Demand	Medium Demand	High Demand
Subcontract	0	15	25
Expand	25	0	20
New Plant	125	130	0

After calculating the opportunity losses, the next step in the minimax regret approach is to determine the maximum regret for each decision option as follows:

Subcontract: 25
Expand: 25
New Plant: 125

Next, we select the option that has the smallest maximum regret. In this case subcontracting and expanding both have the smallest maximum regret of 25.

Spreadsheets can be used to perform all of the calculations illustrated in this example problem. A spreadsheet illustrating these calculations is shown in Figure 12-1 and the formulas that were entered into this spreadsheet are shown in Figure 12-2. To develop the spreadsheet, the payoff table was first entered in columns B-D. In column E the formulas corresponding to the Laplace approach were entered. Specifically, a formula that calculates the average of each row was first entered and then a formula that returns the maximum average was entered in cell E10. In a similar fashion, in rows 6-8 of column F a formula that returns the maximum payoff for a given row was first entered, and in cell F10 a formula that returns the largest maximum value was entered. Column G corresponds to the maximin approach. Thus, in rows 6-8 of column G a formula that returns the minimum payoff for a given row was entered and then a formula that returns the maximum of these minimum payoffs was entered in cell G10. Note that setting up a spreadsheet to perform these calculations is greatly simplified by using the copy command. Specifically, the formulas entered in row 6 can be copied to rows 7 and 8. Likewise, the formulas entered in cell E10 can be copied to cells F10 and G10. Copying formulas is generally much quicker than keying in formulas and can reduce errors associated with entering formulas.

At the bottom of the spreadsheet shown in Figure 12-1 is the regret matrix for the payoff table at the top of the spreadsheet. Each cell in the regret matrix contains a formula that calculates the opportunity loss or regret for each decision under each state of nature. This is done by determining the maximum value of each column (state of nature) and subtracting the actual payoff for a particular decision given this state of nature. Notice in Figure 12-2 how absolute cell addresses were used in the formulas to calculate the opportunity losses. Using absolute cell addresses permitted entering the formula once in cell B18 and then copying this formula to all the other cells in the regret matrix (i.e., cells C18..D20, and B19..B20). In rows 18-20 of column E, a formula that returns the maximum opportunity loss for its respective row was entered. This formula was entered in cell E18 and then copied to cells E19..E20. Finally, to complete the calculations required for the minimax regret approach, a formula that returns the minimum maximum regret was entered in cell E22. Examination of the spreadsheet shown in Figure 12-1 shows that the same results were obtained with the spreadsheet as were obtained by performing these calculations by hand.

Figure 12-1

A	A	B	C	D	E	F	G
1	**Plant Capacity Desision**						
2							
3							
4		*Low*	*Medium*	*High*			
5		*Demand*	*Demand*	*Demand*	*LaPlace*	*Maximax*	*Maximin*
6	*Subcontract*	100	125	150	125.0	150	100
7	*Expand*	75	140	155	123.3	155	75
8	*New Plant*	-25	10	175	53.3	175	-25
9							
10	***Solution Value***				125	175	100
11							
12							
13							
14	**Regret Matix**						
15							
16		*Low*	*Medium*	*High*			
17		*Demand*	*Demand*	*Demand*	*Minimax*		
18	*Subcontract*	0	15	25	25		
19	*Expand*	25	0	20	25		
20	*New Plant*	125	130	0	130		
21							
22	***Solution Value***				25		

Figure 12-2

A	A	B	C	D	E	F	G
1	**Plant Capacity Decision**						
2							
3							
4		*Low*	*Medium*	*High*			
5		*Demand*	*Demand*	*Demand*	*LaPlace*	*Maximax*	*Maximin*
6	*Subcontract*	100	125	150	@AVG(D6..B6)	@MAX(D6..B6)	@MIN(D6..B6)
7	*Expand*	75	140	155	@AVG(D7..B7)	@MAX(D7..B7)	@MIN(D7..B7)
8	*New Plant*	-25	10	175	@AVG(D8..B8)	@MAX(D8..B8)	@MIN(D8..B8)
9							
10	***Solution Value***				@MAX(E8..E6)	@MAX(F8..F6)	@MAX(G8..G6)
11							
12							
13							
14	**Regret Matix**						
15							
16		*Low*	*Medium*	*High*			
17		*Demand*	*Demand*	*Demand*	*Minimax*		
18	*Subcontract*	@MAX($A:B$6..$A:B$8)-B6	@MAX($A:C$6..$A:C$8)-C6	@MAX($A:D$6..$A:D$8)-D6	@MAX(D18..B18)		
19	*Expand*	@MAX($A:B$6..$A:B$8)-B7	@MAX($A:C$6..$A:C$8)-C7	@MAX($A:D$6..$A:D$8)-D7	@MAX(D19..B19)		
20	*New Plant*	@MAX($A:B$6..$A:B$8)-B8	@MAX($A:C$6..$A:C$8)-C8	@MAX($A:D$6..$A:D$8)-D8	@MAX(D20..B20)		
21							
22	***Solution Value***				@MIN(E20..E18)		

Example Problem 2: Decision Making Under Risk

Referring to example problem 1, management has concluded a market analysis study that indicates that the probability that demand will be low is 30%, demand will be medium is 50%, and that demand will be high is 20%. What is the expected value for each option and what is the expected value of perfect information?

Solution:

Recall that the expected value for decision alternative i is calculated as:

$$E(D_i) = \sum_{j=1}^{n} P(S_j)V(D_i,S_j)$$

Using the payoff table from example problem 1 and the added probability information we can compute the expected values for each option as follows:

Subcontracting: .3(100) + .5(125) + .2(150) = 122.5
Expand: .3(75) + .5(140) + .2(155) = 123.5
New Plant: .3(-25) + .5(10) + .2(175) = 32.5

The expand option should be chosen since it has the highest expected value.

The expected value of perfect information (EVPI) is the difference between the expected payoff under perfect information and the expected payoff of the optimal decision without perfect information. We just determined that the expected payoff of the optimal decision without perfect information is 123.5 which corresponds to the expand option. To calculate the expected payoff with perfect information we weight the highest payoff associated with each state of nature by the state of nature's probability. In this example, the highest payoffs for the three states of nature are 100 for low demand, 140 for medium demand, and 175 for high demand. Weighting these payoffs by their respective states of nature yields:

Expected Payoff With Perfect Information = .3(100) + .5(140) + .2(175) = 135

Finally, the EVPI is calculated by subtracting the payoff of the optimal decision without perfect information from the expected payoff with perfect information as follows:

EVPI = 135 - 123.5 = 11.5

Recall that another way to calculate the EVPI is to compute the expected opportunity loss (or expected regret) for the best decision. The expected opportunity loss is calculated as follows:

$$EOL(D_i) = \sum_{j=1}^{n} P(S_j)R(D_i, S_j)$$

Plugging the opportunity loss values that were calculated in example problem 1 into this formula yields:

Subcontract: .3(0) + .5(15) + .2(25) = 12.5
Expand: .3(25) + .5(0) + .2(20) = 11.5
New Plant: .3(125) + .5(130) + .2(0) = 102.5

The best option (i.e., the option with the lowest expected opportunity loss) is to expand. Note that the expected opportunity loss of the expand option and EVPI calculated previously are both equal to 11.5.

A spreadsheet that calculates the expected value and the expected opportunity loss of the three plant capacity options is shown in Figure 12-3. This spreadsheet was developed by making minor modifications to the spreadsheet shown in Figure 12-1. The formulas that were entered into this spreadsheet are shown in Figure 12-4. Notice how the absolute cell addresses were used for the formulas entered in cells E6..E8 and cells E18..E20. Specifically, using absolute cell addresses permitted entering the formula in cell E6 and then copying this formula to cells E7..E8 and cells E18..E20.

Example Problem 3: Multistage Decisions

A company is considering inspecting batches of a critical component before it is released to the shop floor to be assembled into the company's final products. Historical data suggests that 10% of the batches contain sufficient numbers of bad parts that the batch should be sent to the rework department before being released to the shop floor. Also, historical data suggests that the probability that there is an 80% probability that the sampling procedure will conclude that a batch of materials is defective when in fact it is defective and there is a 10% probability that the sampling procedure will conclude that a batch is defective when in fact it is not defective. Likewise, there is a 20% chance that the sampling procedure will indicate that a batch is not defective when in fact it is, and a 90% chance that the sampling procedure will indicate that a batch is not defective when in fact it is not defective. Finally, accounting records indicate that it costs $250 to rework defective batches before they are released to the shop floor and it costs $175 to send nondefective batches to the rework area. Additionally, it costs $500 if defective batches are not initially sent to rework, while it costs nothing if nondefective batches are not sent to rework and immediately released to the shop floor. Develop a decision tree to model this situation to help determine if this company should inspect batches prior to releasing them to the shop floor.

Figure 12-3

A	A	B	C	D	E
1	**Plant Capacity Decision**				
2					
3	*Probability:*	0.3	0.5	0.2	
4		*Low*	*Medium*	*High*	*Expected*
5		*Demand*	*Demand*	*Demand*	*Value*
6	*Subcontract*	100	125	150	122.5
7	*Expand*	75	140	155	123.5
8	*New Plant*	-25	10	175	32.5
9					
10	***Solution Value***				123.5
11					
12					
13					
14	**Regret Matrix**				
15					
16		*Low*	*Medium*	*High*	*Expected*
17		*Demand*	*Demand*	*Demand*	*Value*
18	*Subcontract*	0	15	25	12.5
19	*Expand*	25	0	20	11.5
20	*New Plant*	125	130	0	102.5
21					
22	***Solution Value***				11.5

Figure 12-4

A	A	B	C	D	E
1	**Plant Capacity Decision**				
2					
3	*Probability:*	0.3	0.5	0.2	
4		*Low*	*Medium*	*High*	*Expected*
5		*Demand*	*Demand*	*Demand*	*Value*
6	*Subcontract*	100	125	150	($B$3*B6)+($C$3*C6)+($D$3*D6)
7	*Expand*	75	140	155	($B$3*B7)+($C$3*C7)+($D$3*D7)
8	*New Plant*	-25	10	175	($B$3*B8)+($C$3*C8)+($D$3*D8)
9					
10	***Solution Value***				@MAX(E8..E6)
11					
12					
13					
14	**Regret Matix**				
15					
16		*Low*	*Medium*	*High*	*Expected*
17		*Demand*	*Demand*	*Demand*	*Value*
18	*Subcontract*	0	15	25	($B$3*B18)+($C$3*C18)+($D$3*D18)
19	*Expand*	25	0	20	($B$3*B19)+($C$3*C19)+($D$3*D19)
20	*New Plant*	125	130	0	($B$3*B20)+($C$3*C20)+($D$3*D20)
21					
22	***Solution Value***				@MIN(E20..E18)

Solution:

A decision tree for this problem is shown in Figure 12-5. Reading the tree from right to left we observe that the first decision that must be made is whether to inspect the batches or not to inspect the batches. If the batches are not inspected, then either a defective or nondefective batch is released to the shop. If the batch is not defective, no cost is incurred. On the other hand, if a defective batch is released to the shop, a cost of $500 is incurred.

If the batches are inspected then the results of the inspection will indicate that the batches are defective or not defective. To continue, we make the following definitions:

I_1 = Results of inspection indicate batch is defective
I_2 = Results of inspection indicate batch is not defective
S_1 = The batch is defective
S_2 = The batch is not defective

Regardless of whether the results indicate that a batch is defective (I_1) or not defective (I_2), we must decide whether to send the batch to the rework department or not. Finally, after the decision is made concerning whether or not to send the batch to the rework department, we find out whether the batch was in fact defective (S_1) or not defective (S_2).

As we read the decision tree from left to right, the first piece of information we need are the $P(I_k)$ values. In the problem description we were given information about the $P(I_k|S_j)$ values. For example, we were told that there is a 20% chance that the sampling procedure will indicate that a batch is not defective when in fact it is. Thus, $P(I_2|S_1) = .20$. The table below shows the $P(I_k|S_j)$ probabilities for all values of k and j:

	S_1	S_2
I_1	.8	.1
I_2	.2	.9

Also in the problem we were given the probabilities for the states of nature corresponding to whether the batches were defective or not. For example, we were told that the probability that a batch was defective was 10%. Thus, $P(S_1) = .10$. Using the $P(I_k|S_j)$ values and the $P(S_j)$ values we can calculate the $P(I_k \cap S_j)$ values. Recall that $P(I_k \cap S_j) = P(I_k|S_j)\, P(S_j)$. Once we calculate the $P(I_k \cap S_j)$ values we can calculate the $P(I_k)$ values using the formula:

$$P(I_k) = \sum_{j=1}^{n} P(S_j \cap I_k)$$

The values for $P(I_k \cap S_j)$ and $P(I_k)$ are computed as follows:

Figure 12-5

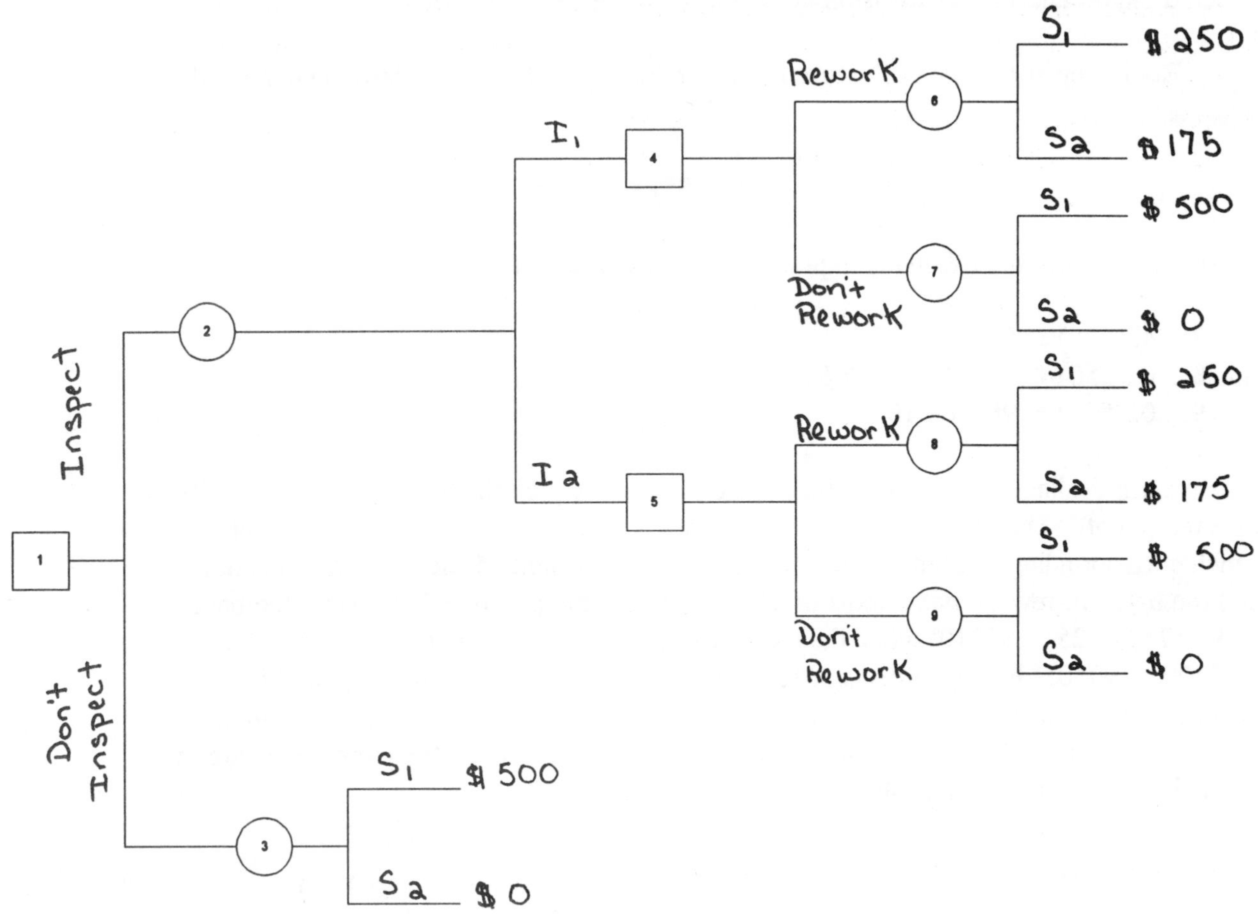

	$\underline{S_1}$	$\underline{S_2}$	$\underline{P(I_k)}$
I_1	.8(.1) = .08	.1(.9) = .09	.08 + .09 = .17
I_2	.2(.1) = .02	.9(.9) = .81	.02 + .81 = .83

The last piece of information we need to complete the decision tree are values for the $P(S_j|I_k)$. For example, we need $P(S_1|I_1)$ which corresponds to the probability that a batch turns out to be defective given that the sample indicated that it was defective. Recall $P(S_j|I_k) = P(I_k \cap S_j)/ P(I_k)$. Thus, the $P(S_j|I_k)$ can be calculated as follows:

	$\underline{S_1}$	$\underline{S_2}$
I_1	.08/.17 = .47	.09/.17 = .53
I_2	.02/.83 = .02	.81/.83 = .98

These probabilities are shown in Figure 12-5.

Now that we have all the probability information, we can fold back the tree working from right to left. Specifically, at each state of nature node we compute the expected payoff and at each decision node we select the best decision.

Beginning at the state of nature node 6 in Figure 12-6 we calculate the expected payoff as:

$$.47(250) + .53(175) = 210.25$$

In a similar fashion, the following expected payoffs are calculated:

node 7: .47(500) + .53(0) = 235
node 8: .02(250) + .98(175) = 176.5
node 9: .02(500) + .98(0) = 10

Since we are dealing with costs, at the decision nodes we pick the branch with the smallest expected payoff. Therefore at decision node 4 with choices 210.5 and 235 we select the branch corresponding to sending the batch to rework. At node 5 the best branch is not to send the batch to rework with a cost of 10. At state of nature node 2 the expected payoff is 44 (.17*210.25 + .83*10) while the expected payoff at state of nature node 3 is 50 (.10*500 + .90*0). Finally at decision node 1 we would choose to use the sampling procedure since the expected the cost of this branch is less than the cost of the branch associated with not using the sampling procedure. In this example, the expected value of sample information is $6 (50 - 44).

Figure 12-6

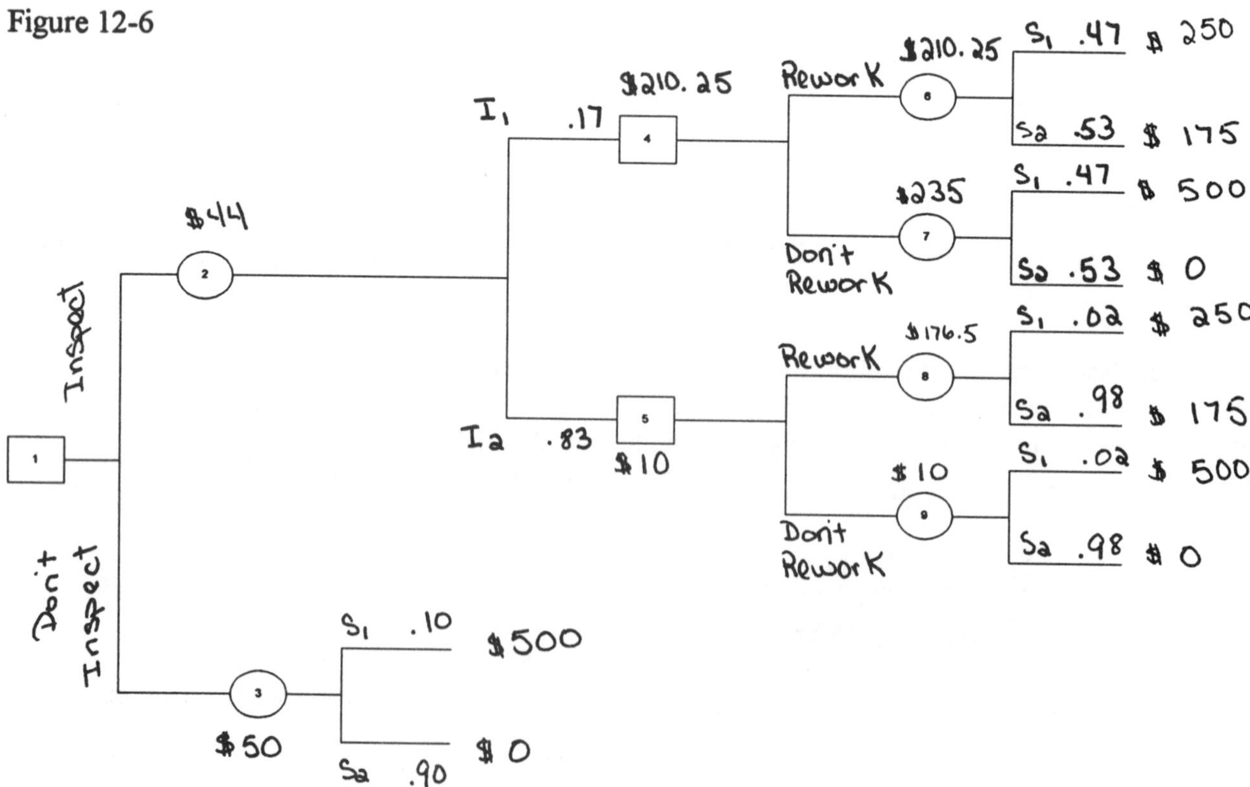

TRUE/FALSE QUESTIONS

1. ___ One way decision analysis differs from other modeling approaches is that it explicitly models the decision process itself.

2.___ In decision analysis problems we typically deal with an infinite number of possible solutions.

3. ___ Decision analysis is particularly appropriate for decisions than recur and therefore can be programmed.

4. ___ States of nature are the outcomes associated with decisions.

5. ___ A matrix that summarizes payoffs with rows corresponding to decisions and columns corresponding to states of nature is called a decision tree.

6. ___State of nature nodes are represented by squares.

7. ___Decision tress are read from left to right.

8. ___ Decisions under risk are situations where the decision maker has probabilities for the states of nature.

9. ___ The Laplace method relies on the assumption that no state of nature is any more likely than another.

10. ___ The maximin criterion is considered to be an optimistic approach.

11. ___ Opportunity losses can only be nonnegative values.

12. ___ In decisions under uncertainty, we assume complete ignorance about the states of nature.

13. ___ In working with decision trees, we always work from left to right.

14. ___ The expected payoff is computed at each decision node in a decision tree.

15. ___ Performing the calculations associated with a decision tree is called folding back the tree.

16. ___ By perfect information, we mean knowing in advance what state of nature will occur.

17. ___ The expected value of perfect information is the same as the expected payoff under perfect information.

18. ___ One way to calculate the expected value of perfect information is to compute the expected opportunity loss for the best decision using the expected value criterion.

19. ___ The expected value of perfect information represents the maximum amount that we could improve our outcome by having better information about the future.

20. ___ Multistage decision trees are applicable to situations in which a decision maker considers acquiring additional information on which to base a key decision.

21. ___ Posterior probabilities are initial probabilities assigned to the states of nature.

22. ___ A solution to a multistage problem is referred to as a decision strategy.

23. ___ Hash marks indicate the path to take at a decision node.

24. ___ The expected value of sample information is always less than or equal to the expected value of perfect information.

25. ___ Utility theory is an approach for assessing risk attitudes quantitatively.

26. ___ The utility function is linear for risk neutral individuals.

27. ___ In AHP, the top level corresponds to the overall objective of the decision process.

28. ___ A critical issue with AHP is the consistency of judgments specified in the pairwise comparison matrices.

ANSWERS:

1. T, 2. F, 3. F, 4. T, 5. F, 6. F, 7. T, 8. T, 9. T, 10. F, 11. T, 12. T, 13. F, 14. F, 15. T, 16. T, 17. F, 18. T, 19. T, 20. T, 21. F, 22. T, 23. F, 24. T, 25. T, 26. T, 27. T, 28. T

CHAPTER 13

REVIEW

Computer simulation involves designing a logical computer model of a system or decision problem and conducting computer-based experiments with the model to describe, explain, and predict the behavior of the system. Simulation outputs are generated by sampling from distributions of the probabilistic variables. Based on repeated sampling, simulation generates outputs that show the variation in a system's performance or the uncertainty in decision problems.

Because simulation models are descriptive, they do not provide optimal solutions to problems by themselves. Rather, the decision maker uses the simulation as a tool to evaluate the effects of changes made to the controllable variables on the system's performance or other outcomes.

A major advantage of using simulation experiments is that proposed systems can be evaluated without actually building them. In addition, decision makers can experiment with existing systems without disturbing them and can test the limits of a system without damaging or destroying it. On the other hand, using simulation requires that the way a system operates is fully understood. Thus, a large amount of effort in simulation modeling is needed to collect high quality data.

Simulation analysis has been used extensively in manufacturing systems design, in transportation planning, in financial planning, in health care systems, and numerous other areas.

Building a simulation model involves: 1) formulating the problem, 2) developing a conceptual model, 3) collecting data, and 4) developing a logical model.

A simulation model translates a set of controllable and uncontrollable inputs into system performance measures. A *scenario* is a specification of the controllable inputs. The purpose of using simulation is to compare the performance of different scenarios so that conclusions can be drawn as to which scenario is the best.

After the problem has been formulated, the next step is to develop a conceptual model. One type of conceptual model is a flowchart of the system or process under consideration. After the conceptual model has been developed, relevant data are collected. It is important that the data collected reasonably describe the population. Finally, to perform a simulation, the conceptual model must be translated into a logical simulation model that computes the performance measures for each scenario. Simulation models can be implemented using spreadsheets, a general-purpose computer programming language, or a special-purpose simulation modeling language.

Performing a simulation involves two activities: 1) developing mechanisms for generating probabilistic outcomes in the simulation, and 2) recording and summarizing information from which to compute performance measures from the simulation. Generating probabilistic outcomes is typically accomplished by grouping numbers in proportion to the probabilities. *Monte-Carlo simulation* is the process of simulation by sampling from probability distributions using random numbers.

Because the random numbers used in a simulation represent a sample from an infinite population, the output of a simulation model is also a sample from some infinite population of outcomes. Therefore, we expect to obtain different results each time a simulation is run with a different sequence of random numbers. Thus, analyzing the results of a simulation study often involves attempting to characterize the population of outcomes so that statistical statements can be made about the performance measures in which we are interested. How the results of a simulation experiment are interpreted depends on: 1) how many times we run the simulation model, and 2) the length of each run.

A single simulation experiment is called a *run*. Because any simulation exhibits variability, we should never draw conclusions on the basis of a single simulation run. Making valid statistical statements about the performance measures requires that the simulation experiment be *replicated* i.e., repeated several times.

The best way to compare two systems is to make paired comparisons of the results using *common random numbers*. The major advantage of this approach is that the observed differences between the systems are more likely to be due to the controllable factors than to random noise.

The longer a simulation is run, the more accurate will be the estimate of the average value.

Risk is the inability to predict the outcomes or consequences of a decision. *Risk analysis* is an approach that is aimed at developing a probability profile of key decision variables. Monte-Carlo simulation is an effective approach for performing risk analysis.

Simulated outcomes from arbitrary probability distributions are called *random variates*.

SOLVED PROBLEMS

Example Problem 1: Simulating an Inventory Ordering Policy with a Spreadsheet

Sandwiches Inc. has collected data over the past 120 days concerning the number of 12 inch submarine sandwiches it sells each day as summarized below:

Demand	Number of Days
75	18
80	30
85	24
90	36
95	12

Thus, on 30 of the 120 days, Sandwiches Inc. sold eighty 12 inch sandwiches. The manager estimates that each time a customer has to be turned away because the shop has run out of 12 inch buns costs $1.25 in lost contribution to overhead and profits and customer ill will. On the other hand, because bun freshness is critical to satisfying customers, any unused buns are disposed of at the end of the day. The buns costs $.50 each.

Each night the manager places an order for buns from a local bakery which delivers the buns the following morning. Currently, 90 buns are ordered each night. Develop a simulation model that can be used to compare order quantities of 90, 95, and an order quantity based on a three day moving average. Also, develop the simulation models so that the average daily costs are calculated on the basis of 15 day periods.

Solution:

The first step in developing a simulation model for this problem is to determine how random numbers can be used to simulate the demand for 12 inch sandwiches. The calculations needed to make this determination are summarized below:

Demand	Number of Days	Probability	Cumulative Probability
75	18	18/120 = .15	.15
80	30	30/120 = .25	.40
85	24	24/120 = .20	.60
90	36	36/120 = .30	.90
95	12	12/120 = .10	1.00

If random numbers are generated between 0 and 1, we can assign them in the following fashion to simulate the demand for 12 inch sandwiches (note: RN = the random number generated between 0 and 1):

Random Number Interval	Outcome
$.000 \leq RN < .150$	75 sandwiches demanded
$.150 \leq RN < .400$	80 sandwiches demanded
$.400 \leq RN < .600$	85 sandwiches demanded
$.600 \leq RN < .900$	90 sandwiches demanded
$.900 \leq RN < 1.000$	95 sandwiches demanded

Now we are ready to develop a spreadsheet to simulate this situation. Figure 13-1 contains a Lotus 1-2-3 spreadsheet that was developed to simulate different scenarios for ordering the 12 inch buns. Figure 13-2 shows the formulas that were entered into the spreadsheet shown in Figure 13-1. Before entering the formulas into the spreadsheet, the recalculation mode was set to manual. This can be done in one of two ways: entering the command /**W**orksheet**G**lobal**R**ecalc**M**anual (/WGRM) or by selecting the menu items Tools-User Setup-Recalculation and then selecting manual.

At the top of Figure 13-1 the random number range (or interval) was entered for each possible outcome. Thus, the range A4..C8 will serve as a vertical lookup table. In cells B10 and B11 the costs for purchasing buns and the costs of not having enough buns were entered. In the future if these costs change, only the values entered in these cells will need to be changed and no changes will have to be made to the formulas.

The bottom half of Figure 13-1 contains the formulas to execute a 15 day simulation. Each row, beginning with row 16, corresponds to the simulation of a single day. The first column contains a label to identify the day. The second column contains the formula **@RAND** to generate a number from a uniform distribution between 0 and 1. The third column contains a formula that determines the demand for 12 inch subs based on the random number generated using the @VLOOKUP function. Recall, the syntax of this function is @VLOOKUP(CELL, TABLE RANGE, OFFSET). The CELL argument is the cell in the spreadsheet that contains the value that is compared to the values in the first column of the vertical lookup table. The TABLE RANGE identifies the location of the vertical lookup table. When the closest but not larger value is found in the first column of the table, the value in the same row and the OFFSET number of columns over is returned. Note the first column in the table has an offset of 0, the second column has an offset of 1, the third column has an offset of 2, and so on.

Column D corresponds to the number of subs ordered the night before. Thus, this column corresponds to the controllable decision variable and different specifications for this variable correspond to different scenarios. Finally, column E contains a formula that calculates the daily cost. The logic for this formula is that if we order more buns than are needed then the costs for the day is the number of left over buns that must be disposed of times the $.50 per bun. On the other hand, if we run out of buns, then the daily costs is the number of buns we are short times $1.25. To capture this logic, the @IF function is used as is shown in Figure 13-2.

As can be observed from Figure 13-1, the simulation run of 15 days resulted in an average daily cost of $3.58. In Figure 13-3 the scenario associated with ordering 95 buns each day was simulated by entering 95 in cells D16..D30. This single simulation run resulted in an average daily cost of $4.50. Similarly, Figure 13-4 shows a spreadsheet corresponding to the scenario where a 3 day moving average is used as the order quantity for the next day. Since three days of historical data are needed to determine the order quantity, the current order quantity of 90 was entered for days 1-3. Then, beginning with day 4, the order quantity was based on an average of the last three daily demands. Figure

Figure 13-1

A	A	B	C	D	E
1	**12 Inch Bun Ordering Policy Simulation**				
2					
3	*Random Number*	*Range*	*No. 12" Subs*		
4	0.00	0.15	75		
5	0.15	0.40	80		
6	0.40	0.60	85		
7	0.60	0.90	90		
8	0.90	1.00	95		
9					
10	Bun Costs	$0.50			
11	Shortage Costs	$1.25			
12					
13					
14		*Random*		*No. 12"*	*Daily*
15	*Day*	*Number*	*No. 12" Subs*	*Subs Ordered*	*Cost*
16	1	0.380	80	90	$5.00
17	2	0.674	90	90	$0.00
18	3	0.302	80	90	$5.00
19	4	0.641	90	90	$0.00
20	5	0.986	95	90	$6.25
21	6	0.828	90	90	$0.00
22	7	0.345	80	90	$5.00
23	8	0.104	75	90	$7.50
24	9	0.201	80	90	$5.00
25	10	0.004	75	90	$7.50
26	11	0.552	85	90	$2.50
27	12	0.498	85	90	$2.50
28	13	0.522	85	90	$2.50
29	14	0.384	80	90	$5.00
30	15	0.656	90	90	$0.00
31					
32	**AVERAGE DAILY COST**				$3.58

Figure 13-2

	A	B	C	D	E	F	G	H	I
1	12 Inch Bun Ordering Policy Simulation								
2									
3	Random Number	Range	No. 12" Subs						
4	0.00	0.15	75						
5	0.15	0.40	80						
6	0.40	0.60	85						
7	0.60	0.90	90						
8	0.90	1.00	95						
9									
10	Bun Costs	$0.50							
11	Shortage Costs	$1.25							
12									
13									
14		Random		No. 12"	Daily				
15	Day	Number	No. 12" Subs	Subs Ordered	Cost				
16	1	@RAND	@VLOOKUP(B16,$A$4..$C$8,2)	90	@IF(D16>C16,(D16-C16)*$B$10,(C16-D16)*$B$11)				
17	2	@RAND	@VLOOKUP(B17,$A$4..$C$8,2)	90	@IF(D17>C17,(D17-C17)*$B$10,(C17-D17)*$B$11)				
18	3	@RAND	@VLOOKUP(B18,$A$4..$C$8,2)	90	@IF(D18>C18,(D18-C18)*$B$10,(C18-D18)*$B$11)				
19	4	@RAND	@VLOOKUP(B19,$A$4..$C$8,2)	90	@IF(D19>C19,(D19-C19)*$B$10,(C19-D19)*$B$11)		{EDIT}{HOME}^{DOWN}		
20	5	@RAND	@VLOOKUP(B20,$A$4..$C$8,2)	90	@IF(D20>C20,(D20-C20)*$B$10,(C20-D20)*$B$11)		/XGG19~		
21	6	@RAND	@VLOOKUP(B21,$A$4..$C$8,2)	90	@IF(D21>C21,(D21-C21)*$B$10,(C21-D21)*$B$11)				
22	7	@RAND	@VLOOKUP(B22,$A$4..$C$8,2)	90	@IF(D22>C22,(D22-C22)*$B$10,(C22-D22)*$B$11)				
23	8	@RAND	@VLOOKUP(B23,$A$4..$C$8,2)	90	@IF(D23>C23,(D23-C23)*$B$10,(C23-D23)*$B$11)				
24	9	@RAND	@VLOOKUP(B24,$A$4..$C$8,2)	90	@IF(D24>C24,(D24-C24)*$B$10,(C24-D24)*$B$11)				
25	10	@RAND	@VLOOKUP(B25,$A$4..$C$8,2)	90	@IF(D25>C25,(D25-C25)*$B$10,(C25-D25)*$B$11)				
26	11	@RAND	@VLOOKUP(B26,$A$4..$C$8,2)	90	@IF(D26>C26,(D26-C26)*$B$10,(C26-D26)*$B$11)				
27	12	@RAND	@VLOOKUP(B27,$A$4..$C$8,2)	90	@IF(D27>C27,(D27-C27)*$B$10,(C27-D27)*$B$11)				
28	13	@RAND	@VLOOKUP(B28,$A$4..$C$8,2)	90	@IF(D28>C28,(D28-C28)*$B$10,(C28-D28)*$B$11)				
29	14	@RAND	@VLOOKUP(B29,$A$4..$C$8,2)	90	@IF(D29>C29,(D29-C29)*$B$10,(C29-D29)*$B$11)				
30	15	@RAND	@VLOOKUP(B30,$A$4..$C$8,2)	90	@IF(D30>C30,(D30-C30)*$B$10,(C30-D30)*$B$11)				
31									
32	AVERAGE DAILY COST				@AVG(E30..E16)				

Figure 13-3

A	A	B	C	D	E
1	**12 Inch Bun Ordering Policy Simulation**				
2					
3	*Random Number*	*Range*	*No. 12" Subs*		
4	0.00	0.15	75		
5	0.15	0.40	80		
6	0.40	0.60	85		
7	0.60	0.90	90		
8	0.90	1.00	95		
9					
10	Bun Costs	$0.50			
11	Shortage Costs	$1.25			
12					
13					
14		*Random*		*No. 12"*	*Daily*
15	*Day*	*Number*	*No. 12" Subs*	*Subs Ordered*	*Cost*
16	1	0.508	85	95	$5.00
17	2	0.238	80	95	$7.50
18	3	0.874	90	95	$2.50
19	4	0.571	85	95	$5.00
20	5	0.842	90	95	$2.50
21	6	0.359	80	95	$7.50
22	7	0.198	80	95	$7.50
23	8	0.768	90	95	$2.50
24	9	0.788	90	95	$2.50
25	10	0.397	80	95	$7.50
26	11	0.907	95	95	$0.00
27	12	0.281	80	95	$7.50
28	13	0.518	85	95	$5.00
29	14	0.451	85	95	$5.00
30	15	0.997	95	95	$0.00
31					
32	**AVERAGE DAILY COST**				$4.50

Figure 13-4

A	B	C	D	E
12 Inch Bun Ordering Policy Simulation				
Random Number Range		No. 12" Subs		
0.00	0.15	75		
0.15	0.40	80		
0.40	0.60	85		
0.60	0.90	90		
0.90	1.00	95		
Bun Costs	$0.50			
Shortage Costs	$1.25			
Day	Random Number	No. 12" Subs	No. 12" Subs Ordered	Daily Cost
1	0.394	80	90	$5.00
2	0.698	90	90	$0.00
3	0.512	85	90	$2.50
4	0.613	90	85	$6.25
5	0.293	80	88	$4.00
6	0.962	95	85	$12.50
7	0.509	85	88	$1.50
8	0.401	85	87	$1.00
9	0.553	85	88	$1.50
10	0.923	95	85	$12.50
11	0.863	90	88	$2.50
12	0.195	80	90	$5.00
13	0.667	90	88	$2.50
14	0.854	90	87	$3.75
15	0.510	85	87	$1.00
AVERAGE DAILY COST				$4.10

13-5 shows the formulas that were entered to calculate the three day moving average. Note that since a fraction of a bun cannot be ordered, the 3 day moving average was rounded to zero decimal places using the @ROUND Lotus function. The syntax of this function is @RAND(x,n) which rounds x to n places.

Of course, we should never make decisions on the basis of the results obtained from a single run of a simulation model. Obtaining additional replications of the simulation models developed is easily accomplished. Specifically, the simulation models are replicated each time the F9 function is pressed. Figure 13-6 summarizes the results of 10 replications of each of the models developed where Q stands for the order quantity. Note that since each replication simulates 15 days, 10 replications of a model represent 150 simulated days. Also shown in Figure 13-6 is the sample mean (calculated as the mean of the average daily costs) and the standard error. Note to calculate the standard error the @STDS function and not the @STD function should be used since we are calculating the sample standard deviation and not the population standard deviation. The sample means and standard errors shown in Figure 13-6 can be used to construct confidence intervals to determine if the observed differences between the three ordering policies are statistically significantly different.

Example Problem 2: Using a Continuous Distribution in Spreadsheet Simulation

Develop a simulation model for the previous example where the demand is based on a normal distribution with a mean of 85 12 inch subs per day and standard deviation of 10. Compare ordering policies of Q = 90 and Q = 85 using the common random number approach.

Solution:

A spreadsheet for this situation is shown in Figure 13-7. Figure 13-8 shows the formulas that were entered into this spreadsheet.

At the top of Figure 13-7 the parameters for this problem were entered. The bottom two-thirds contain the formulas that generate the random numbers and compute the daily costs for the two ordering policies considered. Column A contains labels to identify the day. Column B contains a formula that generates random z values (i.e., random values from a normal distribution with a mean of 0 and variance of 1). This formula is based on the formula given in the text book for generating normally- distributed variates with mean of 0 and variance of 1 as follows:

$$z = \sqrt{-2 \ln R_1} \cos (2\Pi R_2)$$

Entering this formula required using the @SQRT, @LN, and @COS Lotus functions in addition to the @RAND function as can be seen from Figure 13-8.

Figure 13-5

A	A	B	C	D	E	F	G	H
1	**12 Inch Bun Ordering Policy Simulation**							
2								
3	*Random Number*	*Range*	*No. 12" Subs*					
4	0.00	0.15	75					
5	0.15	0.40	80					
6	0.40	0.60	85					
7	0.60	0.90	90					
8	0.90	1.00	95					
9								
10	Bun Costs	$0.50						
11	Shortage Costs	$1.25						
12								
13								
14		*Random*		*No. 12"*	*Daily*			
15	*Day*	*Number*	*No. 12" Subs*	*Subs Ordered*	*Cost*			
16	1	@RAND	80	90	$5.00	{EDIT}{HOME}^{DOWN}		
17	2	@RAND	90	90	$0.00	/XGF16~		
18	3	@RAND	85	90	$2.50			
19	4	@RAND	90	@ROUND(@AVG(C18..C16),0)	$6.25			
20	5	@RAND	80	@ROUND(@AVG(C19..C17),0)	$4.00			
21	6	@RAND	95	@ROUND(@AVG(C20..C18),0)	$12.50			
22	7	@RAND	85	@ROUND(@AVG(C21..C19),0)	$1.50			
23	8	@RAND	85	@ROUND(@AVG(C22..C20),0)	$1.00			
24	9	@RAND	85	@ROUND(@AVG(C23..C21),0)	$1.50			
25	10	@RAND	95	@ROUND(@AVG(C24..C22),0)	$12.50			
26	11	@RAND	90	@ROUND(@AVG(C25..C23),0)	$2.50			
27	12	@RAND	80	@ROUND(@AVG(C26..C24),0)	$5.00			
28	13	@RAND	90	@ROUND(@AVG(C27..C25),0)	$2.50			
29	14	@RAND	90	@ROUND(@AVG(C28..C26),0)	$3.75			
30	15	@RAND	85	@ROUND(@AVG(C29..C27),0)	$1.00			
31								
32	AVERAGE DAILY COST				$4.10			

Figure 13-6

Summary of 10 Replications of Each Simulation Model

	Average Daily Cost		
Replication	Q = 90	Q = 95	Q = 3 Day Mov. Avg.
1	$3.58	$4.50	$4.10
2	$4.00	$5.00	$7.30
3	$2.83	$4.17	$4.80
4	$3.50	$4.33	$4.32
5	$2.25	$5.50	$4.93
6	$3.17	$5.33	$6.77
7	$2.08	$4.33	$3.93
8	$4.25	$5.00	$5.98
9	$4.33	$6.17	$4.35
10	$2.33	$4.83	$3.73
Sample Mean	3.23	4.92	5.02
Standard Error	0.22	0.16	0.32

Figure 13-7

A	A	B	C	D	E
1	**12 Inch Bun Ordering Policy Simulation**				
2					
3					
4	Mean	85.0			
5	Std. Deviation	10.0			
6	Bun Costs	$0.50			
7	Shortage Costs	$1.25			
8					
9					
10	Monte-Carlo Simulation				
11					
12		Random		Daily Cost	Daily Cost
13	Day	z value	No. 12" Subs	Q = 90	Q = 85
14	1	-1.208	73	$8.50	$6.00
15	2	-0.358	81	$4.50	$2.00
16	3	1.389	99	$11.25	$17.50
17	4	-1.161	73	$8.50	$6.00
18	5	-1.278	72	$9.00	$6.50
19	6	0.323	88	$1.00	$3.75
20	7	-0.191	83	$3.50	$1.00
21	8	0.386	89	$0.50	$5.00
22	9	-0.049	85	$2.50	$0.00
23	10	-0.686	78	$6.00	$3.50
24	11	-1.026	75	$7.50	$5.00
25	12	-0.096	84	$3.00	$0.50
26	13	0.310	88	$1.00	$3.75
27	14	-0.656	78	$6.00	$3.50
28	15	0.136	86	$2.00	$1.25
29					
30	**AVERAGE DAILY COST**			$4.98	$4.35

Figure 13-8

	A	B	C	D	E
1	12 Inch Bun Ordering Policy Simulation				
2					
3					
4	Mean	85.0			
5	Std. Deviation	10.0			
6	Bun Costs	$0.50			
7	Shortage Costs	$1.25			
8					
9					
10	Monte-Carlo Simulation				
11					
12		*Random*		*Daily Cost*	*Daily Cost*
13	*Day*	*z value*	*No. 12" Subs*	*Q = 90*	*Q = 85*
14	1	@SQRT(-2*@LN(@RAND))*(@COS(2*@PI*@RAND))	@ROUND(+$B$5*B14+$B$4,0)	@IF(90>C14,(90-C14)*$B$6,(C14-90)*$B$7)	$6.00
15	2	@SQRT(-2*@LN(@RAND))*(@COS(2*@PI*@RAND))	@ROUND(+$B$5*B15+$B$4,0)	@IF(90>C15,(90-C15)*$B$6,(C15-90)*$B$7)	$2.00
16	3	@SQRT(-2*@LN(@RAND))*(@COS(2*@PI*@RAND))	@ROUND(+$B$5*B16+$B$4,0)	@IF(90>C16,(90-C16)*$B$6,(C16-90)*$B$7)	$17.50
17	4	@SQRT(-2*@LN(@RAND))*(@COS(2*@PI*@RAND))	@ROUND(+$B$5*B17+$B$4,0)	@IF(90>C17,(90-C17)*$B$6,(C17-90)*$B$7)	$6.00
18	5	@SQRT(-2*@LN(@RAND))*(@COS(2*@PI*@RAND))	@ROUND(+$B$5*B18+$B$4,0)	@IF(90>C18,(90-C18)*$B$6,(C18-90)*$B$7)	$6.50
19	6	@SQRT(-2*@LN(@RAND))*(@COS(2*@PI*@RAND))	@ROUND(+$B$5*B19+$B$4,0)	@IF(90>C19,(90-C19)*$B$6,(C19-90)*$B$7)	$3.75
20	7	@SQRT(-2*@LN(@RAND))*(@COS(2*@PI*@RAND))	@ROUND(+$B$5*B20+$B$4,0)	@IF(90>C20,(90-C20)*$B$6,(C20-90)*$B$7)	$1.00
21	8	@SQRT(-2*@LN(@RAND))*(@COS(2*@PI*@RAND))	@ROUND(+$B$5*B21+$B$4,0)	@IF(90>C21,(90-C21)*$B$6,(C21-90)*$B$7)	$5.00
22	9	@SQRT(-2*@LN(@RAND))*(@COS(2*@PI*@RAND))	@ROUND(+$B$5*B22+$B$4,0)	@IF(90>C22,(90-C22)*$B$6,(C22-90)*$B$7)	$0.00
23	10	@SQRT(-2*@LN(@RAND))*(@COS(2*@PI*@RAND))	@ROUND(+$B$5*B23+$B$4,0)	@IF(90>C23,(90-C23)*$B$6,(C23-90)*$B$7)	$3.50
24	11	@SQRT(-2*@LN(@RAND))*(@COS(2*@PI*@RAND))	@ROUND(+$B$5*B24+$B$4,0)	@IF(90>C24,(90-C24)*$B$6,(C24-90)*$B$7)	$5.00
25	12	@SQRT(-2*@LN(@RAND))*(@COS(2*@PI*@RAND))	@ROUND(+$B$5*B25+$B$4,0)	@IF(90>C25,(90-C25)*$B$6,(C25-90)*$B$7)	$0.50
26	13	@SQRT(-2*@LN(@RAND))*(@COS(2*@PI*@RAND))	@ROUND(+$B$5*B26+$B$4,0)	@IF(90>C26,(90-C26)*$B$6,(C26-90)*$B$7)	$3.75
27	14	@SQRT(-2*@LN(@RAND))*(@COS(2*@PI*@RAND))	@ROUND(+$B$5*B27+$B$4,0)	@IF(90>C27,(90-C27)*$B$6,(C27-90)*$B$7)	$3.50
28	15	@SQRT(-2*@LN(@RAND))*(@COS(2*@PI*@RAND))	@ROUND(+$B$5*B28+$B$4,0)	@IF(90>C28,(90-C28)*$B$6,(C28-90)*$B$7)	$1.25
29					
30	AVERAGE DAILY COST			@AVG(D28..D14)	$4.35

In column C, the z values generated in column B were converted to normal random variates with mean of 80 and standard deviation of 10 using the following formula:

$$x = \sigma z + \mu$$

with $\mu = 80$ and $\sigma = 10$. Finally, in columns D and E, formulas that calculate the daily costs of ordering 90 buns and 85 buns, respectively, were entered. Notice that for a given day, the same random number is used to determine the daily costs for that day regardless of which order size is used. To illustrate, on day 4 a demand of 72 subs was generated. Thus on day 4 there was a surplus of 17 buns (90-73) associated with a 90 bun order quantity, and a surplus of 12 buns (85-73) with the 85 bun order quantity. The daily costs for day 4 were calculated to be $8.50 (17*.50) for the 90 bun order quantity, and $6.00 (12*.50) for the 85 bun order quantity. Using the same random numbers to compare two or more scenarios is called the common random number approach and has the advantage that observed differences between different scenarios are more likely to be due to the controllable factors than due to random noise. Note that while the formulas entered in column E are not shown in Figure 13-8, they are exactly the same as the formulas entered in column D except that the 90 was replaced with an 85 in the column E formulas.

TRUE/FALSE QUESTIONS

1. ___ Simulation models can by themselves provide optimal solutions to problems.

2. ___ Simulation models are examples of prescriptive models.

3. ___ Simulation models are usually implemented on a computer because of the large number of calculations involved.

4. ___ An advantage of using simulation is that proposed systems can be evaluated without actually building them.

5. ___ A large amount of effort in simulation modeling involves the collection of high quality data.

6. ___ Simulation models are most useful in situations involving dynamic interactions between elements of the system and for systems which have many probabilistic elements.

7. ___ Any specification of the controllable inputs defines a replication.

8. ___ A scenario is a conceptual model that can be best characterized as a managerial description of the process.

9. ___ Simulating complex systems usually requires special computer programming languages.

10. ___ If a problem can be solved analytically, then simulation is not appropriate.

11. ___ Pseudorandom number refers to a computer-generated random number.

12. ___ Truly random phenomena cannot occur in nature.

13. ___ The process of simulation by sampling from probability distributions using random numbers is often called Monte-Carlo simulation.

14. ___The term Monte-Carlo simulation was coined by scientists who worked on the development of the atom bomb.

15. ___ If a simulation model is properly designed, we would not expect different results each time the simulation model is run with a different sequence of random numbers.

16. ___ Because of variability, the interpretation of simulation results requires statistical analysis.

17. ___ How a simulation experiment is interpreted depends only on how many times the models is run and not on the length of each run.

18. ___ A single simulation experiment is called a run.

19. ___ If a simulation model is properly designed then it is acceptable to draw conclusions on the basis of a single run.

20. ___ Replicating a simulation experiment means repeating the experiment several times.

21. ___ A disadvantage associated with using common random numbers is that random noise across alternative scenarios is increased.

22. ___ The longer a simulation is run, the more accurate will be the estimate of the average value.

23. ___ Simulated outcomes from arbitrary probability distributions are called random variates.

Answers:

1. F, 2. F, 3. T, 4. T, 5. T, 6. T, 7. F, 8. F, 9. T, 10. T, 11. T, 12. F, 13. T, 14. T, 15. F, 16. T, 17. F, 18. T, 19. F, 20. T, 21. F, 22. T, 23. T

CHAPTER 14

REVIEW

Static simulation models are independent of time whereas dynamic simulation models depend on time and therefore incorporate a simulation clock to maintain a log of events. Although simple dynamic simulation models can be implemented on spreadsheets, sophisticated simulation languages are usually needed to implement complex problems.

Dynamic simulation models often involve the processing of customers at service facilities. Customers in dynamic simulation models might be people, manufacturing jobs, paper work that needs to be processed, patients, and so on. Facilities in dynamic simulation models include things like workers, machines, work stations, material handling equipment, and so on. One important issue in developing a dynamic simulation model is specifying the times when customers arrive for service. This can be done in one of two ways: either specify the actual time that customers arrive for service, or specify the times *between successive arrivals*. The advantage of the second approach is that we only need to know the time the last customer arrived to generate the arrival time of the next customer. A key question to ask in developing any model is: What do we need to know to compute the performance measures we want?

Event driven simulation models operate by moving the simulation clock forward to the time at which the next logical event occurs.

Simulation models can be implemented on computers in one of three ways: 1) with a spreadsheet, 2) with a general-purpose programming language, and 3) with a special-purpose simulation language. Translating a logical flow chart that is written correctly into a computer programming language is generally not that difficult. However, using general-purpose programming languages requires that specialized routines for generating stochastic outcomes, computing statistical measures, monitoring simulated time, and so on be developed and coded. Numerous simulation models have be written in general-purpose languages such as FORTRAN, C, BASIC, and PASCAL.

Special-purpose *simulation languages* automatically perform typical simulation functions such as generating random numbers, collecting statistical information, producing summary reports, and advancing the simulation clock. Among the most popular simulation languages are SLAM (Simulation Language of Alternative Modeling), SIMAN, GPSS (General Purpose Systems Simulator), and SIMSCRIPT. In particular, SLAM models are developed by combining *network symbols* that perform certain logical operations into a network diagram that corresponds to a conceptual model of the system being studied.

A simulator is a parameter-driven simulation that requires no programming. The user simply inputs a set of data that describes the system. Most simulators have been developed for specific applications such as manufacturing applications or network communication applications. SIMFACTORY II.5, XCELL+, WITNESS, and ProModelPC are popular manufacturing simulators. To create a simulation model of a manufacturing system using a simulator, one must consider the types of parts moving through the system, the types of processing stations in the system, the capacity of the stations, the processing times of the parts at each station, the order or routing in which the parts visit the stations, and the scheduling of part arrivals. Also, machine downtime, labor requirements, and material handling equipment may be considered.

One important and challenging task associated with simulation modeling is ensuring the accuracy of the model and convincing the end user that the model is a valid representation of the real system being studied. *Verification* refers to the process of determining if the simulation program performs as intended. In other words, is the simulation model free from logical errors and bugs? *Validation* is concerned with determining whether the conceptual model accurately represents the real system under investigation.

Validation typically consists of three steps: 1) developing a model with high face validity, 2) validating the model assumptions, and 3) validating the model output. A model is said to have *face validity* when the model seems reasonable to those who understand the real system. The most objective and scientific means of validation is to compare the output of the model with data from the real system for the same inputs.

SOLVED PROBLEMS

Example Problem 1: Using a Spreadsheet to Develop a Dynamic Simulation Model

Car Lube Inc. provides two basic services: oil changes or combined oil and transmission fluid service. Historical records indicate that 80% of the customers purchase only the oil change while 20% purchase the combined oil and transmission fluid service. Car Lube's facilities include a garage with a single bay. Thus, only one car can be serviced at a time. The time to change a car's oil is 12 minutes while the time to perform the combined oil and transmission fluid service is 20 minutes. Finally, a recent study indicates that the customer interarrival time can be approximated with a uniform distribution over the range of 5 to 20 minutes. Develop a spreadsheet to simulate the arrival and servicing of 20 customers.

Solution:

A spreadsheet to simulate this situation is given in Figure 14-1 and representative formulas for this spreadsheet are shown in Figure 14-2. The top of Figure 14-1 contains the model assumptions. Cells A13..C14 correspond to a vertical lookup table that is used to determine the customer service times given that 80% of the customers purchase just the oil change while the other 20% purchase the combined oil and transmission service.

Figure 14-1

Car Lube Service Time Simulation						
Formulas and Assumptions						
Interarrival time is uniform between 5 to 25 minutes						
Type of service has the distribution and service time:						
Service	Probability	Time (min.)				
Oil	0.8	12				
Oil and Transmission	0.2	20				
Lookup Table						
Random number range		Serv. Time				
0	0.8	12				
0.8	1	20				
Customer Arrival	Time of Arrival	Time Serv. Begins	Service Time	Service Finished	Wait Time	Time in System
1	7.2	7.2	12	19.2	0.0	12.0
2	17.0	19.2	12	31.2	2.2	14.2
3	35.7	35.7	20	55.7	0.0	20.0
4	51.2	55.7	12	67.7	4.5	16.5
5	67.8	67.8	12	79.8	0.0	12.0
6	74.0	79.8	12	91.8	5.8	17.8
7	85.2	91.8	12	103.8	6.7	18.7
8	100.7	103.8	12	115.8	3.1	15.1
9	115.5	115.8	12	127.8	0.4	12.4
10	133.7	133.7	12	145.7	0.0	12.0
11	149.8	149.8	20	169.8	0.0	20.0
12	169.9	169.9	12	181.9	0.0	12.0
13	180.0	181.9	12	193.9	1.9	13.9
14	193.2	193.9	12	205.9	0.7	12.7
15	214.1	214.1	12	226.1	0.0	12.0
16	234.3	234.3	12	246.3	0.0	12.0
17	257.6	257.6	20	277.6	0.0	20.0
18	276.7	277.6	12	289.6	0.9	12.9
19	294.9	294.9	12	306.9	0.0	12.0
20	318.8	318.8	12	330.8	0.0	12.0
Averages					1.3	14.5

Figure 14-2

Car Lube Service Time Simulation								
Formulas and Assumptions								
Interarrival time is uniform between 5 to 25 minutes								
Type of service has the distribution and service time:								
Service	Probability	Time (min.)						
Oil	0.8	12						
Oil and Transmission	0.2	20						
Lookup Table								
Random number range		Serv. Time						
0	0.8	12						
0.8	1	20						
Customer Arrival	Time of Arrival	Time Serv. Begins	Service Time	Service Finished	Wait Time	Time in System		{EDIT}{HOME}^{DOWN}
1	5+((25-5)*@RAND)	+B18	@VLOOKUP(@RAND,$A$13..$C$14,2)	+C18+D18	+C18-B18	+E18-B18		/XGI17~
2	+B18+(5+((25-5)*@RAND))	@MAX(B19,E18)	@VLOOKUP(@RAND,$A$13..$C$14,2)	+C19+D19	+C19-B19	+E19-B19		
3	+B19+(5+((25-5)*@RAND))	@MAX(B20,E19)	@VLOOKUP(@RAND,$A$13..$C$14,2)	+C20+D20	+C20-B20	+E20-B20		
4	+B20+(5+((25-5)*@RAND))	@MAX(B21,E20)	@VLOOKUP(@RAND,$A$13..$C$14,2)	+C21+D21	+C21-B21	+E21-B21		
5	+B21+(5+((25-5)*@RAND))	@MAX(B22,E21)	@VLOOKUP(@RAND,$A$13..$C$14,2)	+C22+D22	+C22-B22	+E22-B22		
6	+B22+(5+((25-5)*@RAND))	@MAX(B23,E22)	@VLOOKUP(@RAND,$A$13..$C$14,2)	+C23+D23	+C23-B23	+E23-B23		
7	+B23+(5+((25-5)*@RAND))	@MAX(B24,E23)	@VLOOKUP(@RAND,$A$13..$C$14,2)	+C24+D24	+C24-B24	+E24-B24		
8	+B24+(5+((25-5)*@RAND))	@MAX(B25,E24)	@VLOOKUP(@RAND,$A$13..$C$14,2)	+C25+D25	+C25-B25	+E25-B25		
9	+B25+(5+((25-5)*@RAND))	@MAX(B26,E25)	@VLOOKUP(@RAND,$A$13..$C$14,2)	+C26+D26	+C26-B26	+E26-B26		
10	+B26+(5+((25-5)*@RAND))	@MAX(B27,E26)	@VLOOKUP(@RAND,$A$13..$C$14,2)	+C27+D27	+C27-B27	+E27-B27		
11	+B27+(5+((25-5)*@RAND))	@MAX(B28,E27)	@VLOOKUP(@RAND,$A$13..$C$14,2)	+C28+D28	+C28-B28	+E28-B28		
12	+B28+(5+((25-5)*@RAND))	@MAX(B29,E28)	@VLOOKUP(@RAND,$A$13..$C$14,2)	+C29+D29	+C29-B29	+E29-B29		
13	+B29+(5+((25-5)*@RAND))	@MAX(B30,E29)	@VLOOKUP(@RAND,$A$13..$C$14,2)	+C30+D30	+C30-B30	+E30-B30		
14	+B30+(5+((25-5)*@RAND))	@MAX(B31,E30)	@VLOOKUP(@RAND,$A$13..$C$14,2)	+C31+D31	+C31-B31	+E31-B31		
15	+B31+(5+((25-5)*@RAND))	@MAX(B32,E31)	@VLOOKUP(@RAND,$A$13..$C$14,2)	+C32+D32	+C32-B32	+E32-B32		
16	+B32+(5+((25-5)*@RAND))	@MAX(B33,E32)	@VLOOKUP(@RAND,$A$13..$C$14,2)	+C33+D33	+C33-B33	+E33-B33		
17	+B33+(5+((25-5)*@RAND))	@MAX(B34,E33)	@VLOOKUP(@RAND,$A$13..$C$14,2)	+C34+D34	+C34-B34	+E34-B34		
18	+B34+(5+((25-5)*@RAND))	@MAX(B35,E34)	@VLOOKUP(@RAND,$A$13..$C$14,2)	+C35+D35	+C35-B35	+E35-B35		
19	+B35+(5+((25-5)*@RAND))	@MAX(B36,E35)	@VLOOKUP(@RAND,$A$13..$C$14,2)	+C36+D36	+C36-B36	+E36-B36		
20	+B36+(5+((25-5)*@RAND))	@MAX(B37,E36)	@VLOOKUP(@RAND,$A$13..$C$14,2)	+C37+D37	+C37-B37	+E37-B37		
Averages					@AVG(F37.	@AVG(G37..G18)		

Beginning in row 16 of Figure 14-1 is a table that keeps track of when the customers arrive, when the actual service begins, the customer service time, and when the service is completed. Also, the table contains formulas that calculate how long each customer had to wait after arriving before the service began and how long a customer spent in the system.

As shown in column A of Figure 14-1, the table simulates the arrival of 20 customers. In column B the arrival time of each customer is computed. Recall that the interarrival time was determined to be uniformly distributed over the range of 5 to 25 minutes. Also, recall that uniform random variates can be generated over the range [a, b] using the formula $U = a + (b-a)R$, where R is a random number with a uniform distribution between 0 and 1. If we begin the simulation at time zero then the first arrival would be computed as: $5 + (25-5)R$. Replacing R with the Lotus @RAND function yields the formula 5+((25-5)*@RAND) which was entered in cell B18 to generate the time of the first customer arrival. Since we are using the time between arrivals to generate the next arrival, the time of the second customer arrival would be the time of the first customer arrival plus $5 + (25-5)R$. Thus, the following formula was entered into cell B19 to generate the time of the second arrival: +B18+(5+((25-5)*@RAND)). This formula was then copied to cells B20..B37.

Column C contains formulas that determine when the service begins for a particular customer. For service to begin, two events must happen: 1) the customer must have arrived, and 2) the service must have been completed for the prior customer. Thus, the time service begins for a customer is the maximum of when that customer arrives and when the service is completed for the preceding customer. Since no customers are processed before the first customer arrival, service begins for the first customer at the same time of his/her arrival. Therefore, in cell C18 the formula +B18 was entered. The time the second customer begins service is equal to the larger of the time the second customer arrives or the time when the service has been completed for customer 1. The time that customer 2 arrives is calculated in cell B19 and the time the service is completed for customer 1 is calculated in cell E18. Thus, the formula to calculate when customer 2 begins service (cell C19) was @MAX(B19, E18). The formula entered in C19 can be copied to cells C20.. C37.

Column D contains formulas to calculate the service time for each customer. To calculate the service time, the vertical lookup table in cells A13..C14 was used. This table assigns an 80% probability to a customer having a 12 minute service time and a 20% probability of a customer having a 20 minute service time. Notice how the @RAND function was used directly in the @VLOOKUP function.

Column E contains formulas to calculate the service completion time for each arriving customer. Service completion times were computed by adding the service time to the time service begins.

In columns F and G the wait time and time in system for each customer, respectively, are computed. The wait time is computed as the difference between the time service is started and the time the customer arrived. Likewise, the time a customer spends in the system is calculated as the difference between the time the service is completed and the time the customer arrived. Additionally, in row 39 the average wait time and time in system are calculated.

The spreadsheet shown in Figure 14-1 can be used to investigate relatively simple questions such as how long it takes to process 20 customers or what the average wait time and time in system are. In addition, the effect of buying labor saving equipment can also be investigated. For example, assume that a new piece of equipment can be purchased that reduces the oil change time to 10 minutes and reduces the combined oil and transmission service time to 15 minutes. A spreadsheet reflecting these changes is shown in Figure 14-3. Comparing Figure 14-1 to Figure 14-3 we observe that the average wait time was slightly higher after the change (1.6 versus 1.3 minutes) while the average time in system was slightly lower (12.6 versus 14.5 minutes). Of course, we should never draw conclusions on the basis of a single simulation run especially since common random streams were not used and we have no way of knowing whether these differences are due to random noise. The proper way to compare these two systems would be to replicate each model at least 20 or 30 times in order to develop confidence intervals to test to see if the differences detected are statistically significant.

While spreadsheets are capable of modeling relatively simple relationships, investigating more complex relationships is difficult with spreadsheets. For example, in the spreadsheets given in Figures 14-1 and 14-3 we simulated the processing of 20 arrivals. Suppose on the other hand we wanted to simulate the entire day the garage was open. To do this we would need a simulation model that would keep generating arrivals until it was time to close the garage. While this can be done with macros, doing it in a spreadsheet is a little awkward. Or suppose we wanted to keep track of the number of customers that were in the system at any given time. Again doing this in a spreadsheet is probably possible, but would be complicated to implement. Thus, due to these limitations, in most cases it is preferable to use general-purpose programming languages or if available special-purpose simulation languages to develop dynamic simulation models.

Example Problem 2: Simulation Model Coded in BASIC and SLAM

For comparison purposes, in this example we show the BASIC code and SLAM code for the simulation model developed in the previous example.

BASIC Program for Car Lube Service Time Simulation

Below is a sample program written in True Basic for the Car Lube Simulation. The program was written to demonstrate how BASIC can be used to simulate a problem and therefore could have been coded more efficiently with fewer lines of code.

Figure 14-3

	A	B	C	D	E	F	G
1	**Car Lube Service Time Simulation**						
2							
3	*Formulas and Assumptions*						
4							
5	Interarrival time is uniform between 5 to 25 minutes						
6	Type of service has the distribution and service time:						
7	Service	Probability	Time (min.)				
8	Oil	0.8	10				
9	Oil and Transmission	0.2	15				
10							
11	Lookup Table						
12	Random number range		Serv. Time				
13	0	0.8	10				
14	0.8	1	15				
15							
16		Time of	Time Serv.	Service	Service		Time in
17	Customer Arrival	Arrival	Begins	Time	Finished	Wait Time	System
18	1	17.6	17.6	10	27.6	0.0	10.0
19	2	31.9	31.9	10	41.9	0.0	10.0
20	3	40.6	41.9	15	56.9	1.3	16.3
21	4	56.8	56.9	10	66.9	0.1	10.1
22	5	64.2	66.9	15	81.9	2.8	17.8
23	6	79.0	81.9	10	91.9	3.0	13.0
24	7	100.8	100.8	10	110.8	0.0	10.0
25	8	115.4	115.4	10	125.4	0.0	10.0
26	9	134.8	134.8	15	149.8	0.0	15.0
27	10	147.1	149.8	10	159.8	2.6	12.6
28	11	169.6	169.6	10	179.6	0.0	10.0
29	12	190.4	190.4	10	200.4	0.0	10.0
30	13	202.4	202.4	10	212.4	0.0	10.0
31	14	208.6	212.4	10	222.4	3.8	13.8
32	15	230.4	230.4	10	240.4	0.0	10.0
33	16	249.2	249.2	10	259.2	0.0	10.0
34	17	271.0	271.0	10	281.0	0.0	10.0
35	18	284.4	284.4	15	299.4	0.0	15.0
36	19	292.9	299.4	10	309.4	6.5	16.5
37	20	298.3	309.4	10	319.4	11.1	21.1
38							
39	*Averages*					1.6	12.6

```
! Car Lube Service Time Simulation
! Dimension Arrays
DIM AT (0 TO 20) ! ARRAY TO STORE ARRIVAL TIMES
DIM STB(0 TO 20) ! ARRAY TO STORE WHEN SERVICE TIME BEGINS
DIM STF(0 TO 20) ! ARRAY TO STORE WHEN SERVICE TIME FINISHES
DIM WT(20)      ! ARRAY TO STORE CUSTOMER WAITING TIMES
DIM TIS(20)     ! ARRAY TO STORE TIMES IN SYSTEM
! Initialize Variables
LET AT(0) = 0
LET TOTAL_WT = 0
LET TOTAL_TIS = 0
RANDOMIZE ! GENERATE DIFFERENT VALUES FOR EACH SIMULATION RUN
! GENERATE THE ARRIVAL TIMES FOR 20 CUSTOMERS
FOR ARRIVAL = 1 TO 20
  LET AT(ARRIVAL) = AT(ARRIVAL - 1) + (5 + (20*RND))
NEXT ARRIVAL
! SIMULATE SERVICING THE 20 ARRIVALS
FOR ARRIVAL = 1 TO 20
  !CALCULATE WHEN SERVICE TIME BEGINS
  LET STB(ARRIVAL) = MAX(AT(ARRIVAL), STF(ARRIVAL - 1))
  !DETERMINE TYPE OF SERVICE
  LET R = RND
    IF R < .8 THEN LET ST = 12 ! 80% CHANCE OF JUST OIL CHANGE
    IF R >= .8 THEN LET ST = 20 ! 20% CHANCE OF OIL AND TRANSMISSION
SERVICE
  ! CALCULATE TIME WHEN SERVICE FINISHED
  LET STF(ARRIVAL) = STB(ARRIVAL) + ST
  ! CALCULATE WAIT TIME AND TIME IN SYSTEM
  LET WT(ARRIVAL) = STB(ARRIVAL) - AT(ARRIVAL)
  LET TIS(ARRIVAL) = STF(ARRIVAL) - AT(ARRIVAL)
NEXT ARRIVAL
! COMPUTE SUMMARY STATISTICS
FOR X=1 TO 20
  LET TOTAL_WT = TOTAL_WT + WT(X)
  LET TOTAL_TIS = TOTAL_TIS + TIS(X)
NEXT X
LET AVG_WT = TOTAL_WT/20
LET AVG_TIS = TOTAL_TIS/20
! PRINT SUMMARY STATISTICS OF SIMULATION RUN
PRINT "AVG. TIS = "; AVG_TIS; "AVG. WT = "; AVG_WT
END
```

The comments after the exclamation point (!) should make the program self-explanatory to those who are familiar with the BASIC programming language.

SLAM Program for Car Lube Service Time Simulation

Below is a sample program written in SLAM for the Car Lube Simulation. The purpose for showing this program is not to teach you how to develop simulation models in a special-purpose simulation language. Rather it is to demonstrate the advantages of using such special-purpose simulation languages. Specifically, notice that when compared to the BASIC program how few lines of code were needed. In addition, this SLAM program does everything the BASIC program does and more. For example, this SLAM program would automatically generate summary statistics such as the percent idle time, the maximum number of customers in the system and the maximum number of customers waiting for service. Obtaining this information with a general-purpose programming language would require adding substantially more lines of code.

```
GEN,SHAFER,CAR LUBE,2/7/95,30;
LIM,1,1,100;
NETWORK;
        CREATE,UNFRM(5,25),0,1,20;
        QUEUE(1);
          ACT/1,12,0.8,TERM;
          ACT/1,20,0.2,TERM;
TERM  TERM;
         END;
```

TRUE/FALSE QUESTIONS

1. ___ Simulation involves primarily generating random numbers and replicating numerical outcomes on spreadsheets.

2. ___ Because of the power offered by spreadsheets, sophisticated simulation languages are no longer needed to implement complex dynamic simulation models.

3. ___ If the operation of the system is independent of time, we have a dynamic situation.

4. ___ A simulation clock is used to maintain a log of events.

5. ___ In a dynamic simulation model customers might represent people or manufacturing jobs.

6. ___ Specifying the time between successive arrivals is preferred to specifying the actual times that customers arrive for service.

7. ___ In event-driven simulation, the simulation clock is moved forward in even increments to simulate the passage of time.

8. ___ A logical correctly written flow chart for a simulation model should translate easily into a computer programming language.

9. ___ Because of the availability of special-purpose simulation languages, simulation models are rarely written in general purpose programming languages.

10. ___ One of the drawbacks of using special-purpose simulation languages is that the programmer must include all the details for file management, advancing time, computing statistics, and so on.

11. ___ A simulator is a parameter-driven simulation that requires no programming.

12. ___ Because of their narrow scope, some simulators require the analyst to make some crucial approximations in modeling the real system.

13. ___ Verification is concerned with determining whether the conceptual model is an accurate representation of the real system under investigation.

14. ___ The most objective and scientific means of validation is to compare the output of the model with the data from the real system for the same inputs.

15. ___ Face validity refers to the extent a model seems reasonable to those who understand the real system.

Answers:

1. F, 2. F, 3. F, 4. T, 5. T, 6. T, 7. F, 8. T, 9. F, 10. F, 11. T, 12. T, 13. F, 14. T, 15. T

CHAPTER 15

REVIEW

Management scientists refer to waiting lines as *queues* and the analysis of waiting lines is called *queuing theory*. Queuing theory applies to situations where customers arrive to a system, wait, and receive service. The objectives of queuing theory are to improve customer service and reduce operating costs.

Queuing systems consists of three elements: 1) customers, 2) servers, and 3) a waiting line or queue. Customers arrive to the system according to some *arrival process*. While the arrival process can be deterministic or stochastic, most arrival processes are stochastic. Stochastic arrival processes are usually described by a probability distribution representing the number of arrivals during a specific time interval, or by a distribution that represents the time between successive arrivals. In addition, the *arrival rate* may be constant or may vary with time. The set of potential customers is referred to as the *calling population*.

Modeling customer arrivals can be complicated by three behaviors often exhibited by customers. For example, customers can *renege* or leave a queue before being served. Also, in systems with multiple queues, customers can *jockey*, or switch queues. Lastly, an arriving customer may decide that the line is too long and therefore *balk*, or decide not to join the queue.

Just as customer arrivals occur according to some process, service occurs according to a *service process*. Again, like customer arrivals, service times may be deterministic or stochastic. In the case of stochastic service processes, the service times are described by some probability distribution. Modeling service processes can be complicated by service times depending on the type of customer and by having multiple servers.

The order in which customers are served is defined by the *queue discipline*. The most common queue discipline is first-come, first-served (FCFS).

Three common queuing configurations are: 1) a single queue feeding one or more parallel servers, 2) several parallel servers fed by their own queues, and 3) a combination of several queues in series.

The inputs to a queuing model are the arrival process, service process, queue discipline, and system configuration. The purpose of using queuing models is translate these inputs into measures of system performance. Used in this way, queuing models are descriptive. In general, system performance is evaluated on the basis of two measures: 1) the quality of service provided to the customer, and 2) the efficiency of the service operation and the cost of providing the service. The quality of service is often measured by average waiting times in the queue (W_q), the average time spend in the system (W), and percentage of customers (or jobs) completed by their deadline. Measures for the efficiency of the service include the average queue length (L_q), the average number of customers in the system (L), average throughput, server utilization, and the percent of customers who balk or renege.

A *Poisson process* can be used to model customer arrivals if it can be assumed that 1) customers arrive independent of each other and arrive one at time, 2) past arrivals do not influence future arrivals, and 3) the probability of an arrival does not vary over time. The parameter λ is called the *mean arrival rate* and is expressed in dimensions of customers per unit time. The *mean interarrival time* between successive customers is the reciprocal of λ. Furthermore, if the arrival process is Poisson, then the distribution of the interarrival times has an exponential probability distribution. Also, the number of arrivals over a period of time T is Poisson with mean λT.

In queuing models it is often assumed that service times follow an exponential distribution. The *mean service rate* (μ) represents the average number of customers served per unit of time and $1/\mu$ represents the average service time. For many situations assuming exponential service times is reasonable and provides the added benefit of simplifying the mathematics required in calculating system performance measures.

By convention, queuing models are characterized using the notation A/B/s, where A represents the arrival distribution, B represents the service time distribution, and s is the number of servers. Additionally, the following symbols are used to specify the arrival and service time distributions: M for exponential distribution (or Poisson process), G for general service time distribution, GI for general arrival distribution, and D for deterministic service times or arrival processes.

The simplest queuing model is the M/M/1 model. This model is valid as long as $\lambda > \mu$, otherwise the server will not be able to keep up with demand. All analytical queuing models including the M/M/1 model provide only *steady state* values of the operating characteristics. Steady state means that the probability distribution of the operating characteristics does not vary with time. The time it takes for a system's queues to build up and reach steady state is called the *transient period*. Since mathematical queuing models provide only steady state results, determining how long it takes to reach steady state requires other methods of analysis.

An important relationship in queuing theory is known as Little's Law and states that for any steady state queuing system, $L = \lambda W$. Similarly, it can also be shown that $L_q = \lambda W_q$.

The M/G/1 model is applicable to situations where the arrivals are Poisson and the service times are arbitrary. To use the M/G/1 model, all we need to know is the mean service time $1/\mu$ and the variance of service time.

In models with multiple servers, λ must be less than $s\mu$ or the queue will grow to infinity. In models with a finite calling population, the mean arrival depends on the number of customers in the system. To model situations with finite calling populations, it is assumed that the arrival rate of each customer follows a Poisson process with mean λ.

Simulation analysis of queuing systems is particularly applicable for a number of reasons. First, mathematical queuing models require restrictive assumptions such as Poisson arrivals and exponential service times. Second, queuing models in general are rather difficult to formulate and solve even when the distribution of arrivals and departures is known. Third, in many actual situations, customers arrive in batches. Fourth, service systems often vary the number of servers. Finally, analytical queuing models only provide steady state values for operating characteristics.

SOLVED PROBLEMS

Example Problem 1: M/M/1 Queuing System

To illustrate the analysis of an M/M/1 queuing system, we extend the Car Lube Inc. example presented in example problem 1 of Chapter 14 of this study guide. In the present problem we assume that Car Lube Inc. operates a single bay garage for the purpose of performing oil changes on cars. Historical data indicates that the arrival of cars follows an exponential distribution with a mean of 4 arrivals per hour and that service times follow an exponential distribution with mean of 6 cars serviced per hour. Analyze this situation with the appropriate queuing theory tools. Further, management is interested in determining the benefits associated with increasing the service rate to 8 cars per hour in increments of .5.

Solution:

A spreadsheet to analyze this problem is shown in Figure 15-1 and representative formulas are shown in Figure 15-2. In cell B3 the current value of λ=4 was entered while in cell B4 the value of μ=6 was entered. In rows 6-10 the typical measures of queuing system performance were entered. To facilitate entering the formulas for these performance measures, cell B3 was given the range name **L** (for λ) and cell B4 was given the range name **U** (for μ). Assigning the cells these range names permitted entering the formulas in a form similar to the formulas provided in the text.

Recall, the formula for the average number in the queue (L_q) was given as:

$$\frac{\lambda^2}{\mu(\mu-\lambda)} = \frac{4^2}{6(6-4)} = 1.33$$

Figure 15-1

A	A	B	C	D	E	F
1	**Car Lube M/M/1 Queueing Model and Sensitivity Analysis**					
2						
3	Lambda	4	4	4	4	4
4	Mu	6	6.5	7	7.5	8
5						
6	Average number in queue	1.33	0.98	0.76	0.61	0.50
7	Average number in system	2.00	1.60	1.33	1.14	1.00
8	Average time in queue	0.33	0.25	0.19	0.15	0.13
9	Avg. waiting time in system	0.50	0.40	0.33	0.29	0.25
10	Probability system is empty	0.33	0.38	0.43	0.47	0.50

Figure 15-2

	A	B	C	D	E	F
1	**Car Lube M/M/1 Queueing Model and Sensitivity Analysis**					
2						
3	Lambda	4	4	4	4	4
4	Mu	6	6.5	7	7.5	8
5						
6	Average number in queue	1.33	0.98	0.76	0.61	0.50
7	Average number in system	2.00	1.60	1.33	1.14	1.00
8	Average time in queue	0.33	0.25	0.19	0.15	0.13
9	Avg. waiting time in system	0.50	0.40	0.33	0.29	0.25
10	Probability system is empty	0.33	0.38	0.43	0.47	0.50

Using the defined range names, the following formula was entered in cell B6 to calculate L_q: +L^2/((U*(U-L))). Likewise, the formula to compute the average number in the system (L) was given as:

$$\frac{\lambda}{\mu-\lambda} = \frac{4}{6-4} = 2.00$$

Again, using the defined range names, the following formula was entered in cell B7 to calculate L: +L/(U-L). The remaining formulas for cells B8..B10 were entered in a similar fashion. The results indicate that given the present operating conditions, on average 1.33 customers will be waiting for service and an average of 2 customers will be in the system (i.e., both waiting for service and receiving service). Additionally, customers spend an average of .33 hours (19.8 minutes) waiting for service, and spend an average of .5 hours (30 minutes) in the system (both waiting for and receiving service). Lastly, 33% of the arriving customers would not have to wait to receive service (i.e., the probability that the system is empty is .33).

In columns C-F, sensitivity analysis was conducted for the service rate μ while holding the arrival rate λ constant. Specifically, the service rate was increased in increments of .5 up to a service rate of 8 cars/hour. To calculate the performance measures for these alternative levels of λ, the formulas entered in cells B6..B10 were copied to cells C6.. F10.

Finally, Figure 15-3 contains a spreadsheet to demonstrate how spreadsheets can be used to simulate a queuing system and Figure 15-4 shows the formulas that were entered. Specifically, the spreadsheet shown in Figure 15-3 is a slight modification of the spreadsheet presented in Figure 14-1. These modifications involved generating interarrival times from an exponential distribution (previously they were generated from a uniform distribution) and generating service times from an exponential distribution (previously they were generated from a discrete distribution). To generate a random variate with an exponential distribution (E) with mean m, we use the formula E = -m*LN(R), where R is a random number from a uniform distribution between 0 and 1. The arrival rate of 4 customers per hour is equivalent to an interarrival time between customer arrivals of 15 minutes. Thus, to generate interarrival times with an exponential distribution and mean of 15 we would use the formula: E = -15*LN(R). This formula was entered in cell B13 of the spreadsheet shown in Figure 15-3 as: -$B$8*@LN(@RAND), where cell B8 was used to store the mean interarrival rate. Since the arrival time of the second customer is equal to the arrival time of the first customer plus a randomly generated interarrival time, the formula: +B13+(-$B$8*@LN(@RAND)) was entered in cell B14 to generate the arrival for the second customer. The formula entered in cell B14 was then copied to cells B15..B22.

Service times were generated in a similar fashion. Specifically, to generate random exponentially distributed service times with a mean of 10 the following formula was

Figure 15-3

A	A	B	C	D	E	F	G
1	**Car Lube Service Time Simulation**						
2							
3	*Formulas and Assumptions*						
4							
5	Interarrival time is exponential with mean of 15 minutes						
6	Service time is exponential with mean of 10 minutes						
7							
8	Interarrival time	15					
9	Service time	10					
10							
11		Time of	Time Serv.	Service	Service		Time in
12	Customer Arrival	Arrival	Begins	Time	Finished	Wait Time	System
13	1	9.9	9.9	12.5	22.4	0.0	12.5
14	2	10.7	22.4	20.0	42.4	11.7	31.8
15	3	30.4	42.4	3.4	45.8	12.1	15.4
16	4	34.7	45.8	23.3	69.1	11.1	34.4
17	5	35.7	69.1	2.0	71.1	33.3	35.4
18	6	36.2	71.1	2.1	73.2	34.9	37.0
19	7	36.8	73.2	9.0	82.2	36.4	45.4
20	8	46.4	82.2	5.0	87.2	35.8	40.8
21	9	49.7	87.2	10.8	98.0	37.5	48.3
22	10	55.0	98.0	2.2	100.2	43.0	45.2
23	11	77.4	100.2	1.5	101.7	22.7	24.2
24	12	104.2	104.2	10.1	114.4	0.0	10.1
25	13	132.3	132.3	16.9	149.3	0.0	16.9
26	14	135.7	149.3	36.9	186.2	13.6	50.5
27	15	154.6	186.2	3.1	189.3	31.6	34.7
28	16	160.1	189.3	6.3	195.6	29.2	35.5
29	17	166.8	195.6	21.1	216.7	28.8	49.9
30	18	171.3	216.7	10.5	227.2	45.4	55.9
31	19	189.2	227.2	3.7	230.8	37.9	41.6
32	20	212.6	230.8	11.5	242.4	18.3	29.8
33							
34	*Averages*					24.2	34.8

Figure 15-4

A	A	B	C	D	E	F	G
1	**Car Lube Service Time Simulation**						
2							
3	***Formulas and Assumptions***						
4							
5	Interarrival time is exponential with a mean of 15 minutes						
6	Service time is exponential with mean of 10 minutes						
7							
8	Interarrival time	15					
9	Service time	10					
10							
11		Time of	Time Serv.	Service	Service	Wait	Time in
12	Customer Arrival	Arrival	Begins	Time	Finished	Time	System
13	1	-$B$8*@LN(@RAND)	+B13	-$B$9*@LN(@RAND)	+C13+D13	+C13-B13	+E13-B13
14	2	+B13+(-$B$8*@LN(@RAND))	@MAX(B14,E13)	-$B$9*@LN(@RAND)	+C14+D14	+C14-B14	+E14-B14
15	3	+B14+(-$B$8*@LN(@RAND))	@MAX(B15,E14)	-$B$9*@LN(@RAND)	+C15+D15	+C15-B15	+E15-B15
16	4	+B15+(-$B$8*@LN(@RAND))	@MAX(B16,E15)	-$B$9*@LN(@RAND)	+C16+D16	+C16-B16	+E16-B16
17	5	+B16+(-$B$8*@LN(@RAND))	@MAX(B17,E16)	-$B$9*@LN(@RAND)	+C17+D17	+C17-B17	+E17-B17
18	6	+B17+(-$B$8*@LN(@RAND))	@MAX(B18,E17)	-$B$9*@LN(@RAND)	+C18+D18	+C18-B18	+E18-B18
19	7	+B18+(-$B$8*@LN(@RAND))	@MAX(B19,E18)	-$B$9*@LN(@RAND)	+C19+D19	+C19-B19	+E19-B19
20	8	+B19+(-$B$8*@LN(@RAND))	@MAX(B20,E19)	-$B$9*@LN(@RAND)	+C20+D20	+C20-B20	+E20-B20
21	9	+B20+(-$B$8*@LN(@RAND))	@MAX(B21,E20)	-$B$9*@LN(@RAND)	+C21+D21	+C21-B21	+E21-B21
22	10	+B21+(-$B$8*@LN(@RAND))	@MAX(B22,E21)	-$B$9*@LN(@RAND)	+C22+D22	+C22-B22	+E22-B22

entered in cell D13: -$B$9*@LN(@RAND), where cell B9 was used to store the mean service time. Once this formula was entered in cell D13, it was copied to cells D14.. D22. The formulas determining the time service begins (column C), the time service is finished (column E), the wait time (column F), and the time in system (column G) required no modifications and are discussed in the solution to example problem 1 in Chapter 14.

Example Problem 2: Queuing Model for a Finite Calling Population

Eight workers at company XYZ share an office copier. On average each worker needs to use the copier once per hour. A recent time study indicates that the time it takes to run a typical job on the copier is exponentially distributed with mean of 5 minutes. Additionally, the time study indicated that the arrivals to the copier followed a Poisson distribution. Calculate the typical system performance measures for this office.

Solution:

A spreadsheet that calculates the typical system performance measures for a finite calling population is shown in Figure 15-5 and representative formulas are shown in Figure 15-6. Note that we have a finite calling population because there are only 8 workers who use the copying machine and once they join the queue to use the copier or are in the process of using it, they can no longer be included as potential arrivals.

Cell B3 contains the arrival rate given as each employee needing the copier one time per hour. The service rate of 12 jobs per hour was entered in cell B4. Note that 5 minutes per job is equivalent to 12 jobs per hour. Finally, 8 was entered in cell B5 corresponding to the number of people in the population.

To facilitate entering the formulas for the system performance measures, cell B3 was given the range name **L** (for λ), cell B4 was given the range name **U** (for μ), and cell B4 was given the range name N (representing the number of people in the population). Additionally, since several of the performance measures include the value of P_0 (the probability that the system is empty) in their calculation, cell B11 was given the range name **P0**. The only formula that requires explanation is the formula for P_0. Recall that this formula is computed as follows:

$$P_0 = \frac{1}{\sum_{n=0}^{N} \frac{N!}{(N-n)!}(\lambda / \mu)^n}$$

This formula is complicated by the fact that we need to sum a relatively complex term in the denominator. The easiest way to sum a number of terms like this is to use the Lotus @HLOOKUP (horizontal lookup) function. This function works the same as the

Figure 15-5

A	A	B	C	D	E	F	G	H	I	J
1	**Office Copier Queueing Model**									
2										
3	Lambda	1								
4	Mu	12								
5	Number in population	8								
6										
7	Average number in queue	0.495								
8	Average number in system	1.072								
9	Average time in queue	0.071								
10	Avg. waiting time in system	0.155								
11	Probability system is empty	0.423								
12										
13										
14	Lookup table	0	1	2	3	4	5	6	7	8
15		1	0.667	0.389	0.194	0.081	0.027	0.007	0.001	0.000
16		1	1.667	2.056	2.250	2.331	2.358	2.365	2.366	2.366

Figure 15-6

A	A	B	C	D
1	**Office Copier Queueing Model**			
2				
3	Lambda	1		
4	Mu	12		
5	Number in population	8		
6				
7	Average number in queue	+N-((((L+U))/L)*(1-P0))		
8	Average number in system	+B7+(1-P0)		
9	Average time in queue	+B7/((N-B8)*L)		
10	AvG. waiting time in system	+B9+(1/U)		
11	Probability system is empty	1/(@HLOOKUP($N,B14..J16,2))		
12				
13				
14	Lookup table	0	1	2
15		((@FACT($N)/(@FACT($N-B14))*(($L/$U)^B14)))	((@FACT($N)/(@FACT($N-C14))*(($L/$U)^C14)))	((@FACT($N)/(@FACT($N-D14))*(($L/$U)^D14)))
16		+B15	+B16+C15	+C16+D15

@VLOOKUP function except that instead of moving down rows and then across the offset number of columns, it moves across columns first and then down the offset number of rows. We will use this function to calculate the sum of this term in steps. Specifically, in the first step (row 15) we calculate the term for a specific value of n (where n varies from 0 to N). To illustrate, in cell B15 the term is calculated for n=0 (cell B14) as follows:

$$\frac{N!}{(N-n)!}(\lambda / \mu)^n = \frac{8!}{(8-0)!}(1/12)^0 = 1$$

Likewise, in cell C15, the equation is calculated for n=1 (cell C14) as follows:

$$\frac{N!}{(N-n)!}(\lambda / \mu)^n = \frac{8!}{(8-1)!}(1/12)^1 = 0.667$$

In a similar fashion, the term is calculated for n=2 through 8 in cells D15 to J15, respectively. Row 16 is used to compute the sum of this term from 0 to N. To illustrate, cell F16 contains the sum of this term from 0 to 4. Referring back to cell B11, the @HLOOKUP function moves across row 14 to the appropriate column based on N entered in cell B5, and returns the value two rows down. Notice that once the formula was entered in cell B15, it can be copied to cells C15..J15. As this example illustrates, the @HLOOKUP function can serve as a useful tool for summing complex terms.

TRUE/FALSE QUESTIONS

1. ___ The analysis of waiting lines is called queuing theory.

2. ___ The customers in queuing models are always people.

3. ___ A queue does not have to be visible to study it.

4. ___ Most arrival processes are deterministic.

5. ___ Arrival rates can be constant or may vary with time.

6. ___ The calling population is the set of potential customers.

7. ___Failed machines in a factory awaiting repair would be an example of an infinite population.

8. ___ Once customers join a line, they may not always stay in the same order that they arrived.

9. ___ A customer is said to renege if when they arrive at the system they determine that the line is too long and decide not to join the queue.

10. ___The time it takes to serve a customer may be deterministic or stochastic.

11. ___ Service times could depend on the type of customer.

12. ___ First-come, first-served is an example of a queue discipline.

13. ___ Queuing models are prescriptive in nature.

14. ___ If λ is the mean arrival rate, the mean interarrival rate is the reciprocal of λ.

15. ___ While assuming exponential service times is often reasonable, it also complicates the mathematics involved in calculating performance measures.

16. ___ Queuing models in general are rather difficult to formulate and solve even when the distribution of arrivals and departures is known.

17. ___ The M/M/1 is considered to be a complex queuing model.

18. ___ When $\lambda = \mu$, any variation that exists in the arrival or service pattern will result in the queue building up indefinitely.

19. ___ Mathematical queuing models provide only steady state results.

20. ___ The M/G/1 model applies to situations in which we have Poisson arrivals and arbitrary service times.

21. ___ In situations with a finite calling population, the mean arrival rate depends on the number of customers in the system.

22. ___ In general, queuing systems do not lend themselves well to simulation analysis.

23. ___ It is possible that a system would not reach steady state until after it closes.

24. ___ Steady state averages can provide important insights about the behavior of queuing systems during transient periods.

25. ___ Simulation can be used to model nearly any queuing system regardless of the assumptions made.

Answers:

1. T, 2. F, 3. T, 4. F, 5. T, 6. T, 7. F, 8. T, 9. F, 10. T, 11. T, 12. T, 13. F, 14. T, 15. F, 16. T, 17. F, 18. T, 19. T, 20. T, 21. T, 22. F, 23. T, 24. F, 25. T